D0982560

Between Two Streams

Between Two Streams
A Diary from Bergen-Belsen

ABEL J. HERZBERG

*Translated from the Dutch
by Jack Santcross*

I.B.Tauris Publishers
LONDON · NEW YORK

in association with
The European Jewish
Publication Society

Published in English in 1997 by I.B.Tauris
Victoria House, Bloomsbury Square,
London WC1B 4DZ

In the United States of America and in Canada
distributed by St Martin's Press
175 Fifth Avenue, New York NY 10010

Reprinted 1997

Copyright © 1989 by the Estate of Abel J. Herzberg, Amsterdam,
Em. Querido's Uitgevrij B.V.

English translation copyright © 1997 by Jack Santcross

Published in association with The European Jewish Publication
Society.

The European Jewish Publication Society is a registered charity
which gives grants to assist in the publication and distribution of
books relating to Jewish literature, history, religion, philosophy,
politics and culture.

A full CIP record for this book is available from the British Library

A full CIP record for this book is available from the Library of
Congress

ISBN 1 86064 121 0

Set in Monotype Ehrhardt by Ewan Smith, London

Printed and bound in Great Britain by WBC Ltd, Bridgend,
Mid Glamorgan

Contents

Translator's Note

The train that brought Abel J. Herzberg to Bergen-Belsen had left Westerbork on 11 January 1944. Among its passengers was a boy who barely a fortnight earlier had celebrated his ninth birthday in Westerbork – some nine months after his arrest in Amsterdam.

The train that carried Abel J. Herzberg away from Bergen-Belsen on 10 April 1945, less than a week before the British arrived, also carried away the boy who had been a fellow passenger on the inward journey.

At the time of these events, the boy understood little of what was happening to him. Though even if he had understood, he would not have been able to describe his experiences because from the time of Holland's occupation in May 1940 until well after the war he received very little schooling. Nevertheless, he had felt all the pain and had experienced every torment described in this diary.

Many years later the boy was no longer sure what was true or imagined. He could only feel pain, anger and sadness. Then he read this diary, and knew that everything he remembered had been true. Nothing had been imagined.

That boy, now a man, is the translator of this diary, fifty years after entering Bergen-Belsen.

Though unable to write my personal account of what had taken place, I still wanted somehow to honour all those who had failed to survive those horrors, in particular the children. Since this diary had not yet been translated into English, I felt I could do no better than be the means by which Abel J. Herzberg could give his account to readers of English.

Apart from correcting a few misspelled German words I have followed the original Dutch text as closely as possible.

To make the diary more accessible to readers, I have added a number of explanatory footnotes for which I take full responsibility.

I hope I will be found to have done justice to the author and his diary, and apologise for any oversights. The task has been an honour for me, and is my personal salute to Abel J. Herzberg.

Jack Santcross
Wembley, February 1994

Biographical Note

Abel Jacob Herzberg was born in Amsterdam in 1893 and grew up in a non-orthodox but religious home.[1] His father was a broker in uncut diamonds. Around 1880 his parents emigrated from Lithuania to Holland; his mother with her family, and his father by himself. They met in Amsterdam, where they got married. Although they had fled from the pogroms against the Jews, his mother remembered with nostalgia her former homeland and the strongly religious Jewish community there. 'The essence of the stories my parents told me, was that they were Jews. It was a recurring theme. It stood in the foreground. It not only meant they were foreigners, but that even in their home country they had never been anything but foreigners. Although they came from Russia, and their families had lived there for many centuries, they were not Russians and were also never recognised there as such. That is why they left there.' That is what Abel Herzberg wrote to his eight-year-old grandson in letters first published in Dutch in 1964 under the title *Brieven aan mijn kleinzoon*.[2] Elsewhere he wrote: '1908, I was not fifteen yet, a Zionist congress was being held in the Arts and Sciences Hall in The Hague. My parents went there and took me with them. There, on Zwarte Weg, I saw for the first time in my life a Jewish flag, and I knew we were not dreaming. Except that we had to wait forty years, forty bitter years, and that was something we did not know.'

During the First World War he enrolled as a volunteer in the

---

[1] This biographical note was written by Renata Laqueur and appeared in *Schreiben im KZ, Tagebücher 1940–1945*, ed. Martina Dreisbach (Niedersächsischen Landeszentrale für politische Bildung, Hanover 1991). It has been translated from the German and edited by Jack Santcross.

[2] *Letters to my grandson.*

Dutch army even though he did not have Dutch nationality. He served for three and a half years because he considered it a duty to his new homeland.

After the war he studied law, worked in the courts, and then set himself up in Amsterdam as a lawyer specialising in administrative law.

In the 1930s he played a prominent role in the Dutch Jewish community. He was also editor of *De Joodse Wachter*[3] and from 1934 to 1939 chairman of the Dutch Zionist Association.

After the occupation of Holland in 1940, Abel Herzberg, his wife Thea and their three children were forced to go into hiding. Their first hiding place seemed to them to be too insecure. In the second refuge in Blaricum, the Herzbergs came to realise what it meant to wipe out their existence, as it were, while simultaneously endangering the lives of other people. The family were unable to endure this way of life and took the risk of returning to Amsterdam. In March 1943 they were arrested by the Germans. The family was interned in Barneveld. Before they were taken to Westerbork transit camp, Thea Herzberg managed to smuggle the children out of the camp and take them to safety on a nearby farm.

From September 1943 until January 1944 Abel and Thea Herzberg were imprisoned in Westerbork. In the middle of January they were transported to Bergen-Belsen. In April 1944, 172 prisoners – among them the Herzbergs – were told they could leave for Palestine in exchange for interned Germans. They were moved into separate huts, were exempted from forced labour, and were not maltreated. After five weeks, though, they were returned to the 'normal' camp without any explanation, together with fifty other prisoners. At the same time, Abel Herzberg decided to keep a diary with the intention of expanding the notes 'later'. They cover the period from 11 August 1944 to 26 April 1945.

In the summer of 1945, Abel and Thea Herzberg returned to Amsterdam. Their three children had also survived. Their son and

---

[3] *The Jewish Watch.*

eldest daughter, twenty-one and nineteen years old, immediately emigrated to Palestine. The youngest daughter remained with her parents in Holland. Herzberg's diary was first published in the journal *De Groene Amsterdammer.*

In the letters to his grandson he wrote: 'Who in those days had expected that those who migrated to Palestine would found a state there for the third time and that those who migrated to America would become their financiers? Both were equally poor and equally inexperienced. *We* expected it. We were sure of it. As a child I discussed with both my uncles, who themselves were still only youngsters then, what the uniform of Jewish soldiers should look like. And we were quite serious.'

After the war Abel Herzberg wrote many books: novels, stories, dramas. Most of them had as their theme the persecution of the Jews. He wanted to keep alive both the knowledge of what people were capable of and the debate about how one could prevent it from happening again.

In the 1970s he spoke out for the release of several German war criminals, not from a sense of compassion, but because he was convinced that revenge was inhuman.

He received numerous honours and prizes. In 1965 he was made Knight of the Order of Orange-Nassau, and in 1974 he was awarded the Dutch prize for literature for his collected works. Abel Herzberg died in May 1989.

For these biographical details I wish to express my thanks to Tamir Herzberg, the author's grandson, to whom he wrote the above-mentioned letters.

Renata Laqueur

Introduction

I wrote this diary in Bergen-Belsen camp, where I was a prisoner from mid-January 1944 until the evacuation fifteen months later. After having worked for quite some time in all kinds of internal and external working parties, I was summoned for exchange to Palestine. For a few weeks I experienced the joy of beckoning freedom before being sent into slavery again, together with a number of others of whom only a few survived. Soon afterwards, clandestinely of course, I began to record the notes contained in this book.

These notes were meant as a guide for a full account of what had happened. This I had intended to write after the liberation, should I live to see it. But after the liberation the future was of greater interest than the past. For a number of years the diary was left on one side until the manuscript, which had been typed in the meantime, was brought to the attention of the editors of *De Groene Amsterdammer*.[1] They published it almost in its entirety in the edition of 6 May 1950, which was devoted to the commemoration of the surprise attack on Holland in May 1940 and the liberation of the country five years later. At the time it seemed best to leave unaltered what had been written in the camp so that a by now rather faded memory should not distort facts and moods.

Thereupon, the diary was published as a diary in unabridged form, including all errors and contradictions, omitting only a few passages that contained superfluous repetitions for the reader. Comments added to one or two points are indicated as such on the relevant page. For obvious reasons all names have been replaced with initials, as was done earlier in *De Groene*.

---

[1] Independent Dutch weekly newspaper founded in 1877.

A few factual details about Bergen-Belsen camp may help the reader understand the diary better.[2] Bergen-Belsen consisted not of a single camp of uniform character, but of a series of different categories of camps. There was a large concentration camp for political prisoners (*Häftlinge*) and a small internment camp for Jews with – as far as we could determine – American nationality, who therefore did not need to wear a yellow star and whose treatment, given German conditions, could be called normal. Subsequently, new temporary camps kept being added, populated by unknown transports from unknown destinations. Towards the end of the war it seemed as if all the prisoners who had been evacuated from the cleared German camps were being concentrated in Bergen-Belsen, so that its population grew to ten times as many as the available space allowed for, resulting in unimaginable chaos and misery. Whereas in the beginning the inhabitants of the different camps of Bergen-Belsen had almost no contact with one another, now old and new prisoner transports were brought together. This greatly encouraged the spread of infectious diseases, particularly spotted fever.[3] One of the oldest and most significant camps in Bergen-Belsen was the so-called *Sternlager*, named after the yellow star that, unlike other prisoners, Jewish prisoners had to wear. It is this camp that the diary deals with. The Germans called it a *Vorzugslager*,[4] which it was, for it was intended for Jews who, as an exception to Adolf Hitler's 'Vernichtungspolitik',[5] were to be not exterminated but kept alive to serve as material for exchange against Germans abroad – Palestine in the first place, but also elsewhere overseas.

This *Sternlager* in Bergen-Belsen was intended, therefore, as a kind of depot where, compared with the *Häftlinge*, the prisoners did indeed enjoy significant advantages. Their heads were not shaven, they kept their clothes and blankets and even a little luggage, and

---

[2] (Author's note): Interested readers are referred to the outstanding and scholarly monograph on the camps entitled 'Bergen Belsen' by Eberhard Kolb, published in 1962 by Verlag für Literatur und Zeitgeschichte, Hanover.

[3] Typhus – a disease that is transmitted by lice.

[4] Camp for privileged people.   [5] Extermination policy.

families were not torn asunder. Though they naturally lived in separate huts, men and women could meet each other daily. Not least because of its mixed character, the camp differed significantly from normal concentration camps.

The exception to the extermination policy was made partly out of fear of reprisals that neutral or Allied states might take against German nationals, and partly out of consideration that they could probably rid themselves of a number of Jews this way more economically than by robbing them of their life in gas chambers or with murderous hard labour. That personal speculation among various National Socialist leaders – first of all Heinrich Himmler – should have played an important role here, especially after the tide on the battlefield had turned against Germany, may be taken as fact. In any case, the Jews who were transported to Bergen-Belsen from Holland and from many other occupied countries were those whom the Germans had credited with having a certain value on the international market in human beings. The attempt to keep certain groups of Jews in Bergen-Belsen (and elsewhere) for exchange or emigration was – at least in part – kept secret from Hitler and even symbolised a kind of sabotage of his policies. This applies in particular to Hungarian Jews, for whom a separate camp had been established in Bergen-Belsen and whose situation there was tolerable. In the *Sternlager* this sabotage – if indeed it existed at all – was in turn sabotaged, with the well-known result that 70 per cent of the internees[6] in this camp for privileged persons died (that is, if death in Bergen-Belsen can be called 'dying'). Of the remaining 30 per cent many were indeed exchanged for German nationals or taken secretly across the German frontier by official National Socialist authorities (that is to say, without the prior knowledge or approval of the leaders at the top). The rest pulled through with tuberculosis or other chronic diseases unless they had managed to obtain extra food for themselves through special duties, such as working in the kitchen.

---

[6] The SS had promised those who were sent to the *Sternlager* of Bergen-Belsen that they would be treated as internees, not as prisoners.

3

Of those who had been privileged to enjoy all the delights of Bergen-Belsen from beginning to end, very few – but more women than men – managed to remain in good physical condition. For them, too, captivity could not have lasted very much longer. Psychological resistance was generally stronger, but a discussion of this now would anticipate the diary.

This diary is published out of respect for those who did not return from the camps. It is out of duty to them that the living will not cease to recount what happened there. A duty in particular, therefore, to those among the dead who in their deepest misery knew how to live their life at the highest level attainable to mankind.

This account of Bergen-Belsen is called *Between Two Streams*.[7] The title occurs several times in the diary, where it is explained. Two streams manifested themselves in the camp – and not only there: National Socialism and Judaism. Not only persecutors and persecuted, powerful and powerless, took part in this lugubrious drama. Two irreconcilable principles of life fought invisibly in the visible battle.

---

[7] Mesopotamia (Greek for 'between the rivers'). Name given to the land lying between the Tigris and Euphrates rivers.

Diary

11 August 1944 At half past eleven, just as the working parties were returning, a sudden announcement: general roll-call. Those who had not been assigned work are eating. Much consternation. No one knows what is in store this time, not even the *Ältestenrat*[1] know, or they say they do not know. People guess, and the guesses range from the composition of a transport destined for Palestine to the distribution of an extra ration of cheese. Meanwhile, people make their way, some reluctantly, dragging their feet, all with fear in their hearts, most of them driven by an irrepressible curiosity that enables them to conquer their extreme reluctance. Perhaps it will be something good after all. Lately, optimism has predominated. Perhaps, one person says to another, the war has ended ... the unfortunate man laughs and hopes, despite disbelief. The children, too, arrive on the muster ground, but are sent back. Suddenly a *Scharführer*[2] shouts: 'Genug, alle anderen zurück.'[3] The LW (*Lagerwache*, a kind of police force established by the prisoners themselves) takes charge: 'Genug, alle anderen zurück.' The confusion grows. Apparently, they intend to form a new working party. People start to back away. Most remain standing though. There is much curiosity. Soon it is satisfied. Solomon S. is sentenced to four weeks' harsh punishment in the bunker.[4] He stole shoes from the warehouse to the detriment of the SS. That is what the SS are saying, at any rate. The sentence must be made public now. Hence the roll-call. However, S. has already served thirty days' bunker for the same offence. He has only just been released, together with D. and two others. They say they did

---

[1] Council of senior prisoners. [2] SS lance-sergeant.
[3] Enough, everyone else go back. [4] Solitary confinement.

not steal. The *Scharführer* from the warehouse had allowed them to give a pair of old shoes to some poor wretch. The *Scharführer* was found out and denies it. Naturally, the Jews are not believed now; on the contrary, they are accused of insulting the SS. They served their sentence, but now they must return to the bunker. Besides them, Hans S. has to go too. He had called to order a *Kapo*[5] who had abused and hounded the Jews. A *Scharführer* had heard of it, or perhaps the *Kapo* himself had reported it. S. served six days. They had accused him of sabotage and had given him a confession to sign. He had refused to sign it. He was released from the bunker. With a sense of relief, he returned to the hut. Now he has been re-arrested. More bunker? In the evening, they come to collect his luggage. We know better then: KZ (*Konzentrationslager*).[6] KZ means Mauthausen,[7] Mauthausen means death.

S. is a young man, aged about twenty-five. Strong, honest, sincere. One of the best *Chaluzim* (Palestine pioneers). He is married with a child who celebrated its first birthday a few weeks ago. His wife and child feel 'down'. With a sentimental look in his eyes he told me he wished he could have been present on his child's birthday. Its first one. We talked about the second birthday. It is something you must not do here. You must not make any plans. You must just carry on toiling, toiling. One day, somewhere, a glimmer will appear ...

And always there are some who delude themselves. The luggage had been collected for inspection. But then they bring his food to the gate. The *Scharführer* refuses to accept it. 'No need,' he says. 'S. is being interrogated.' Then we know there can be no further doubt.

12 August The *chasan* (cantor) of a *shul* (synagogue) in Cracow sang. People debate the quality of his voice. Albanians, Africans and Dutch pray the same prayers. Judaism is a single religion. There is hardly any difference, not even in part.

---

[5] A prisoner who is appointed to wield authority over his fellow prisoners and thereby becomes a member of the camp staff.
[6] Concentration camp.
[7] Concentration camp in Austria known for its hard labour in the stone quarries.

Albanians, Africans and others sing Hebrew songs under the direction of Z. and Z.'s children. East and West will meet. Modern songs. A discussion takes place about appointing a magistrate to deal with the prompt adjudication of breaches at work and of discipline. It is needed badly. Getting Jews to respect group discipline is not easy. Jews also make bad rulers. They still have to learn it. It is a difficult subject. The discussion dissolves into a personal quarrel which is settled again an hour later. Naturally, there is immediately the jurisprudential point of view, the opportunistic one. Opportunism relating to theory. Questions of prestige are at stake — questions of eligibility and disputes about them. Someone says something. Someone stands up and leaves the discussion, another supports it. A third does exactly the opposite. The supporters form a faction against the non-supporters. There is criticism. There is no magistrate.

There are parcels, though. I get sardines from Portugal. A blessing! The censor has opened a tin. We must finish it therefore. We hand it round and make friends, eat from it ourselves and finish our reserve of bread. In August it is hot on the Lüneburger Heide.[8]

For the first time in months I have eaten my fill. There were large quantities of mussels — but many of them stink. They stink of the latrines. It is better to ignore it though. We are hungry and stinking mussels are quite tasty enough. This afternoon we also fished the potatoes out of the soup. They gave us raw onions and we made a potato salad with chopped mussels and onions. Friends had some limonsecco.[9] Consequently, we are having a wonderful meal. I even managed to get sated and am therefore contented and optimistic.

13 August B., a Greek, is in charge of the food distribution. The *Scharführer* let him choose between onions and jam. Naturally, B. chose the jam. So we got the onions. The camp is teeming with raw onions now and everywhere it stinks of onions and more onions. It

---

[8] Luneburg Heath.
[9] Perhaps a brand name, or dried lemon, lemon powder?

is not pleasant, but healthy. There are still some mussels left, enough for another meal.

The food is abominable. Turnips, with I know not what kind of leaf. Everything is underdone and unpalatable. We struggle through it courageously. An hour after we have eaten, we are hungry again – hunger, hunger. So tonight the onions and mussels will taste wonderful. The mussels are fresh and do not stink.

It is Sunday today. On Sundays we work only in the morning but in view of the war situation they have revoked the free Sunday afternoon. Last week it was the same. We had to carry on working till nine then, and to keep in practice, they repeated it on Monday and Tuesday. The women who work in the shoe and clothing in-dustries are exhausted. No rest this afternoon. And the laundry ... who will do the laundry? And who will prepare some food? And who will spend an hour or so talking with the children? We live for a newspaper.

By the grace of God they allow the women to return to camp this afternoon. T., however, is working in the kitchen. Probably it will carry on till eight. She is filling herself on carrots now. It is worth a day's work to her. I can see her through the barbed wire fence sitting in the hot sun.

14 August Hut 13 is being punished. During roll-call, they had not stood orderly and still. Once again roll-call had lasted one and a half hours because someone had miscounted in hut 28. Apparently hut 13 had got tired. Now they must stand in the cold, because it is chilly today. Today we heard that Dr. and Do. have also been sent to the KZ. No one knows why.

Two kinds of people exist. In normal society you cannot tell them apart because their characters and true differences find no means of expressing themselves. Through the complexity of life, one gets trapped on sidetracks, and both the researcher and subject alike take these sidetracks. Sometimes you think you can get the measure of a person by observing their behaviour, but you are wrong. All you are doing is observing an incidental action or an incidental inaction, a detail, a nuance. At other times you think you have formulated some incredibly significant standards by which to judge others, or have discovered a very important yardstick with which to measure their worth or worthlessness. You completely fail to notice then that you are dealing with trivia, that you have been seized by the fascination of details that are only of secondary importance. When you discover a very tiny facet of life that no one has ever discovered before, you think you have achieved something. Here, though, life is simple and problems are reduced to primary proportions. In the past – at least that is what I seem to remember – the problem of eating presented itself in an infinite variety. There was the question of what to eat, with whom, when, et cetera, et cetera. How many books have not been written about eating, how many fine minds have not racked their aesthetic heads over the question of whether it is possible to draw conclusions about someone from the way they cut their bread or their meat, placed the pieces in their mouth, chewed or swallowed and similar details. How many fine minds have not thought that they could amuse others with this, or be of service to them. I fear that once you have been here you will have the lasting impression that all this belongs merely to our 'civilisation', that is to say, to the conventions that society has adopted for itself, and in fact, to lies. For why have conventions been adopted? To make life more agreeable, better, more bearable? Probably, but does it in fact mean anything other than that one wants to cover up man's true nature, that one shuns his nakedness? Our clothes, too, we wear not just because we are cold, but also to make a pretence of something that does *not* exist and to hide something that *does* exist. And all too often concealment itself has become a veritable art, its purpose being to draw attention to and accentuate *what* is being concealed. What sophistication man manages to display in the process.

Not here. Here civilisation no longer exists and consequently, no sophistication either. As for eating, all I have to say is: there is hunger on one side of our body, namely the inside, and fodder on the outside. Now the problem is: how to make the fodder reach the stomach. That is all. You have a fodder dish which is brown. It is a little impractical for a snout, else it could easily be used for pigs. You have a spoon, why? Because if you slurped from your fodder dish you might make a mess, and that would be a pity.

Bread arrives in large hunks. Eyes stare greedily and enviously to see if one hunk is larger than another. When you are standing in a queue and notice that a smaller hunk is about to be handed out, just when it comes to your turn, you slip away and let the next man bear the loss. You join the rear of the queue, and try your luck again.

And everyone expects from the other that which lives and roars most strongly inside him. To grab more than his inadequate share, as much more as he needs to still his hunger, that hollow feeling in his stomach. Are there no restraints any more then? There are, but they are not moral restraints, they are opportunistic ones. And you can see it now: everything you once learned about them and observed, stemmed from wealth. When you left the largest piece of meat for another with whom you were sitting at table, you did so because you were already sated. And when you gave something away, you did so because you were unable to finish what you had. You do not believe it, do you, man of society, you incredibly wealthy man! You, who have a house, and in that house a room, and in that room a table, and at that table a chair on which you sit, just sit normally on your backside. When you have no house, though, and no room and no table and no chair, but only a trough that you hoist above your bunk, because below you there are two more people sleeping in their cages, then you will *know* what people are like. People are creatures who hate you because you still occupy the top bunk of a three-tier bunk bed on which you can sit, whereas they can only recline. They drag their trough somewhere to a bench where they spoon, slurp, gobble up, nice-nice, and all they have to say is: today the soup is thin and yesterday it was thicker, and the hut leader picks out the pieces for himself and his wife, and we get the liquid, and to secure the top bunk of a three-tier bunk bed you need connections and protection, and did you notice how the food distributor stirred in the container? They are all scum.

Who is scum? Scum is someone who manages to obtain a crumb

more than another. What is honesty? The conviction that in the long run it is *more advantageous* to distribute everything equally. And who is honest? Whoever lacks elbows, smartness, know-how, the ability to obtain more for himself than his proper share. The weak are honest. Perhaps that is how it is in society, too. But it goes unnoticed. *Erst kommt das Fressen und dann kommt die Moral.*[10]

And yet ...

And yet I have seen people who, locked in some deep, incomprehensible loneliness – bearing the traits of a perverse determination in their faces – acted differently towards their fellow beings. Perhaps they were afraid of that dreadful feeling of remaining alone and were therefore looking for open-handedness, in the literal sense of the word. When I think of them, I see them as people rising high above the murky common herd, even though they were usually withdrawn, unnoticed, and belonged to the simple toilers and heavers. A camp for Jews is a sad, cheerless, grubby place on earth, somewhere on the heath, where everything that lives, or bears or brings life, has been hacked down, uprooted or burned. There is sand, grit and dust, but nothing, nothing else. On it stand a number of rows of grey-green huts. Not a tree grows there, no flower, not even grass, everything has one hue, one colour – the colour of colourlessness. The shrine is the muster ground, and the muster ground is really just a large area of nothingness, sand, grit and dust. Nowhere in the camp is there shade. On the muster ground shade is a forgotten word. In the summer it is scorching there. Nowhere in the camp is there paving or drainage. When it rains, the muster ground becomes either flooded, or a floating mass of mud and mire. With broken, half-rotten shoes on their feet, the people of Israel stand waiting for hours. In winter, shivering with cold, or soaked from the rain. Men, women and children. Roll-call is like a religious rite, or at least a sacred act for that bunch of inferior anthropoids who, partly unfulfilled by the human ideals that their teachers and priests taught them, and partly out of genuine indignation at all

---

[10] 'First food, then morality' – from the *Threepenny Opera* by Bertolt Brecht.

manner of fine cant, have invoked with pounding hearts a stark and lewd heathendom which taught them that the absolute binding power of ethics and morals was nonsense, and that in principle, whatever was advantageous would always be permitted. We will dissect these presumptuous and immodest creatures in greater detail. For the moment one sees them occupied each morning at roll-call, counting, counting, counting.

The camp is surrounded by a double fence of barbed wire. This fence is guarded day and night by sentries, armed with rifles and search lights. Around this camp, surrounded by barbed wire and sentries, are more barriers. More sentries with loaded rifles and accompanied by guard dogs. Escape from a camp is impossible. Besides, who would wish to escape? Where to?

15 August The fifteenth of August nineteen hundred and forty-four. *Forty-four!* Who could have imagined there would still be war then? Every autumn we lived in hope ... this year the last one ... Next year ... and it became 1944 and still we do not know anything. Because what is one of the worst torments of our life? What does it mean to have been taken prisoner and interned in a camp? We exist beyond time, beyond life, beyond space. As long as he lives in society, every person in his own way is a small cog in the large machinery of society. He receives motion and passes motion on, and however modest his role, something moves because of him! But we? We are nothing any more. We have been lifted out of the universe, we receive nothing, and we give nothing. No influence reaches us from outside, no influence flows out from us. Not a single force acts upon us, no counter force emanates from us. All that exists is the desire – we sense it – to destroy us. We experience it as a natural law, as we experience the laws of gravity, of cold and heat, and we resist with bitterness, with silence, with avoidance, by preserving our physical strength to the utmost, by being frugal with our movements. It drives the others to a frenzy sometimes. However, we do not walk if we can drag our feet, and if we can stay in bed five seconds longer, we do not make them a present of them. For the rest, though, life is something from which we are cut off. And – only a prisoner will understand this – that means yearning, hankering after freedom.

Prisoners like us receive no news. It is forbidden to read newspapers; transgressions are punished severely and collectively. Whoever gets hold of a newspaper can say goodbye.

Thus we do not know what is happening in the world.

Yet the camp is not so isolated for things not to happen there that reflect events in the world outside. A distant echo gets through. That is how we know that the large transport that arrived in the night is a symptom of the downfall of the Third Reich. In the past few days they erected a large tent camp next to ours. We saw them at work, the *Häftlinge* from the adjoining KZ. The men, barely clad and many barefoot, were beaten in the customary way by their *Kapos*. Nothing, I believe, is more humiliating to mankind than the labour of such *Häftlinge*. They toiled not like animals, but like slaves, which is far worse. Naturally, the good paterfamilias will take such a statement for rhetoric, and when the war is over and a few years have elapsed, no one will understand any longer that this was far from being rhetoric but was hard literal truth. Compassion for animals, or at least care in handling animals, gave way to an incomprehensible, quite irrational hatred. The *Kapo* beats, with a stick, a whip, a riding crop, a length of rubber, and if he has nothing else, with his cap. He beats constantly. He beats and he shouts. The *Häftling* may not offer any resistance and must not retaliate. Any attempt to do so means bunker, without food, even harder labour, sometimes the noose. He does not retaliate, but one can see how adept they have become during their years of captivity at avoiding the blows. The men carry a red cross on their backs and a red stripe on their sleeves and trousers. Sometimes they wear blue and white striped prison uniform, all torn, patched and torn again. Grey with dirt, most of them have no shoes. Many are barefooted. Whoever has a pair of wooden soles tied to his feet with a leather strap is rich. They are shaven bald, pale and gaunt from hunger and wretchedness. Yet they work much harder than we do. They are driven and beaten much harder.

No doubt they envy us. They experience the same agonising hunger. We know that they are dying in their hundreds, at a much faster rate than we are. They do seem to receive parcels though. They also have newspapers.

We are forbidden to talk to them. Punishment for infringement is again very severe. To talk means KZ. KZ means saying goodbye.

The *Häftlinge* had set up the tent camp. Our men had carried the straw, and last night and this morning a transport of women and children moved into the ten or twelve huge tents. Who are they? It is happening in the adjoining camp. We can see it. Yet no one knows anything, that is how isolated we are. All kinds of conjectures are circulating, and most of them amount to: refugees from Poland or East Prussia. One thing we do know then: it is a sign of dis-integration and we will not get away from here. We must wait for the chaos. Will we have to swap places with these women and move into tents? Those who like to surrender to gloomy predictions believe it. It strengthens our resistance, though. Whoever wants to know how that manifests itself should go to hut 12 on Sunday evenings when the French, Albanian and Serbian Jews are the guests of the Greeks, and there is singing. Then there is excitement and life in the group. A freedom song, and the rhythm is accompanied by hand-clapping and stamping of feet. The SS finally leave us in peace. They are out of sight. Only the sentry in the tower can hear us and is probably becoming annoyed and may report us. Yet the song wells up and the full vitality, the stubborn power of the Jewish nation, breaks through. French and Greek, Serbian and Russian songs are sung, most are incomprehensible, but everyone knows their meaning: 'Il faut se tenir.'[11] They will not get the better of us. Then, at the end, the Greek national anthem resounds and after that ... Hebrew, *Ha-Tikvah*.[12]

No one had announced it, and naturally they are not Zionists. Perhaps they hardly know what it is. Nevertheless, they all join in – in the only language they have all learnt (?), knowing that whatever

---

[11] One must keep one's spirits up.   [12] The Hope. Anthem of the Zionist movement. Now also the Israeli national anthem.

may divide them, a common fate has brought them together, and that in spite of themselves, a common force lives within them to change this fate. They are not Zionists, but the song sounds too real and too spontaneous not to recognise how great and profound a respect they have for the idea of their own national system and national objective.

The women in the new camp have no camp dishes to eat off. They eat out of old tin cans. It is the end of the Third Reich.

17 August Yesterday there were parcels. For those who receive them parcels are a blessing. But if you are expecting a parcel – and which of us is not expecting a parcel? – and you do not receive it, the parcel distribution serves only to depress you and to remind you again of the full extent of your wretchedness. It is not even the food that you are yearning for and that has passed you by again. How welcome would be an ounce of butter, a couple of spoonfuls of sugar, a packet of oatmeal, an apple or a couple of cigarettes! Given the total inadequacy, the monotony or tastelessness of the food here, just for once you would get close to feeling sated, for one day your stomach would function more normally again, your saliva would not keep sticking in your throat and give you a sour and irritating cough. That is exactly how it would all be, but it is not the most important. The most important is the greeting from living people, loved ones who are thinking of you. And when week after week, month after month, you do not receive it, your worries increase and you begin to torment yourself with memories. Where are the children? How are they? Why is there never, *never* a word from them, a greeting from them, a parcel? Where are they now? Are they still alive? When you lie on your bunk at night it robs you of your sleep, where are the children sleeping now?

I have a nine-year-old daughter. Have the Germans, those guardians of European culture, locked her away, taken her to Poland? Quite a few young children were deported by themselves. Here in BB (Bergen-Belsen), too, there are young children all alone.

Your entire former life unfolds before you again then. You see your house, the streets where you once lived, the park where you used to play as a child. How did all this come about? And why, oh why? You think of your friends, what are they doing now? Of brothers and sisters in Poland. Where can they be?

When you receive a parcel, you receive a little comfort, a little hope. When you do not receive a parcel, the bile rises in your throat.

Now, there has also been no news in the past few days. We know literally nothing any more. Apparently, the women who arrived in the adjoining camp have come from Poland. At least, that is what most people assume. They are reported to be saying that everything is going well, that Warsaw no longer exists but has gone up in flames, and that the Americans have landed in Toulon. Everyone now asks everyone else: have the Americans landed in Toulon? Everyone shrugs his shoulders. Who knows?

In the camp to the left of ours seventeen hundred Hungarian Jews have been accommodated. Barbed wire separates us. As a matter of fact, barbed wire seems to be a Germanic predilection. Wherever you stand or go there is barbed wire. All high-grade stuff: good quality, rust-free. With long, thickly planted barbs. Horizontal and vertical barbed wire. Perhaps the ancient Germans used to have barbed beards. The macaroni of the Third Reich.

According to reports a transport of three hundred Hungarian Jews will shortly be leaving for Switzerland. They had promised us Austausch[13] and we have been waiting for it since January, that is more than seven months ago. At the end of April they selected a group of two hundred and fifty people who were taken to another hut and were destined for exchange. We were among them. We waited there for six weeks, each day looking forward to our deliverance. The treatment there was better than here. We were not required to work there. Once a day the SS would arrive for roll-call. After five minutes they would leave again. Without cursing, without shouting.

After six weeks the commandant arrived with a couple of *Schar-*

---

[13] Exchange.

*führer*s to give us instructions for the journey. A list was read out. We had been dropped. The others could leave. Together with our luggage we were sent back to the hell again. I shall never forget the tension as the list was called off. To complete the effect the Americans appeared in the sky and the 'Fliegeralarm'[14] order was given. The reading was suspended. After its resumption, the list was drawn up. On completion, it emerged that a few were unable to leave because of illness or because they did not want to be parted from their relatives who were remaining behind. Who will take their place?

Again we are not among them. I had given up Westerbork,[15] the protection of Barneveld[16] – for nothing.

I know all too well what postponement means. Camp – slavery – hunger – brutal treatment – continuous humiliation – roll-call – the SS. Being cut off from all news. Captivity. Wretchedness fills us to the point of nausea. It means spending another winter here – illness, perhaps death, and what a death!

On the morning of departure of the chosen ones, when all the luggage was packed and already taken outside, the message came: the journey had been postponed. Once again a period of waiting begins. Again staring out anxiously from day to day, from week to week.

A new transport is arriving. British Jews from North Africa. Almost natives. The hut has to be cleared. The chosen ones, too, are being rejected again. Back to the camp – roll-call – work – humiliation – slavery – work – SS. Abuse and ranting.

A few die. A few more drop out again. We are promised the first vacant places. Then when it comes to a new selection, others get them.

---

[14] Air-raid alert.   [15] Internment camp in the north-east of Holland to which most Dutch Jews were brought before being deported to the east.

[16] Some 640 people, mostly intellectuals and their families, had obtained (temporary) exemption from deportation. They were interned in a country house (De Schaffelaar) in Barneveld and a villa (De Biezen) in Ede; both towns situated between Amersfoort and Arnhem. On 29 September 1944, the internees of these two 'camps' were given half an hour's notice to prepare themselves for transfer to Westerbork. Twenty-two younger members managed to escape. (Dr J. Presser, *Ondergang*, Staatsvitgeverij, The Hague 1965.)

A group of Jews is leaving for Palestine, most of whom have no interest in Palestine, nor want to have any interest in it. They use the exchange to escape from the misery. Once they are out of the misery they will start abusing the Zionists again, in so far as they are not already doing that *now*. Moreover, most of those who are leaving are completely useless. Aged, sick, handicapped. A band of near corpses is being exchanged.

We may stay behind and watch all our hopes go up in smoke. A hope borne since childhood – for forty years. For us there remains the misery, the roll-call, the labour, the humiliation, and the SS. And for how long still? For how long?

Now, a second transport, the Hungarians, recently arrived, are also leaving before us. Our response is: hold on. On what grounds might we have a better claim than other Jews?

18 August Last night I watched a new transport of Polish women arrive. It was a strangely mild August evening whose infinite beauty penetrates even to here. For although they have robbed us of the world, they have not succeeded with the sky. The clouds and the moon remain our witnesses. Oh, if only they could speak! But they cannot speak. They remain silent and embody the silence as it were. That silence which is full of mysteries, of whisperings of the past, filled with an endless melancholy that evokes an almost intolerable longing. The depths of sorrow become fathomless.

In this silence the Polish women file past. This, too, takes place without any sound. It is as if shadows are passing by, as if a film is being projected with the sound turned off. Not a word is spoken. Not a sound is heard. Their feet shuffle silently along the ground. If you look more closely you will notice that a significant number of them are walking barefoot. If ever a film is made of this period and the director wants to capture the effect of the infinite wretchedness of evacuation, let him revert to the silent film. Turn the music off too. Show only their eyes. Because not only are there no words with which to convey the misery of the dispossessed, no other sound is capable of it either – silence, silence, a bewildering silence.

A woman collapses in front of us. No shouting, no sob, no sigh. Several others bend over her. Not a word is spoken. No questions, no answers. People tug and pull at the collapsed woman. Then suddenly the raucous voice of the SS screeches through the air: 'Auf, auf. Marsch, marsch. Schnell, schnell.'[17] They lift her up, the funeral procession continues on its way. Women, children, one or two pushing a pram. Many carry a bag on their back. There is a child among them holding a dog on the end of a piece of rope.

We, dispossessed Jews, look on. Women from Warsaw file past in the silent evening ... Europe 1944. 'Alle Männer raus!'[18] Extra roll-call ...

The last few days have been stifling hot. I do not understand anything about the food here. Some of it can hardly be called food fit for human consumption. They feed us on cabbage leaves. As a result half the camp has diarrhoea. Some of the food is excellent. Many a person in Holland would envy us our evening porridge. We have diarrhoea, we shrug our shoulders. We just carry on eating. When you have diarrhoea, there is not a single remedy. When you have less than 39.5° fever, you just turn up for roll-call. During the night you need to get up five or six times. Naturally there is no light in the huts; it would shine out. One can hardly find the toilet in the dark. A queue of four or five people has formed. The floor, the walls, are indescribably filthy.

The camp is full to bursting now. Yet still more people keep arriving. Our bunks are three-tiered now. The atmosphere is stifling in this heat. Even so ... after two days you get used to that too.

The Polish women are living in tents on straw, without mattresses. They have no eating utensils. We were asked if we would relinquish some of ours. No one responded.

It is swarming with fleas now. Lice, too, have arrived on the scene. But we? We think of the Polish women and feel profoundly contented. We are living in palaces.

---

[17] Up, up. March, march. Quickly, quickly.
[18] All men outside!

19 August It has turned hot now. A burning, searing, scorching heat. By way of a surprise, we were given mussels today. The SS are probably having peaches and melon. All summer we have not seen a single flower, fruit or berry. Some of the mussels are tainted, but even in the height of summer hungry people do not throw rotting mussels away. My left-hand neighbour is sitting on his bunk together with his son making a kind of mussel pâté. As I clamber onto my bunk to do some writing, a stench like fish rotting in a sewer wafts up to me. By way of compensation, I have on my right a direct view of the toilet which during the day may be used only by the sick, and is therefore frequented constantly by the dysentery patients. My bed itself is a battlefield for fleas. Entire armies of them attack us at night and rob us of our sleep, zealously supported by the lice cavalry. By day, the camp is merciless. No shade anywhere. A thick cloud of dust hangs between the huts, chokes one's throat and coats everything with a grey layer.

At half past ten the Jews with South and Central American papers had to present themselves. Officials from Berlin had arrived who read out some names. Such ceremonies always portend the composition of a transport. When, where to, who? No one tells us anything. We are objects, merchandise, to whom nothing is told, therefore, and who are not asked anything either. Just wait and see how they will dispose of your life.

In every country that it marched into in its clumsy boots the Third Reich immediately began to carry out the most sacred item of its manifesto: the extermination of the Jews.[19] As far as we know it happened in more or less the same way throughout Western Europe. In Eastern Europe they took the easy way. There they slaughtered the Jews. *Sans phrase.*[20] In Western Europe they did make exceptions. The exceptions included the establishment of a Jewish intermediary

---

[19] (Author's note): Subsequently it appeared that what follows is not quite correct. As nothing in the diary is being altered, inaccuracies are not being corrected either. It contains what was believed in the camp, rightly or wrongly.

[20] Without exception. (Possibly an allusion to '*La mort sans phrase*', attributed to Sieyès in the National Convention (1792–95) when (on 17 January 1793) it was about to vote on the sentence to be imposed on Louis XVI.)

organ. In Holland it was called De Joodse Raad voor Amsterdam.[21]

What was the purpose of such bodies? Naturally, they imagined all sorts of things. Probably they lived under the illusion that with clever manoeuvring they could save something or, as it was called: 'could prevent worse', or could delay the measures being put into effect. Once history had run its full course we knew the truth. The Jewish Councils were nothing more than burial societies, considered essential by the Third Reich for burying the Jewish communities that were doomed to die or had already been murdered. Executive organs, therefore, of planned or completed policies. As such, the Jewish Councils fulfilled their tasks to perfection. They made but one mistake: they imagined the undertaker could come to a compromise with death. Nothing lies further from the truth. Death is relentless, merciless. All that an undertaker can do is bury, and that can be organised better or worse. In Holland the organisation was beyond all praise. It was a real pleasure to be buried by the Jewish Council. Evacuation from the province to Amsterdam or removal to the ghetto, or a repose in Westerbork was – special circumstances aside – considered an excursion. That should not be thought of lightly! Burial is a necessity and an undertaker a useful creature. He must just know his place, and above all he must not assume the role of 'leader' of mankind. The Jewish Councils did not always and everywhere know their place, and sometimes overestimated their ability and importance.

In Bergen-Belsen, as in every Jewish camp, we also have such a Jewish council. Here it is called *Ältestenrat*. It, too, is primarily the executor of decisions made by the Germans. Members of the *Rat*[22] must dance to the tune of the Third Reich more than others. At the head of the *Ältestenrat* is the *Judenälteste*.[23] He is appointed and dismissed by the commandant. Consistent with the principles of leadership, the other members of the *Rat* are likewise not elected by the internees but appointed by the commandant on the recommendation of the *Judenälteste*. The *Judenälteste* here is a Greek, a strongly

---

[21] The Jewish Council for Amsterdam.   [22] Council.   [23] Senior Jew.

built fair-haired man who – unlike the other internees – has not lost an ounce of his former weight despite a really incredibly hard working day trotting almost non-stop behind every SS man (*Rotten-*, *Schar-* or *Sturmführer*)[24] who at any given moment may want to unburden himself of whatever is on his mind. The origin of this situation is quite simple. The *Judenälteste* receives three times as much to eat as anyone else and is proud of it. The commandant had promised it to him, and not only to him, but also to his family. Moreover, the *Judenälteste* has quite a few other sources of income of which he can be less proud. This has earned him the reputation of being 'corrupt', but I do not think he is given his dues with this qualification.

For our *Judenälteste* is not so much corrupt, as a kind of robber chief. We know that throughout the ages certain types exist who never vary inwardly and know only how to adapt themselves outwardly to the changing circumstances. One of these types is the robber chief from the heroic epic. In modern society one encounters him in numerous places that he manages to infiltrate and exercise his influence in for a shorter or longer period. Well-paid positions are often filled by men who differ not in the slightest psychologically from the earlier robber chief. Politics is a very popular hunting ground for the robber chief, which largely explains the surprisingly rapid diffusion of Fascist and National Socialist ideas. The robber chief is a much sought after, well-paid advertising agent. In short, wherever what is required is not so much ability as the ability to pretend having it, wherever impudence, adroitness and the use of elbows can help to achieve the objective.

21 August It is still sweltering. Fire is falling out of the sky. All day there is no shade to be found anywhere here. In the crammed huts, where 350 people are crowded together in three-tier bunks (instead of 150 in two-tier bunks, for which they were intended), it is so

---

[24] *Rottenführer* – SS lance-corporal; *Scharführer* – SS lance-sergeant; *Sturmführer* – SS lieutenant.

stifling that we can hardly sleep at night! Diarrhoea and other intestinal and gastric complaints are spreading ever wider. Exhaustion is becoming more and more prevalent although the work is decreasing and the work groups are getting smaller. Discipline is becoming noticeably more relaxed. Last night, when everyone was eating, there was suddenly a general roll-call. It was half past six. The working parties were returning. Again some tension. Two people were sent to a concentration camp by order of the *Reichssicherungshauptstellen*[25] in Berlin. They had stolen potatoes from the warehouse. The impression made by such an announcement is profound but of short duration. With the prospect of a rapid end one immediately gets over such things.

Only rarely have we had heat, blazing heat and extra roll-call. Yesterday, first in the morning and then, when it did not tally, again in the afternoon. Then, by way of a surprise, as the saying goes, a third one in the evening. Taken together, the first two roll-calls lasted a good three hours. At roll-call this morning, a few of the children were noisy. An extra hour of standing in the blazing heat. Two thousand people, mostly women and children.

Again thousands of Polish women are passing by. Again that ominous silence. It is the middle of the day, it is blazing hot. The women – this time young, strongly built ones – are carrying heavy bundles. They seem not to be tired. Most of them are barefooted, but otherwise they are well dressed. It is rumoured that they are going to work on the land, and this has a semblance of truth. We stand watching. Some say: they plundered us bare. As far as the Jewish question is concerned, the Polish nation did indeed side all too eagerly with Germany. From time immemorial the Poles have been renowned and experienced pogrom initiators, the economic boycott against the Jews was popular in Poland. But anyone with a little more insight will feel his heart sink. This, then, is the result of more than a hundred years of social movement. Here before your eyes you can see how human labour is organised, and it strikes a

---

[25] The correct name in German is *Reichssicherheitshauptamt* – State Security HQ.

very bitter note to think that the proletariat went on strike against a cut in wages of a few pence yet accepts and remains silent about the loss of all its rights as labourers, as human beings. Indeed, would a similar loathsome, dishonourable slavery have been possible without the co-operation (and the spontaneous and enthusiastic co-operation) of the German proletariat?

As for us – a new catastrophe is hanging in the air. We have been told that if the *Bettenbau*[26] does not improve or if the huts are not orderly and spotlessly clean, entire huts will be deported. Next to roll-call, *Bettenbau* is the second most sacred relic of the German Reich: a means *par excellence* with which to badger and torment. The shattering effect of such an announcement is impossible to imagine. Deportation from huts means separation of husbands and wives, perhaps even of women and children. The Polish women, too, are separated from their children. The immense emotional, but also material, misery of such a parting needs no explaining. Words can only weaken it. Good news reaches us from France. We understand the joy in the free world, but know that unless the Allies arrive very soon, we will be lost. Lost in sight of the harbour.

23 August Every day there is blazing heat. There is not enough water. Yesterday I had to wash myself at night, in the dark. In the daytime the taps are dry. One or two give a trickle. And the wash-rooms that do have water are crammed. In 21–22 (hut numbers) the washroom, equipped for at most three hundred people, is now being used by eighteen hundred women. The SS say they know all about the things requiring attention in the camp, but are at a loss to know what to do about it. They advise absolute cleanliness! The Third Reich is afraid of infectious diseases. How are they meant to be held at bay then? It is swarming with flies here.

Today more transports of Polish women arrived, this time without any luggage, without hats or coats. Most of them are shaven bald. Unlike the other transports, they walk in rows of five, so beloved by

---

[26] Bed making.

the SS, and are clad in uniform dresses. Each time there is one who carries a bucket.

We are given tinned beetroot. Apparently the Third Reich needs tins for the Polish women. They also give us roe and minced fish. How we are meant to poach or fry them remains a problem for now. We will probably have to eat them raw then. It is all paid for with our own money held by the canteen.

There were rumours about the fall of Paris yesterday. The mood is more hopeful than ever. We know nothing for certain, but we do know that world history has taken a decisive turn. The Third Reich is humbug.

My neighbour has high fever again. It is remarkable how young people sometimes have much less resistance.

24 August The Polish women who arrived yesterday are said to be Jews from around Auschwitz. In any case, they are certainly workers. It is also said that behind the Russian camp is a Jewish camp with eighteen hundred Jews. No sooner has it been said than it is corrected again. There are eight thousand Jews. And this, too, is amended again. The entire Lüneburger Heide is strewn with Jewish camps. There could be hundreds of thousands. Who knows?

I spoke of 'it', but even in Westerbork people did not speak of 'it'. With the self-mockery that is characteristic of the Jews, one speaks of the IPA, which stands for Jüdische Presse Agentur.[27] Obviously, the air is constantly filled with rumours. People then say: 'the IPA says ...' and everyone listens willingly. One then asks: 'is it truth or is it IPA?' The standard reply is: 'I obtained it from reliable sources.' Naturally the IPA carries on then. When the Greeks send a news item into the world, it is called Gripa, and when a Pole does it: Pipa. The IPA is never believed but always listened to. The need for news is so great that people even want news which they know to be unreliable. To give the matter some foundation, it is said that in the end the IPA nevertheless always proves to be right, but that is

---

[27] Jewish Press Agency.

the biggest IPA of all. Every day the IPA makes guesses and sometimes it guesses correctly. The inventiveness of prisoners completely
cut off from the outside world is astounding. The following riddle
is set for later generations: what is the Hebrew translation of
Wahrheit und Dichtung?[28] Answer: Emeth we ipa (*Emeth* = truth, *we*
means and).

The food is getting worse and worse. Today it is abominable. A
mishmash of red cabbage, carrots, turnips, onions and a few potatoes
boiled in water, without fat, of course, and almost no meat. It tastes
revolting. On the other hand, we are given all sorts of supplementary
food, although of doubtful quality: hard roe, soft roe and beetroot.
Only the beetroot is delicious. The weather continues to be very hot.
We have now reached the point where, for the sake of a little water,
minor scuffles take place in the washrooms. Such things are then
adjudicated by our court.

A most remarkable institution exists here: we have an autonomous
judiciary. Formally, the matter is as follows: consistent with the
principles of leadership, the *Judenälteste* is judge, and empowered to
hand out punishment. Apart from the SS, of course, who can intervene and punish at all times and in every matter, but hardly ever do
so where it concerns relations within the camp. To this extent,
therefore, there is a limited degree of independence here. Well now,
the *Ältestenrat* has called into being an advisory body to advise the
Judenälteste in all punishable matters. The *Judenälteste* is wise enough
strictly to follow its advice, and as the body in question, called the
Rechtskommission,[29] consists of absolutely scrupulous individuals, and
is led by lawyers with many years of experience who fulfil their task
with the utmost gravity and care, the judicial commission has
managed to earn much authority for itself. Anyhow, it is a body
whose objectivity and integrity is hardly held in doubt.

The *Rechtskommission* deals with the most diverse matters, of a
criminal as well as a civil nature, and the problems it faces are more
difficult, and for the lives of those who are brought before it, of

---

[28] Fact and fiction.   [29] Judicial commission.

greater importance, than even the most experienced lawyer will have experienced. I myself am a founding member of the commission and have therefore been judge. Originally, I was its secretary and chairman, but lately I have been the *Judenälteste's Sachwalter*[30] in judicial matters and am responsible, therefore, for the entire judicial organisation.

What did we do? First, and in my view most importantly, we drew up a set of principles; the judicial commission and all its branches had to uphold *absolute* propriety and integrity for itself and its members, under all circumstances. No one was allowed to deviate in the slightest to right or to left, under penalty of instant dismissal. We set out with the idea that it was of the utmost importance for the camp that at least somewhere justice and justice alone should be sought in a *practical way*, and that justice and nothing but justice should be administered, impartially and without any self-interest. To assist the judicial commission we formed an investigation team, consisting of six or seven people, to whom exactly the same principles applied.

A tremendous number of antisocial acts occur in a camp such as this, some more and some less serious, yet acts which in their totality can undermine the life and health of numerous camp inhabitants. There can be no doubt, therefore, that we are dealing here with a matter of public danger.

The first to come to mind is theft, a crime which until recently was the order of the day here, and still occurs. Theft of bread, butter, jam, cheese and other foodstuffs in particular was – and is – a veritable curse. Besides, the camp is constantly brought to a state of commotion through the theft of clothing and similar items.

The true significance of theft here should be clearly borne in mind. In normal society it is generally the poor who steal from the rich, someone who needs something from someone who can replace what has been stolen. Here, though – apart from the meagre reserves that some may possess – we are all equally poor, in the sense that we

---

[30] Adviser.

are all dependent on what we are given. And as this means a *minimum* to survive on, indeed too little to live on, theft, particularly of bread or butter, is an attempt on the victim's life! We desperately need all the calories we are given, and if we do not get them, any chance of surviving this ordeal is lost. The thief's excuse of having stolen because he was hungry does not exist here. The victim is just as hungry as he is. Besides, people steal not only from hunger, but also – and not least – so that bread may be traded for cigarettes. Those who are addicted to smoking seem not to eschew any means by which they might procure cigarettes for themselves, not even theft, not even the most cowardly theft: taking bread from children. And if they can procure that bread only through burglary, they will surmount the final scruple, get up in the dead of night, sneak towards a cupboard or suitcase, and break it open. Prior to that, they will have spied on the owner to discover how much bread he has stored away.

All these kinds of thefts are perpetrated by men and women of all ages, from every level of society. Hunger or a craving for cigarettes seizes its slaves without respect of persons. In the end, a kind of general depravity in circumstances such as ours seems unavoidable for numerous people who in normal circumstances would never have resorted to even the slightest dishonesty. Psychological and moral decline, indeed ruination, perplexes us anew each time.

Accordingly, I have seen labourers as well as former big capitalists and businessmen of stature steal. Once, a chief clerk of one of the largest banks was caught cutting slices from a fellow prisoner's bread. A woman of culture, taste and charm had no scruples about getting up in the night to steal butter from the cupboards. Another, whose husband had once managed a major company, had pinched jam from a baby's cot. A third, from a well-known and respected social environment, had searched the beds, for which she had the opportunity as hut nurse, and had taken sugar from bags and jars. A businessman, the manager of a world-famous company, had stolen three rations of bread from one of his acquaintances. On the day of his father's cremation, the son of a very well-known Amsterdammer had appropriated a suitcase with foodstuffs and cigarettes belonging to his best friend, who had taken him into his confidence.

Age, too, made no difference. A boy of sixteen proved to be an accomplished burglar; a man approaching seventy stole whatever he could lay his hands on.

26 August The Polish women in the tent camp next to ours are quite often replaced, and whenever that happens the Jews must clean out the stable. I am referring here to an old and tattered tent, right next to our camp, initially erected as a storeroom for old shoes that we had to cut apart but which – now that the work has almost come to an end – has been converted into a stable for Polish women. The conversion consisted of placing wood shavings on the floor. The rest is 'entrusted to the care of the public', as we once used to read on the immaculate signs that the distinguished City Fathers had placed in the well cared for little parks of the neatly painted little towns. Merciful heaven, when I think of such things as I sit here writing on top of my three-tier bed directly under the roof in a stifling heat, amidst all kinds of worn-out men suffering from diarrhoea and the stench of a toilet wafting up to my nose, I have to say how good, how civil, how small-minded we used to be. Oh, oh, oh, such a tent with Polish women. And oh, oh, oh, a working party of Jews who must clean out such a tent. Not enough men had reported for work yesterday. There is other work, too, quite a few were sick, and then there are always slackers, of course. Consequently, older men between fifty-five and sixty-five also had to go. Naturally, apart from the general exhaustion that we are all struggling with, some of them were also ill. Men who were suffering from a hernia, from angina pectoris, from diabetes, in short, from every illness known about to the point of boredom from behind the screens of everyday life. Clearly, such men are not the most suitable for mucking out a tattered tent that had been occupied by a thousand Polish women. Especially not at the hottest time of the day, in a heat to make you faint even if you were not working, and in a dust that robs you of your breath. What does the Third Reich do in such circumstances?

It seizes a truncheon and a length of rubber and commences to beat. Yesterday three of these lordships did what the Third Reich is wont to do. They indulged themselves.

Apart from that, though, ill-treatment is administered in moderation here. Now and then a few youths are given a few lashes with a whip, beatings that cause a few bloody scratches and bumps, but that is where it ends. With utmost concern we wonder what our people in Poland might be experiencing. All too often we see here how the *Häftlinge* are beaten by their *Kapos*. Poor men!

When we see that, it gives us a further reason not to complain. We realise once more then what a remarkable phenomenon it is that one bears one's undeniably intolerable fate because another's fate is even more intolerable. Is this perhaps why Hitler needs to persecute the Jews? Is he saying to disgruntled nations: 'Look at the Jews, they have it far worse'? In any case, I have repeatedly heard non-Jews, who had every reason to complain, say: 'Anyway, I am glad that at least I am not a Jew.' No matter how much empathy and compassion we may have, other people's suffering always brings us solace. And although we do whatever possible to moderate it, we seem unable to do without it. For if it is not you, poor brother, who is being tormented, it will be me, and if Moses and Abraham are not being tortured, it will be the turn of John and Peter and Charles. Poor Moses, poor Abraham. Government may not always be aimed at preventing or alleviating suffering. Government may very well mean sharing out suffering, and it may be in the interest of the governing powers if it is not done entirely fairly. Now, since time immemorial you people have been perfectly suited to receive the largest share.

Yesterday the IPA spoke of revolution in Romania and the murder of Antonescu.[31] We feel it is true, but are not certain. Today the IPA joyfully announces that a large transport of Palestine candidates will be leaving shortly. People are very happy. As for me, I am extremely worried. I don't trust such announcements. They do indeed point to a transport ... but not to Palestine.

---

[31] Romanian wartime dictator. Sided with Hitler against the USSR in 1941. Was arrested in 1944 and executed.

27 August It is raining. After weeks and weeks of merciless heat, culminating yesterday in a veritable haze of flames that had descended to earth, it suddenly became cooler this morning. Clouds appeared in the sky, first light ones with bright white heads, hazy and fine, then grey and black, large ponderous colossi that impudently slid over the others. But we did not want to believe yet that the alleviating water was about to fall. It did indeed take rather a long time, but now it has rumbled and rolled in the heavens, one bolt of lightning after another shot through the sky and it began to rain. It poured and pelted, abundantly and generously, freely and amply, as if it no longer mattered in the least how much water was being yielded from above. We had longed for a little and received in abundance, more and more, too much, a blessing of water, which did not stop, which engulfed us. The ears of corn will probably be bent now with the weight of the water; disgruntled, the reapers will be saying: 'All or nothing' ... oh the ears of corn, oh the reapers ... how long is it since we last saw them ...

Do you know what I would like to see sometimes? An ordinary person – just a person, walking in the street. I do not need a cinema or a museum. I wish I could look out of the window of a modest house in the Dapperstraat or in the Jan Pieter Heyestraat,[32] such an ordinary commonplace street dating from the end of the last century. That century which, in contrast to our own, as we diligently learned at school, had so little 'social' awareness. Let me stick to my rain though. Although the sun is shining again, it has got cooler. No doubt there will be pressure in the water mains again. In the mornings we will be able to wash ourselves again, and perhaps soon we will also be given a shower again. The flush of the toilets will also work again so that I will no longer have to sit in the stench here on my bed. We will certainly be much happier.

On the other hand, if it continues to rain, what will I do with my legs? You do not get my drift, do you? That is because you do not know the meaning of space. You have a few cubic metres to yourself.

---

[32] Names of ordinary streets in Amsterdam.

You call it a 'room'. In that room you have placed some objects, called chairs and tables, and when you want to eat, you sit yourself at a table on a chair, and in such a way that every person in the room has a chair, and in front of him on the table enough space for his plate and a piece of bread. There are even chairs to spare in the room. When it rains, though ... where and how must I eat then? When the sun shines, we sit outdoors. Outdoors, there are tables, benches and stools. True, there is not enough room for everyone at once, but one can wait, or rather, can let another wait. When it rains, though, we are unable to sit outdoors. Indoors it is like a Jewish warehouse;[33] the coffins in which we sleep are piled three high, with only twenty centimetres between them.

So where must we eat then? We eat together, my wife and I. We sit on her bunk. Below us is a Greek tailor with his wife and child. Fortunately, there is no one above us yet. In my wife's hut the beds are still only two-tiered. Hence the Greek tailor together with his wife and child are able to sit below us, because there is adequate space between the first and second bunks.

If the beds are three-tiered, the legs of the beds have been shortened. The distance between the first two tiers is then at most fifty centimetres, so that one can sit only on the top bunk. If you are lucky, there may even be a further ten centimetres or so of space between your head and the rafters.

But in either case the problem is always one's legs. In our case, the Greek tailor and his wife are not at all pleased that we clamber on top to eat and sit there. The roads are muddy and dirty, and my shoes are like the road! And it is not pleasant to see the shoes of a fellow citizen dangling above your meagre soup, not once, but day after day, week after week, month after month, as they did last winter.

The worthy pastor will say people ought to love one another. But the worthy pastor has a void which he calls a room, *his* room, and he has a chair, *his* chair, and a table, *his* table. I should like to know

---

[33] Where everything is arranged higgledy-piggledy.

what his love for mankind would be like if every morning, every afternoon and every evening my legs were to dangle above his slice of bread, his soup, his gravy, meat, vegetables, potatoes – and dessert. We long for some space. My Greek tailor does protest occasionally, but I think to myself: my dear man, you are an angel. And I am able to think it all the more, because I cannot understand the curses he undoubtedly casts my way.

Are we perhaps not angels here? People complain bitterly about each other. But could it be any different?

They say man is a social animal. Maybe he does live in tribes, but when he is 'free', he nevertheless does not eat communally. Yet even if he does do that, at least he sleeps alone. Certainly, man is a social animal. What he needs, though, is a den or a cave, where he can be alone with his wife and clasp her to his breast.

Man needs bodily warmth. A child needs the hand of its mother, and a man the body of his wife, and the wife the embrace of her husband, his arms, his caresses. Oh, oh, my God, the millions of widows in this world, after the war – lonely in their beds. There is but one cure for sorrow: bodily warmth. When she is crying from loneliness, take her in your arms and kiss her.

Why do we always talk about God, in Whom we should place our trust? God helps only when we help Him. He lives inside us and has given us of His great warmth. Our life is nothing less than His life, and whenever someone is groaning in agony, take from the life that is inside you and give. That is why people marry. It is not good that man should be alone. That is why he looks for a few cubic metres of space, a cave, a den or a room, and places a bed in it, his bed, and he shares his bed and he shares his warmth. Body against body, that is how man sleeps and how he lives. In this seclusion lies his greatest intimacy.

As for us, us? They call this a community. But anyone who does not have a bedroom, a bed and a wife, has no community. Loneliness cries out from us.

Four thousand lonely people, that is our community. Judge them not but forgive them nothing.

When they rob, insult, hurt and hate each other, when they can no longer suffer each other, it is the agony screaming out from them. They are alone. Their parents are dying in Poland and their children are slaves and being tortured; they do not weep, and at night there is no breast on which to seek a little comfort.

28 August When you wake up you cannot recount the dream that disturbed your sleep, however hard you try. All you remember are a few details, but the oppressive feeling that overcame you, the wild fear that took away your breath, has disappeared and become a vague memory. It is the same with the horrors we experience here. Once this period is over, we will have forgotten them, that is to say, we will remember only that they once existed, like a sharp pain that has passed. Indeed, even now, with the prospect of peace, the days we have lived through already begin to resemble a storm that has abated. Our hearts are leaping on account of the coming liberation feast, and a certain calm is descending into the atmosphere – turbid though that may be. A trifle is sufficient to set our minds at rest, and today there was such a trifle: during roll-call they did not count. For the first time in eight months. The sacred temple service has been neglected, and naturally, we are immediately ready to conclude from this that the priests are busy repudiating their God. Have the SS lost their appetite for the war? Do they no longer believe in victory? Is roll-call no longer worth the effort?

There are plenty of signs to believe the opposite. Yesterday a large group was punished with no less than four days' 'Brotentzug'.[34] Once there is peace we will no longer remember what it meant. For the moment we know it means famine, that accursed unappeasable hollow feeling in the stomach, a throat full of saliva that cannot be swallowed, pressure around one's head, dizziness, legs that feel weak, recurring lapses of memory as if flying through impenetrable fog banks.

The group had not worked hard enough; 'der Rote Müller', a sort

---

[34] Withholding of bread.

of dressed up piglet, lazy as a pig on a hot day, fat and puffed up, with a red mouth and greenish slits for eyes, a cigar stump permanently stuck between a pair of clinging jellyfish lips, the *Rote* Müller felt that not enough work had been done. Four days' *Brotentzug* for a group of forty men ...

Rau, an unsavoury creep with a crippled hand, the *Arbeitsdienstführer*,[35] even though such men are normally of a higher military rank than he is – just as there are secret cellars and passages in the castle of the robber baron – Rau, that spy among spies, that persecutor of persecutors, that feared sneak, this time Rau has surpassed even the dull Müller. He has imposed two days' *Brotentzug* – on everyone who arrived late for roll-call.

There had been an air-raid alert. The working parties, dead beat, had been unable to report for duty and had fallen asleep, each on the first bed he could find. After the all-clear had been given, they were woken up and summoned for duty – and in Mr Rau's opinion, had arrived too late. Not that anyone notices when the air-raid alert has ended. A signal of sorts is given, but is inaudible in the camp. Nor does anyone know how soon after the all-clear is given roll-call is held. Mr Rau decides that with the full weight of his authority. Roll-call has started when *he* is present.

A group of boys runs through the camp shouting: 'Luftalarm abgelaufen, Luftalarm abgelaufen. Appell, antreten ... '[36]

Others repeat it. You get up, you arrive too late ... Two days without bread. Various people give you a slice, or lend you one, and that is how you struggle through the misery. A misery that is quite insurmountable when a couple of rations happen to have been stolen from you.

Finally, this morning the cleaning women from hut 13 were punished. The toilet had been dirty. However, there had been no water with which to wash it away, the flush was broken, there was no mop, no broom, and there were dozens of men with diarrhoea ...

---

[35] SS officer responsible for the direction of labour.
[36] All clear, all clear. Roll-call, line up ...

Rote Müller, though, is responsible for cleanliness, and *Rote* Müller punishes ...

29 August Though peace may indeed be approaching, our hunger is getting worse and worse. Imperceptibly, the food is getting less. Less butter, less curd, less jam. Whether it is due to this, or to something else, whether they are the last straws or our mounting impatience, or whether our nervousness is increasing because the war is nearing the Dutch frontiers again causing our homesickness to be revived, the fact is, we are feeling weaker and weaker – disease is on a frightening increase, the number of people who can barely move is growing, and discipline is also slackening.

The Germans have been punishing like madmen of late. It is pouring with *Brotentzug*. Two days, three days, four days. And all these punishments mean one disaster after another. Those who are punished include the sick, lung sufferers, bronchitis sufferers, particularly young, emaciated men. Naturally, the principle that a young man should be put to work before an older one is correct, but it has its limits. The young man, too, has limited strength, but against that, often unlimited hunger. And all too quickly people are ready with the demagogic complaint of: 'The old must work while the young do nothing.' Not even those young chaps can manage seven days a week. And some days! Officially, they work seventy-two hours, that is to say, six days of eleven hours each and Sundays from half past six till a quarter to twelve. Every day reveille at five. Duty roll-call at a quarter to six, work starts at half past six and continues till a quarter to twelve, fall in at half past twelve, finish at half past six. In reality, the working day is much longer. First of all there are groups that must work officially for unlimited periods, for example the kitchen group. They get up at three in the morning and usually return at about five or six in the afternoon, which means fourteen or fifteen hours a day. Sometimes even longer. An eighteen-hour working day is no exception. Not surprisingly, men who work in the kitchen return to the huts and throw themselves onto their bunks. If they are not too exhausted, they sleep like corpses. On the other hand, they are fed superbly and more than adequately. Despite their almost endless work they manage to keep going very well and have a full and healthy appearance. Work in the kitchen is much sought after, therefore.

Then there are all kinds of supplementary work, such as fetching the containers. That means getting up at four and making one's way to the gate at five to heave the 25- and 50-litre containers from the kitchen to the huts. In the evening, container duties often last till nine or even later, depending on the mood of the duty *Scharführer*. If he feels like finishing earlier, the relevant group is in luck, and if not, there is nothing for it but to blame your misfortune on your Jewish birth.

Besides supplementary work, there is also overtime. When one or more wagons of old shoes or old clothes arrive that need to be unloaded, when work has to be completed, when the commandant feels like it, you may be required to work non-stop from half past twelve in the afternoon till half past eight or half past nine at night. Moreover, this good fortune befalls not only the men, but also the women.

In fact, in the kitchen it is normal to work overtime, even on Sundays. However, you do get a free afternoon there occasionally, and by way of a bonus, a mug of soup. Moreover, the kitchen has yet another attraction. You can surreptitiously eat carrots or swedes there or – something very dangerous – steal them. There have been long debates about whether such stealing is socially acceptable. Some condemn it because it means stealing from the camp supplies. This was particularly so last winter with potatoes. In summer, potatoes are rarely stolen because the stoves are not lit, hence there are no means of boiling or roasting them.

Then there is also punishment duty, or something that amounts to the same thing, deprivation of rest. At any moment, the SS may be seized by a fit of madness and start punishing: standing against the fence. Dozens, sometimes hundreds of people at a time must stand against the fence from a quarter to twelve till half past twelve (which means an unbroken working day of more than twelve hours),

or from half past six till ... the *Scharführer* has had enough of it –
eight, nine, ten, or even eleven o'clock at night. People have stood
against the fence without a coat, while it got cold, and without food.
Naturally they collapsed with pneumonia followed by death. The SS
do not even grimace. They are satisfied! And why must you stand
against the fence? Because you had kept your hands in your pockets,
or not removed your cap.

The free Sunday afternoon offers a further opportunity for
punishment. They can withdraw it and do so with pleasure. One can
also make people work, and then preferably not till half past six, but
for one or two hours longer, or make people do drill. 'Antreten,
abtreten, Fünferreihen, im Gleichschritt Marsch.'[37] Such punishment is meted out for all kinds of trivia. Alleged late arrival for roll-
call, low productivity, alleged inadequate cleanliness, incorrect
'Bettenbau', et cetera.

In short, *usually* the working week is much longer than seventy-
two hours, at least, that is how it was last winter. Recently, a certain
lethargy in maintaining discipline has crept in, even among the SS.
They still hand out punishment in every direction, but there is not
enough work any longer. Or they themselves no longer feel like it.

What sort of work do we do? Mainly unstitching old shoes and
cutting out the usable pieces of leather. The work is indescribably
moronic and above all – as can be imagined – very dirty. When the
Scharführer in charge is asked what purpose it serves, his reply is:
'Wir Deutsche sind Habenixe und Ihr Juden sollt helfen durch Eure
Arbeit uns reich zu machen.'[38]

Naturally we take this lesson in German economics very much to
heart. We are blazing with zeal 'to make Germany rich' by unstitching shoes. An unrelenting and dogged struggle for productivity now
develops between the Jews and the *Scharführer*. Clearly, we must be
careful that we cannot be accused of sabotage. Because at the very
least, sabotage means KZ, and concentration camp means being

---

[37] Fall in, dismiss, form rows of five, march in step.
[38] We Germans are have-nots and you Jews will help us become rich through
your work.

tortured to death. At least *some* work has to be done, therefore. The question is only how much or how little.

Some people manage to do almost nothing. A kind of bookkeeping is kept of the quantity of shoes that are collected. The bookkeepers are Jews, but naturally, they can fiddle the figures only to a limited degree. The most ingenious methods are invented with which to fool the *Scharführer*. For example, when shoes are collected, a larger quantity is booked out, and in addition all or some of the shoes already collected are returned to the large pile. Then, when one of these *Scharführer* cannot imagine why there is no productivity and why the work is not getting less, the Jews, too, have a moment of fun again.

Others, though, find the art of idleness less attractive. There are some who just cannot sit still. The work – five, six, seven hours on end – is excruciatingly dull, but to be idle is far worse. We can talk to each other, but only to a very limited extent, and only as far as the *Scharführer* allows it, but about what? The education and interests of the company one finds oneself in are often very diverse. The main topic of conversation is food: the soup was thick, the soup was thin, Brandon found two pieces of meat in his soup, and Flesseman never receives any. The leader of hut so-and-so distributes unfairly, or does not ladle close enough to the bottom of the container. Friends get the thick, and others the liquid. The serving ladle is not full enough. How many potatoes did you lot have? Four small ones. We had one large and two small ones. Again less. Naturally the leader looks after himself first. In hut X they served a heaped spoonful of jam, in hut Y a level spoonful. Yes, but that was a tablespoon and the other a dessertspoon. Naturally every hut leader is discussed in turn, then every dishonesty that was or was not committed, that might be committed and that could be prevented ... That is the conversation, day in, day out, in the morning, in the afternoon, at 7.00 a.m., at 8.00 a.m., at 9.00 a.m. and still at six in the evening.

One must therefore try to form one's own circle, to have at least some kind of distraction, some standard. Sometimes it succeeds.

There is much philosophising, politicising, debating the jewels of Hebrew literature, translating the psalms from memory, or verses by Judah Halevi.[39] At such times we know very well what distinguishes us from the *Scharführer*. I will discuss it in a separate chapter.

30 August Apart from those who find it difficult not to work, there are others who work really diligently. Naturally the Germans do everything possible to boost productivity, both by force and by other means. Eventually they succeed now and then. As far as the former is concerned, they have at their disposal not only punishment but also the whip or the truncheon. The shoes must be carried to the workplaces from a nearby tent, while the material and waste must be carried away. It is done by means of stretchers which are carried by two people, and one of the pleasures of the SS is to flog the bearers. Once we have reached this point, true slave-driver scenes occur. All that one feels then is shame, not for ourselves, but for them.

More effective than the whip are cigarettes. Bonuses are distributed to those who work hardest. Of course, no respectable person accepts such a bonus, but eventually the temptation becomes too great. One should bear in mind that cigarettes mean 'money' here with which one can buy bread and food from others ... and those who have a wife and children, or a wife whose husband and children are starving ...

Real work – up to a point – is done by the *Vorarbeiter*[40] or the *Kapo*. That is the most shameful institution in the system of the SS, who are masters at creating schisms. The *Vorarbeiter* is appointed, and *must* carry out his job. He *must* demand a certain productivity, he *must* force people to work. He may use whatever means he likes thereby, especially beatings. Anyone who strikes back can count on KZ. In our camp, though, there were *never* beatings by Jewish *Kapo*s. Among the *Häftlinge*, on the other hand, it was the rule. The *Kapo*s proved to be worthy tormentors. Ours restrained themselves to the

---

[39] Eleventh-century Spanish Jewish poet and philosopher.
[40] Foreman.

utmost and at heart *never* sided with the Germans. Though from time to time they had to take action, but never in the form of betrayal. But even this was enough for repeated conflicts. The judicial commission had to deal with one or two cases where a camp inhabitant had revolted against the actions of a *Kapo*. Once, a *Kapo* had beaten someone, not to urge him on, but because he had felt insulted. The *Kapo* was found guilty. Naturally, the sentence was quite dangerous. It took the form of an amicable settlement in a civil procedure. By way of compensation, the *Kapo* had to forfeit five rations of bread. The sentence was approved and carried out and was only possible because public opinion had demanded it, unanimously and without exception. The other *Kapo*s were the first to support it.

One can point to all kinds of contrasts among the Jews. Towards the Germans there was complete and absolute solidarity. Nothing – unless it was absolutely unavoidable in the common interest – was ever reported. There were hardly any instances of a *Kapo* or other person trying to win favour with the SS at the expense of a fellow prisoner. With hindsight, this seems obvious. At the time, under the oppression of the regime, it attested to moral courage.

Because that was the worst of all: the oppression. Worse than the long working day and worse than punishment, worse than roll-call, was the endless oppression, the *constant* shouting, snarling, hounding, from early morning till late at night. Almost every day there would still be inspection after the working parties had finally returned and eaten their soup. Those who had not gone to bed yet but were still sitting up had to jump to attention, to listen to the roaring, the braying of the SS louts, learned through propaganda and training.

Once in a while they were drunk. In their own way they could be jovial then, and make some coarse remark or other. On these occasions there were always some who felt it their duty to laugh. Dignity is not always man's strongest quality.

Whenever working parties had to be formed, the Germans would go through the *Ältestenrat*. Nowhere else, of course, can corruption penetrate deeper, and it did indeed occur – although in this respect

I believe one should take great care not to exaggerate. The *Ältestenrat* earned its right to exist mainly through *this* task, where it performed an outstanding job. Whether and how someone was assigned work was naturally a matter of survival. The *Ältestenrat* managed to save hundreds of men and women from total annihilation, particularly later on, when total exhaustion was rapidly on the increase.

The *Ältestenrat* negotiated and formed working parties: Camp Sanitation, *Jugendbetreuung*,[41] and similar tasks. It was of the greatest importance that by these means hundreds of people were able to remain inside the camp and escape for a longer or shorter period the incessant persecution.

For some it did not work. Rabbis were a favourite quarry, especially because they usually sport a beard. A beard is like a red rag to a German bull. Apparently they had forgotten the beards of the Batavians and the Canninefates.[42] Did their lordships not know that Mr Gillette, too, had a Jewish grandmother?

The shoe working party had a long working day, but not heavy work. Outdoor work was far worse. The kitchen needed wood, for which tree stumps were used. How we worked last winter, sawing and chopping the stumps of fir and pine trees – in winter while it snowed, while it hailed, in the frost, eleven hours a day. In the mornings we would report for duty while it was still dark. Oh, that muster ground on a winter's morning still shrouded in a cold night mist. In the evenings we would return in the dark. Who were the 'we' in those days? There were men aged sixty and seventy, and even eighty! I remember a winter's day when a blind person had to join us who was kept standing helpless and alone in the snow for the entire day ... a fortnight later he no longer had to ... We dug sand, we dug trenches, we moved dunghills – and whatever we did, we were snapped at. We loaded and unloaded tree stumps – and were snapped at. The SS would stand watching. For the SS are first and foremost lazy, lazy as pigs. That is how they imagined the world: at

---

[41] Youth care.   [42] Ancient peoples who lived in the Rhine Delta and supplied soldiers to the Roman legions; now part of The Netherlands.

their feet, just as they had subjected us. And each morning we went on our way: how much longer? and returned: how much longer ... ? We had but one question and one desire ... One longing.

Yet nothing happened ... and we also knew nothing. We were alone, strangled by misery.

Once a week, usually on Wednesdays, they herd us to the bath house. We must fall in then in groups of a couple of hundred men, accompanied by the usual shouting and abuse, after which we are shut up in a large shed where we have to undress. Then we wait. A few hundred naked men, like a bunch of corpses. We see each other's humpbacks, crooked legs, sores and patches. Sixty men at a time are admitted to the shower room, where there are twelve to sixteen showers in parallel rows of four. There are no partitions. Four or five of us stand under one shower, push against each other and try to quarrel as little as possible. We manage remarkably well. Afterwards, a few minutes in which to dress, accompanied by shouting, abuse and, where necessary, blows. At no other time does one feel more strongly to have been reduced to the state of animals.

When the women shower, the *Scharführer* goes along too. No one is embarrassed.

For the past few days, though, we have been without water. This led their lordships to a new discovery. Showering at night when there is adequate water pressure. That is how we came to shower at night with roll-call at half past ten. We would get back at half past one. At 5.00 a.m. roll-call again. The last groups returned at 4.00 a.m. The following day the container carriers had to stand against the fence till ten in the evening. The *Scharführer* had been out of sorts. It was a beautiful night. The women laughed, shouted, and sang their many varied folk songs. The men philosophised. This nation *cannot* be broken.

The IPA says Danzig has fallen and, in the west, Liège. How much of it is true? Tomorrow is the Queen's birthday. What will happen in Holland? No one who has not been here will ever understand what it means to be homesick.

43

31 August The Queen's birthday. For as long as I have lived 31 August has been a public holiday. The courts would be in recess and the office closed. I can still remember the Rokin and Damrak[43] with the stalls close together, the paper garlands, the crowds of people dancing and singing, eating pickled cucumbers and ice cream, and the festivities petering out in the evening as the rain came drizzling down. That is how the holiday used to pass by. On 1 September the new year would begin, the winter. There would still be some fine days and we would still go mushroom picking in Gooi,[44] but that was going back, like paying a visit to grandfather, a courtesy towards a summer that had ended. Then there would be a few birthdays, it would be time to don warm clothes, a scarf ... how it has all changed now! What kind of life is it that we have fallen into? My wife has no shoes any longer. It is raining, and after only a few days the ground starts to get muddy. Mercifully someone gives her a pair of clogs. Though 'pair' is an exaggeration. Two left clogs, that is all. Perhaps we will be able to trade a tin of sardines for a pair of shoes. The sardines have probably been sent by the American Joint[45] in Portugal. But now that the lines of communication are broken there will probably be no more sardines either. We did not receive any parcels from Holland, we feel abandoned.

How much longer! The onset of autumn will bring new miseries. Will the Germans hold out much longer? What will they do with us? The most difficult days of our lives lie ahead.

But today is the Queen's birthday. We wished each other many happy returns, knowing what Orange used to mean to Holland and to us.

Liberty – stable relations. Justice, a certainty in our lives. When Orange fell, we lost the foundation to our existence.

Orange will return, but what happened to the historical cer-

---

[43] Names of streets in the centre of Amsterdam, leading off Dam Square.

[44] Heathland and wooded region situated between Amsterdam and Hilversum.

[45] The Joint Distribution Committee. An American Jewish philanthropic organisation (Abel J. Herzberg, *Kroniek der Jodenvervolging, 1940–1945*, Em. Querido's Uitgeverij, Amsterdam 1985, p. 305).

tainties, the unwavering belief in a constant evolution? Holland fell within four days. Three centuries collapsed and Germany remains an evil neighbour.

Will we be going to *Eretz Israel* (the land of Israel)? Will we find peace there? Will the Jewish Nation be able to live there? Come what may, today we are full of good wishes for Holland and for Orange. We have ample reason for it.

Soon I will be dealing with a new case. A man had bought from a widow an overcoat that used to belong to her deceased husband for ... twelve rations of bread. We shall forbid such a transaction. Twelve rations of bread is prohibitive and the woman does not need the coat. By rights she ought to give it to the W (Welfare), but it had been decided to recognise the right of succession. She will have to be satisfied with less bread now. I reckon four rations of bread to be amply sufficient.

Last night we tried a lady from Amsterdam who had stolen salt from her neighbour's bed. She had thought it was powder or sugar. Another woman had fraudulently appropriated a 38-cent shawl from the Bijenkorf.[46] Someone had left it behind in the toilet and when she saw it hanging there, she had pretended it was hers. She was found out.

The judges who sat with the presiding judge were the Chief Rabbi from Salonica and a lawyer from Montenegro. The bench needed a very long time to arrive at a verdict. The first woman received a 'strenger Verweis'[47] and the second was ordered to help for one evening with cleaning the toilets.

They were lucky. Dutch judges would have been much more severe. Nevertheless, those who were found guilty will rail at the 'German' Jews, or 'Jews' in general. I am certain that after the war 'Jews' will be much railed at, especially by Dutch Jews. Those who were found guilty will do this in particular, those who had failed in their duty, who had been lacking in community spirit. Naturally they will try to shift the blame onto others.

---

[46] 'The Beehive', a department store in Amsterdam.   [47] Severe reprimand.

There has indeed been a lack of community spirit. We have a magistrate here. Here is a sample of one week's verdicts.

For having made wooden sandals out of bedboards. This is an extremely dangerous offence. If it comes to the attention of the Germans, the likely result will be KZ because of sabotage, and collective punishment the least that could be expected. When a mattress was burnt recently (afterwards the allegation even proved to be false), the *entire* camp was punished with one day's bread stoppage. The day happened to be a Sunday. However, as bread is always distributed a day in advance except on Sundays, the entire camp, women, children, the sick, the elderly, in short the entire camp without exception, got no bread for twice twenty-four hours.

What should be done when something like that is discovered? A heavy sentence is unthinkable lest the SS should get to hear of it. In the case in question the culprits were a couple of boys aged about thirteen. The matter was reported to the *Jugendbetreuung* and settled with a thorough telling off.

Not turning up for work that had been assigned; in the case in question, cleaning beds. This, too, is a grave matter. If the work remains undone, collective punishment will follow. So the work must be carried out, though by someone other than the person to whom it had been assigned. Naturally the order had come from the Jews. Nobody would dare to ignore orders from the Germans. Eight days' bunker is the least that could be expected. What ought we to do, though? A severe reprimand, in the hope that it will not happen again.

Insulting the 'Lagerwache'. The 'Lagerwache' is a poor imitation of what in society is called 'the police'. It is a kind of orderly unit whose duties consist of forming a cordon when a new transport arrives, maintaining order when food is distributed, mounting guard during an air-raid alert to ensure no one leaves the huts, supervising the regular use of washrooms, et cetera. Naturally the LW reports every transgression, but most of what it reports deals with insults against itself. The LW, though, managed to make itself not particularly popular. Which is not surprising, because between ourselves, one of the main reasons for its creation was the need to get a few exhausted men exempted from work. We managed to persuade the Germans of the desirability of having our own police: their lordships fell for it, and for some time now a number of people have been wandering through the camp wearing a white armband bearing the initials LW. There is nothing these good men – merchants, doctors, lawyers – are less suited for than being coppers. Naturally they commit one tactical error after another. What maddens them is what maddens every Jew who has a job here. As officials they ought to have some power vested in them, but they have no power, and the public knows it, knows the official, and sees quite clearly that behind him there is nothing but a vacuum. The Jewish official suffers, and has always suffered, from a feeling of powerlessness. Not even with the best will in the world can he instil discipline. A discipline that is imperative – hence his shouting, and that shouting, from a sense of powerlessness, makes him grotesque.

Whoever can, mocks him. Whoever receives an order, tries to back out of it. Whoever gets snapped at, becomes abusive. Whoever becomes abusive, is reported. That is how we come to be trying a lady who had said: 'Go away, scoundrel,' and another, who managed to utter the word 'skunk'. It is much in vogue and very wrong to say: 'Watch it, there will be other times.' Such behaviour is called threatening with something like an internal Israeli day of reckoning. The wretched people, driven to their limits, must have at least someone on whom to vent their bitterness.

What does the magistrate do in all these cases? He talks to the people, gives them a dressing down. That has the desired effect. In general, people understand what is and what is not permissible, most offer their apologies, and there the matter rests. If it does not, or if it concerns a more serious matter, or if the offence is repeated, a portion of jam or curd is withheld. Do not be alarmed, this 'portion' is only a spoonful. It is nevertheless a lot in this monotonous society, and its loss is felt quite badly.

In these slanging matches, it is the different groups of Israelites in particular that manage to indulge themselves against each other.

Dutch Jews are naturally much better than German, not to mention Yugoslavian, Montenegran or other Balkan Jews. The natives from North Africa beat their breasts and loudly proclaim their British nationality. The French Jewesses (whose parents, moreover, had been freshly imported into Paris from Poland or Galicia – that is, if they were not born there themselves), exclaim that they understand only French. In this way, every Jew discovers another Jew against whom he can be an anti-Semite. Of course, the *Scharführer* kicks everyone, irrespective of his erstwhile passport. But no one believes the kick is meant expressly for him, and looks for an object to pass it on to.

The magistrate must act with tact, discretion and *jam-Entzug*[48] in these slanging matches. Of course, he cannot resolve the problem of the internal tensions. We are pleased enough when he manages to quell the worst of the quarrels.

The police must also maintain 'Lagerordnung',[49] which means no more and no less than our constitution. For where would it all end if the lady wife of the banker from the Apollolaan[50] were to remain unpunished for making her nightly piddle next to the hut, or if the widow of a former government official were allowed to flout the order to make her bed in the prescribed manner? Could blankets – property of the Third Reich (reflect on it and bow!) – be allowed to be used for a purpose other than that for which they were intended, or the tranquillity in the Altersheim (old people's home) be disturbed?

The Altersheim is a chapter in itself. Initially, everyone had to report for duty, and *everyone* also had to work. There they stood then last winter, the old dears, shivering for hours on end in the snow on the muster ground, clad in rags and blankets to protect them against the biting wind.

They, too, were assigned work, preferably digging sand. Many caught pneumonia, and Goodman Bones rapped on the wooden walls of their hut. Dozens were transported to the crematorium, sometimes three or four a day.

The *Ältestenrat* managed to have those aged sixty-five or older

---

[48] Withdrawal of jam.   [49] Law and order in the camp.
[50] A fashionable avenue in Amsterdam.

housed in two separate huts. There in the old people's home they are now seeing their days out, getting on each other's nerves, cackling and quarrelling, carping and grumbling, and only a few manage to remain true to themselves. They rummage in each other's beds, pinch from each other whatever takes their fancy, and seek to wound each other to the core by striking at each other's weakest spot.

Nowhere else do people hate each other more than in old people's homes, and nowhere on earth is there a more derelict and more unfortunate institution than in a German camp for Jews. They want to make it to the finishing line but are frail and sick, their bodies are undermined, their spirits and their souls are affected. They are worn out. As everywhere, they soil their beds, suffer, ache, and cannot come to rest on the hard palliasses. And when God has delivered them, and from their first or second tier wooden bunk they have said goodbye to the curse of this world, all too often there is someone waiting to steal a watch, an overcoat, or a wedding ring left behind.

They are dragged to the hospital, where there is a mortuary. Observant Jews can indulge themselves there to their hearts' content in funeral rites. Then the refuse cart arrives upon which – packed in a black coffin – they are taken to the crematorium. Those left behind may accompany it as far as the camp gate. A member of the *Ältestenrat* puts in an appearance. A few friends follow the high cart. Then barbed wire marks the division between life and death.

The coachman, a giant of an SS man, smokes his cigarette. He remains so completely invulnerable, so completely unmoved by the event, that he must be an outstanding pupil of his master. Behind the motionless mask of his face he thinks – assuming he is still capable of thinking – of what importance is a human being? At least another Jew less. And when he feels that the coffin is not being loaded onto the cart quickly enough, he shouts: 'Los, los, Sauvolk, rasch, sonst hau' ich euch einen in den Arsch. Ihr glaubt wohl wir hätten Zeit für eure Juden-Kadaver. So was gibt es nicht. Es ist kein General gestorben!'[51]

---

[51] Hurry up, hurry up, you swine, quickly, or I'll kick you in the arse. You must

No, it is not a General who has died. Someone has died who lived a little and vegetated a little, who loved a few people, a wife or a husband and a couple of children, who felt he had a right to a chair, a table and a bed, who knew nothing about war or politics, who was a little selfish and a little generous, a little banal and a little original, a little silly and a little wise, a little hard and a little sentimental, who, because of some mad theory, was found guilty and sentenced to die in prison; a quite ordinary person has died, in loneliness and immeasurably homesick, who would have liked so very much, just once more, just once more to have seen a face, to have heard a voice, of someone who was dear to him.

Who knows their homesickness? They all carry it with them in their hearts and it destroys them from within. But no one knows it of another, or asks it of another. They know only their own misery and are embittered and dissatisfied. They would like a cup of coffee or a piece of chocolate. But there is none. Is there something for the children, perhaps? Do they have toys? The elderly are shrivelled.

Meanwhile Saartje K. enjoys the chance of telling Mr Ezechiel V. that 'in the past' he used to exploit his workers. 'In the past' Saartje K. used to sell flowers. And Mrs V., who now has to sleep shoulder to shoulder with her, all because of their Judaism, makes no secret of it that 'in the past' Saartje used to be happy with an extra ten cents. 'In the past ...' Everyone has brought his weaknesses from 'the past' and a camp for Jews is a melting pot for such weaknesses from the past. Should one not try to hurt each other with it, and not stab each other in the heart, if given the chance?

When one is fighting over a stool, and there happen to be insufficient stools, and after all, one has to sit somewhere, one can have one's fill:

Sir, you are no gentleman.

No, Sir, you are an ill-mannered lout.

Be quiet, Sir, you cannot insult me.

---

think we have all day for your Jewish corpses. Don't kid yourselves. It is not a General who's died.

Bloody German.

Jew.

End: a scene before the magistrate, five, six, seven times a day.
Verdict: *strenger Verweis*, a spoonful of jam.

1 September And it was evening and it was morning: the sixth year
of World War II. The days drag by, the weeks fly past and turn into
months, into years, our life is wasting away. Meanwhile a new generation is growing up.

It is chilly today. Under the bright sky flies an imaginary flag.
The three colours above the beach, above the white dune, above the
Westertoren.[52] The IPA is saying North and South Holland have
been liberated and there is heavy fighting in Zeeland. Could it be
true?

If it is true, it will not have been easy. How many lives did it cost?
I have three children in Holland. And everyone here has something
in Holland. Their hearts are set on Holland. Oh, the clear Dutch
sky, the curling waves at ebb tide, their bulging greed during spring
tide and a westerly wind. Oh, wonderful, peaceful, dear beach, what
have they done to you? That I am not allowed to go there, I can still
understand. But what I do not understand is that I was no longer
allowed to walk in the Weteringplantsoen,[53] even though I used to
play there with the boys from the Jacob van Campen school. Why
am I no longer allowed to buy something from the kiosk where I
used to buy liquorice? Why am I no longer allowed to travel on the
tram on which my bunkmate from Fort, north of Purmerend, is still
a tram conductor? Did we not serve together as conscript gunners
in the 11th Regiment, 'heavy artillery'?

I have no answer for it. It must be the Jewish question I have
talked about throughout my life without understanding that the
Weteringplantsoen and the liquorice and the number 10 tram had
anything to do with it.

But now I know. I also know that it means something quite

---

[52] West Tower.   [53] Wetering Gardens.

different. The Jews who have come here from Poland, the Jews from the Balkans, are recounting: as yet, their accounts still sound vague and dull, but they resound with the death-cry of hundreds of thousands, of millions. The Third Reich was thirsty and even now, on 1 September 1944, it is still not sated.

Yesterday the bench dealt with juvenile cases. A boy had found a coat and had started to wear it instead of handing it in, a girl of sixteen had found a watch and had kept it, and a young native from North Africa had indulged himself in fighting. There were psychiatric reports, the presiding judge was on top form. He spoke of morale, which had to be kept high, and everyone would have been moved to tears had they not felt they were just hollow phrases – even here.

The poor children probably could not help it. The conditional sentence of bunker, *jam-Entzug*, *Brotentzug* they received will probably do the trick. God willing. But God is in no hurry. He has eternity at his disposal in which to improve the world. More's the pity. Would *we* worry about it, if we were immortal? We would not worry about a thing.

In the same vein one might conclude that awareness of history, that is to say, of the immensity of human life, is both a requirement for and a hindrance to world betterment. We are always working for the future. We work *eternally* for the future. But when will that future finally have its turn?

We educate. We always want a better next generation. When will that generation arrive? When will the ideal have been reached so that there will be a contented generation that will no longer want a 'better' generation? Our answer is: never. Time is on our side. Alas we are eternal, for one generation always follows another generation, just like the mountains where one chain follows another. Man runs, clambers and descends, and clambers anew, filled with nostalgia for a deep plain and a distant horizon, but behind the mountains more mountains rise up and behind those mountains more mountains, and ever more mountains. All that remains is the illusion of the horizon. Similarly, mankind retains the illusion of an end, of an absolute future. But mountain upon mountain slides in front of it. One generation arrives and another departs. Perhaps we ought to stop being eternal so that we might begin to reflect. Perhaps we ought to abandon the illusion of a perfect horizon so that we might achieve the reality of a perfect mountain.

In the meantime, though, it becomes evening and it becomes morning. One day there will probably be peace again and then war again. And people like us, people who are convicted of crimes they have not committed, who are persecuted yet are innocent, who look at each other, and whatever we may think of each other, *know* we are innocent, we who with our wives and children are punished day after day by people to whom we can reply only with silent contempt, we who know *their* crimes, *their* immeasurable guilt, their lawlessness, and have discovered the extent to which they have repudiated every human responsibility for us, we who suffer for them, we who are made responsible for their responsibility, we who are accused of everything that belongs to their criminal intent, who are said to want everything that they bring about, who are said to aspire to everything that they wish to achieve, we who are imputed with every wickedness of the mischief-maker and who bleed for their misdeeds, we who know this from our history, again from generation to generation, we the eternal scapegoat, the brother of him who was beaten to death, who are branded with the mark of Cain the fratricide, we are not even satisfied with the illusion of the horizon – but also want to know what lies behind it, like a child that stands at the seaside and asks: Where do the waves come from?

Mum, what is on the other side of the sea?

England.

Do the waves come from England?

The waves break on the English beach just as they do here.

Does the water divide somewhere in the sea then?

No.

Who stands in the middle of the sea directing the waves – you right, you left?

What can possibly be the cause of man's hatred, of war and

peace, of hunger and plenty, and of our wretchedness that always runs parallel with it?

2 September A rainy day with low-hanging, heavy black clouds, gloomy and chilly. It is dark on my bed, and writing is difficult. Everything reminds one of autumn. There are no trees here but I am certain the leaves have already started to fall. At roll-call, we will have to stand in drizzling rain. The mood is growing despondent and bordering on the black.

Yesterday the IPA retracted its announcements about Holland. Last night the retractions were partly retracted again. Apparently Holland has not been recaptured but there have nevertheless been landings which the Germans will say 'had partly failed'. How the IPA knows that, nobody knows. This morning it is being claimed with great insistence that there were landings in Zeeland and South Holland. The Hague is said to have been bombed. There is said to be fierce fighting. The Germans – filled with hatred – are said to be acting mercilessly. There is even talk of five thousand dead.

Enough to make many a person's heart sink, perhaps more from uncertainty than because of the reports.

We, however, are perfectly calm. We must just wait and in any case cannot influence events. Personally, we have been reassured: yesterday we received a parcel from Amsterdam. It was quite undamaged. Some sugar, a honey cake, some cheese spread and a few trifles. We are overjoyed. Although it does not tell us much, we are becoming hopeful again about our relatives in Holland.

Here roll-calls continue. It is starting to rain again and a strong wind is blowing over the muster ground. The rain penetrates everything. Some two thousand people, mostly women and children, stand shivering.

Again roll-call does not tally. Someone is missing. The error cannot be found. All the huts must be re-counted. The numbers of the working parties are checked. We wait: it is pouring and the people grow numb from the cold.

To complete the mood, the death cart arrives on the muster

ground. Three people have died. Young N., a nineteen-year-old, who contracted tuberculosis in Westerbork and has now died here of starvation and exhaustion; F., fifty-one years old, who spent all of the last six years in camps; and a woman, named Polak, with no family or acquaintances here, about whom nobody knows anything. No one on the muster ground even knows her age.

They have come to collect the dead. The hospital hut faces the muster ground. The three coffins are loaded. Behind the cart walk a father and mother, a wife and a son. Behind the bier of the woman, said to have been called Polak, no one walks. Rachel weeps for her children, refuses to be consoled, for they are no longer. A doctor and a nurse from the hospital and a member of the *Ältestenrat* also follow. A few friends and acquaintances of the families steeped in grief want to accompany them as far as the gate. The *Judenälteste* forbids it; it is not allowed. 'Antreten zum Appell!'[54]

It is pouring. People turn their backs to the wind, like horses when it rains. Everyone is silent. A few cry. The raindrops pelt against the soaked clothing. If we do not keep a grip on ourselves all the children will soon start to lament. Till now they have borne up remarkably well. They sang: 'In the name of Orange, open the gate', and: 'I hold you dear, my Holland'. They also played and romped about, and with their natural vitality, rebelled against our sombre mood. Then they began on the Hebrew songs which they had learnt in Westerbork and here. Ancient prayers to new lively tunes:

> Save us, save us
> How good, how good our share
> How pleasant, how pleasant our fate
> And how beautiful, how beautiful our heritage.

Gradually, as it gets colder the children, too, become silent. Most of them press tightly against their mother's skirt or crawl under her raincoat. The people huddle together for a little protection from each other's bodies.

---

[54] Line up for roll-call!

Across the muster ground the plaints of a grieving mother are heard: Oh my child, my child. Another tries to say a few words of comfort. She rests her head on the shoulder of her husband whose only response is to snivel a little. She had nursed her child through many months.

The SS man, a cigarette dangling from his mouth, and without a movement in his face, climbs onto the cart. 'Fort.'[55]

Three dead. The season has started again.

Finally, when the cart has disappeared, a whistle is blown. Roll-call has ended. The children rush through the rain towards the huts. A girl loses a shoe in the mud and starts to cry. 'Daddy, daddy.' With difficulty I manage to rescue the shoe from under the feet of the surging masses. We enter the already overcrowded hut. It is leaking. The previous day's wind has torn the roofing felt loose. But below me, on the second tier, a party is in progress. The little boy, alone here in the camp with his sister, has his birthday today. Someone has given him a slice of bread and jam, and another a slice of bread and a little sugar. I still have a biscuit and a lump of sugar. Now George and his sister Ursul are celebrating a birthday, and believe it or not, the children are happy. According to the custom here, he also gets an extra portion of soup.

3 September I have registered the estate of Miss Polak, who passed away this morning in the society's zoo[56] and was carried away for cremation two hours after her death. We have our own law of succession here. Spouses inherit from each other, parents from children, and the other way round. No one else. There was also a movement that wanted to abolish *all* rights of succession. But, it was argued, why have a law of property and not of succession?

Miss Polak's estate included eight dishes, a yellow one, a blue one, a red one, et cetera. Three blankets, a pair of underpants, a shirt and two small mirrors. The rear bore a portrait of a young boy. Who is he? He is not very handsome.

---

[55] Away. [56] Irony. The author compares B-B to a friendly society's zoological garden.

They are unreal, those greetings from strangers. Recently we discovered some Hebrew letters on a bed frame that arrived here. They appear to be a letter in Yiddish from a son working in a carpenter's shop who wrote to his parents in the hope of it finding them. I am fine, he writes, I also have food. But the letter was unsigned. In the toilet of hut 10 someone found a message in French written in pencil: 'The Jews in Warsaw have all been murdered because they revolted against the Germans. Homage to the heroes.'

That is how we get to hear something about other groups of Jews, add two and two together, and are profoundly worried.

I have settled the matter of the overcoat. It is to be sold for eight rations of bread, payment to be at the purchaser's discretion and title to remain with the seller who is also supplying two pairs of socks. There was serious opposition to intervening in this matter 'on the grounds that it infringed the freedom of the individual'. I care little for this freedom, which is a freedom to exploit. I would like to confiscate *everything* and distribute it according to need – but am glad not to be faced with having to put it into practice.

It is Sunday afternoon. It is very restless in the hut. A couple of boys are lying in bed with their girl friends. It is pouring. It is unbelievably lugubrious. The IPA maintains that there have been landings in Holland and says Finland has capitulated. Let us set sail now to look beyond the horizon at what is happening.

What enormous giant is making ripples on the water?

Abeles asked me: 'Would you like to give a talk in the *Altersheim*?' Before I realised it, I had agreed, against my will. About what though?

Suddenly I thought of 'The unity of the Jewish people'. I cannot imagine how I came to think of it. I had said it without knowing what I meant.

Here one does not find such unity, and I believe in every Jewish camp it will be just as strange a guest as here. In Westerbork, in Barneveld it was also missing. Here, it does not exist.

Indeed, the differences are not as great as they are said to be. The contrast with German Jews in particular is much exaggerated. Malice and even bad faith play a significant role here. Dutch Jews have a need to be anti-German and demonstrate it with great eagerness to German Jews. Perhaps it is already going too far to assume they have a need of it. Probably it is little more than an imaginary self-interest. They need to parade their friendly disposition towards Holland. According to them this includes distancing themselves from every form of Jewish solidarity.

For all that, to say there is no significant difference between Dutch and German Jews has nothing to do with solidarity. Naturally they speak a different language and are therefore distinguished linguistically, but all else that is construed as distinguishing them is mostly artificial. In general, Dutch and German Jews are similar, which is fairly obvious. The characteristics ascribed to German Jews are in the main not characteristics at all, but annoyances or excesses which Dutch Jews have in equal measure. The difference exists in the tendency to ignore or not ignore these annoyances or excesses. Everyone has been able to establish for himself that there were Dutch Jews who assimilated the manners of the SS as if they had never known anything different. As soon as a German Jew adopts these manners, the anti-German instinct, which in reality is an internal Jewish anti-Semitism, has free rein.

The inferiority of German Jews is in reality an inferior Dutch-Jewish invention. To understand this one need only think back for a moment to the enormous intellectual and moral heights that German Judaism in general had attained before the war. There is not a single human endeavour in which they have not attained the most remarkable achievements, to a far, far greater extent for that matter than Dutch Jews. But that has all been forgotten, and is intentionally forgotten.

However, it has to be said that the differences among Jews are wide and striking. Dutch and Polish Jews are already much less alike than Dutch and German, French Jews undoubtedly occupy a position entirely their own, and between European and African Jewry it is difficult to establish any similarity at all. Balkan Jews differ remarkably from Western European, not to mention their individual nuances. A Dutch Jew has far more in common with a Dutch gentile of his class and social status than with a Jew from Albania, Yugoslavia, Greece or Tripoli. Moreover, even class and social contrasts are perhaps not as great as the contrasts between Jews themselves.

Do these Jews then have nothing in common with each other?

Does it exist, Jewish unity? Undoubtedly it does. In the first place, Jews are bearers of a common fate. All the waters of the sea will not wash away the sign of the Jewish star that was forced upon them, and the thousand denials that one is a Jew are outweighed by the fact that one is treated as a Jew. Persecution of the Jews is general, even when the Jew repudiates his descent or fails to accept it.

I do realise that the significance of this is repeatedly underestimated and intentionally belittled. People say it is not for Germans to decide on the unity of communities, but that it depends on what they themselves want. Whoever does not want to be a Jew is not a Jew, and no one can deprive him of that freedom of choice. And, it is said, he *will* not be deprived of it, at least not by anyone other than the Germans. It follows that there is not a Jewish problem, but rather a German one. Beat out the brains of the Germans and the Jewish question will automatically disappear.

I wish it were true, but it is not. First, no apparent fate exists that in one way or another is not anchored within a person. Second, every fate, desired or accursed, freely chosen or forcibly imposed, has lasting inner consequences.

As far as the first is concerned, from the similar treatment that befalls Jews everywhere it must already be concluded that there has to be a factor that is common to all Jews; in other words, it is no use claiming that you are not or do not want to be a Jew, and have nothing to do with Jews, and everything to do with certain non-Jews. As long as Adolf Hitler recognises you as a Jew, you must be recognisable as such, and if you are recognisable, there must be a criterion for this recognition.

Moreover, it is not Adolf Hitler alone who recognises the Jews. It is an exceptionally large historical aberration to believe that he or Germany can lay claim to specialising in the persecution of the

Jews. Hardly a single system has not known this persecution, or at least discrimination. From the past fifty years we recall the very serious pogroms in Russia, Romania and Poland, and the anti-Semitism in the USA. From the past twenty centuries we recall not a single century in which there has not been a fiercer or more deliberate anti-Semitic stance, and not a single country from which anti-Semitism has been entirely absent. As for the second aspect of fate, it is unimaginable that anyone who has experienced what we have experienced should remain the same kind of person as someone who has merely heard about it. Anyone who has worn a star is marked for ever. He becomes different from the person who saw a star being worn.

I am not saying that all nations have not borne their share of general misery, and I do not ask myself, as so many like to do, whose share of this misery was the greater. All I ask myself is whether the share was also a *particular* share, having an independent character. I then see that all Jews, in every country, have borne their share of that country's misery, and that *in addition*, they are burdened with the full weight of their own problems. Jews, who belong to every nationality, were not excluded from any national problems, and after they had absorbed their due percentage of the misfortune spread across the country of their residence, they could start on their own national problem – the Jewish one. They fell in battle in every army, were bombed in every town, suffered hunger wherever there was famine and in addition paid their toll to history as Jews.

And what is the direct result of every affliction that shapes man's soul, determines his behaviour, shapes his thoughts and feelings? The fear of repetition. And when the entire world is afraid that a new Hitler will arise to subject the world, Jews will be no less afraid. But when the entire world has forgotten that a new anti-Semite may arise – and has forgotten it twenty-four hours after the war has ended – Jews will continue to think about it. Their experience has been different. That is why their thinking is different and their politics are different; and their experience was not different from 1933 to 1944, but from time immemorial to the present day. And the fear of repetition of what *they* have experienced marks them as different people from those who experienced something different. Common experience creates common fear, common fear is another word for unity.

4 September 11 o'clock Rain and wind. Rain and wind. At roll-call we were kept standing for two hours and it did not tally. The error could not be found, so this afternoon we are having roll-call again. If it still does not tally then, we will have to stand for a further two hours and have roll-call for a third time. I feel so numb from the cold already that I can barely hold my pencil. We are shivering and have cold feet. Moreover, the intestinal complaints are still spreading.

This morning there were two more for whom the British will arrive too late. That makes seven or eight in September. The hunting season seems to have started. It is the fourth today. Last night a case came up against a young lady who had been unhappy about being moved to another bed and in her fury is alleged to have said: 'If only I had bribed Albala ... !'

Later addition Albala was the *Judenälteste* who had lodged the complaint himself and had demanded punishment. The case was not proven but for judge X., who had to hear the case, it was very difficult to enter into conflict with the *Judenälteste*. By this time he was on his last legs and was living in permanent fear of not making it to the end. He was becoming increasingly careless and forgetful, could hardly lift his feet any more and said he had no strength left for writing. When he wrote he no longer had the energy to round off his letters. He *did not* acquit the young woman but referred the matter to the investigators for further investigation. In the time gained by this move, the *Judenälteste*'s anger subsided and in this way each got his dues. X. was a strictly honest man but assailed by hunger. He once reproached me for not wanting to prosecute someone accused of stealing bread because I believed it had been a 'Fehlhandlung' (an unconscious mistake), caused by hunger. X. did not believe in such a possibility. A few days later he collected my bread during bread distribution. When I asked him for it he said he had not received any. I asked the food distributor if a mistake could have been made. But both swore on oath, the one that he had given it to X., and X. that he had not received it. He went to his cupboard and said: 'Look for yourself.' I replied: 'You look.' He looked and to his utter amazement produced the bread. From that moment on X. understood what 'Fehlhandlung' meant. He really was the last person to appropriate another's bread. If he had discovered it by himself, he would have returned it of his own accord. But not everyone could do that. This illustrates how theft might occur in the camp.

To think then that all of us could so easily finish up in the mouth of the gaping crematorium. Why do we hate each other so?

Today the IPA says: landings in Jutland, and does not retract the landings in Holland. Already for three days there has not been any reliable news.

12 o'clock Rain and wind, rain and wind. After only a few days of rain the ground is sodden and covered with puddles. Those who have whole shoes can call themselves lucky, but after four years of war who still has whole shoes? By now most of the internees have been away from home for two years or longer, and everything they own is gradually wearing out. Shoe repairing is a major problem here, There are plenty of shoe repairers, but no materials. We did manage to bring enough from the 'shoe industry', but where does one find nails? Then there is the stomach of the shoe repairer, which also makes demands. Moreover, the shoe repairer also happens to have a wife and children, and the wife and children also have stomachs and those stomachs, too, make demands, so that whoever wants to have his shoes repaired is well advised to bring a ration of bread. The shoe repairer has been forbidden to accept it, but no one can forbid the shoe repairer to claim that he is short of materials. For that claim is true, and in any event true enough for him to make it when it suits him, and not to make it when it does not suit him. Whoever arrives with a ration of bread arrives with a natural preference, and as with the shoe repairer so with the watch repairer, who never has any lighter fuel until he smells a counter-offer. And the ban that has been imposed on him is not so firm that he does not know how to work around it.

3 o'clock Rain and wind, rain and wind. Round up of all the men. *Everyone* had to fall in and everyone marched out. Everywhere it is very quiet now. Several people were beaten including Dr L.; P. was thrown to the ground and kicked. Nevertheless some of the young chaps managed to get out of it again. They took elderly and sick people with them. There are trains to be unloaded. It is rumoured that there are forty-four wagons laden with huts waiting at the station, and seven with food supplies. An entire camp is said to have been transferred. Here, in the heart of Germany, we are beginning to notice that they are retreating at the front.

IPA: landings in Holland partly failed. Finland capitulated. Slovakia capitulated. Occupation of Fiume. Hesitantly: landings in Jutland.

Here they are unloading swedes, nothing but swedes. For weeks we have been eating swedes. It is little more than boiled wood. It is unbelievable what one can still make with it. Swedes with carrots, with potatoes, with onions. Swedes, swedes. Last winter we ate nothing but swedes for three and a half months, and each day it tasted good.

Now I will return to what I wrote yesterday. I said that a common fate engenders unity, but if you use your eyes here you will see more than this opened book: a flame that radiates from within, from vast distances, from an enormous distance on high.

A very intimate relationship exists between the Jews and a central point in the ordering of the world, a very intimate mutual relationship. When you see a Jew wrapped in his prayer shawl and – as he expresses it himself – crowned with his prayer bindings, and then listen to what his soul is saying and try to understand what he means, you will learn something of the great, the entire life-dominating concept of Israel's God. Indeed, the religion, that is the Jewish unity. I say it, even though I know just as well as everyone else that most Jews have turned their backs on the Jewish religion, and usually ostentatiously at that, as everything that they do to disavow Judaism is done ostentatiously. This is understandable; since Judaism is put on display, its renunciation must take place at least as openly. I say it, even though I myself do not profess the ancient religion, yet still lay claim to my share of Jewish unity.

To this day the Jewish religion is professed by every group of Jews according to exactly the same model. Behold! Two thousand years ago two brothers bade each other farewell. One went this way and the other that way, the one died and the other died, and also their children died and their children's children. And after endless wanderings, the descendants of the one arrived in a town on the North Sea and the descendants of the other roamed about and were beaten back to a town on the Mediterranean Sea, somewhere in the east, in Greece, in Tripoli, in Italy or Yugoslavia – it matters not where. And Adolf, the world's madman, brought them together in camps, and what transpired? They speak different languages, they are dressed differently and have different longings, but when they turn to their God they are so alike within and without that one could substitute the one for the other and not notice it. The same *tallith* (prayer shawl), the same *tefillin* (prayer bindings), the same formulas, in the morning, in the afternoon and in the evening, the same summons on Friday afternoon: Come my friend, let us go to meet the bride, let us welcome the Sabbath.

The same fasts, the same festivals, the same submissiveness. Lord, open my lips and let my mouth utter Your prayer.

Centuries and dozens of centuries are bridged: they sing exactly the same psalms, and over this bridge passes a spirit, a single spirit: the Jewish one.

Yet even this spirit they disavow, and the God of all this worship they have abjured!

It makes no difference: all the world knows, the trees in the forest know and the stones in the street, that *this* was their national achievement and the throb of their heart.

5 September In the morning at a quarter past six, in the afternoon at half past twelve, 'Arbeitsappell'[57] for *all* men below seventy.

---

[57] Duty roll-call.

Everyone has to report for duty, including the sick. There are huts to be unloaded and erected. The huts come from Cracow. The date, 1 September. Cracow must still be in the hands of the Germans then. The IPA has never asserted anything different. The huts have come from a Jewish camp. Inscriptions in Hebrew have been discovered, a piece of a prayer book, et cetera.

The IPA says: landings in Den Helder, advance on Alkmaar, occupation of IJmuiden, Katwijk and the Hook (De Nieuwe Water-weg)[58]. Heavy bombing by eight thousand aircraft followed by the taking of Amsterdam, occupation of Liège and Maastricht, advance on Venlo, occupation of Groningen. Afterwards, it will be interesting to see how much of it is true. We are starting to live in a state of tension here. We are desperate for the liberation. The men who are required to work are being beaten terribly. Fritz, the Red Müller, Count Turd (so named because he is responsible for the latrines) and Rau are hounding the men with a plank of wood.

The men are selected during roll-call. On the slave markets it was never as bad as this.

In the meantime, because of the new work, everything we had built up here relating to the internal organisation is being destroyed. The investigation branch, the judiciary, the youth care service. The magistrate and chief investigator were also taken along and have been 'permanently' assigned. It is enough to drive you mad. To think that we are powerless here while Holland is being liberated. How many victims will there have been? Who is alive, who fell? They say the entire inner city of Amsterdam extending from the Weteringschans has been devastated. I can imagine the Handelmaat-schappij, the Museum square. Especially near the Concertgebouw and the surrounding area. The barracks, the port, that is to say, a significant part of the old Jewish quarter. Also the stations and the docks, particularly Muiderpoort and Central Station. For the rest, the harbour. The Jews have been deported – their houses are being destroyed. Is it luck?

---

[58] The New Waterway.

Do we fare better or worse than the non-Jews? We fare differently.

A different memory, a different fear. A different fear, a different expectation. A different past, a different God.

Who is this God?

The *liturgy* differs, but not the God.

It is the Only one, the Eternal one. The Jews have established monotheism as the truth. It has determined their history both internally and externally.

Because from a psychological point of view there are only two types of religion. Monotheistic and polytheistic. Man, who established the principle that there is only one who determines life and creation, and to whom everyone and everything is accountable, exists. The ruled and the ruler, the slave and the king, the individual and the community, the individual and the state, the family, the priest, the soldier, the prophet and the legislator, the scholar and the poet, the thinker, the dreamer and the doer. There is no one who, in whatever he thinks or does, when he rests or stirs, when he withdraws into himself or turns to his fellow beings, when he descends contemplatively into his soul or tries to interact with the world about him, no one who every second is not accountable to this concept and has to be in harmony with this concept. God is one, universal and eternal, and through his creation he seeks a particular course and a firm objective from the world. God is One, is therefore identical with the requirements of an ethic; the deepest meaning of monotheism, therefore, lies not so much in the experience of God or of the man–God encounter, not so much in mysticism, in the experience of love or forgiveness, as in creating and justifying a moral standard, *justice* for the individual and for the community.

The polytheist is no less religious than the monotheist. His experiences are no less profound, no less intense, and he knows similarly of revelation upon revelation. But for him the unity of God does not exist, for him being and becoming is an eternal struggle between power and power, powers which exist in principle in unlimited numbers. And what is ultimately moral and just? The power that wins. Whoever is strongest, and *proves* that he is so, is right. And whoever manages to gain dominion also has a right thereto. For this polytheist no greater obstacle exists than the question posed to him by the monotheist: 'Is it allowed?' He wants to indulge himself, to give free rein to the forces rising within him, to measure himself against a fellow being, to test the glory of his power on him, and he hates not the fellow being who approaches him with the same intent and against whom he can test himself, but the fellow being who approaches him with the incomprehensible, agonising question: Cain, Cain, where is your brother Abel?

And it is highly debatable whether from a psychological point of view pure monotheists exist at all. It is far more probable that man is a composite of both. According to his desires and interests he is simultaneously the heathen charged with passions and the man bound by the rules of religion, and each moment heathenism and monotheism threaten to clash within him. Probably man has far fewer 'opinions' than is imagined, far fewer principles, in fact he does not know what he desires. Often and with great skill he manages to make a pretence of it and thereby deceive himself and others.

If the truth be known, man is a battlefield of conflicting thoughts, a duologue, and what happens within him is that one or other tendency gains the upper hand. Now the Jew, in the form of his historical appearance, is the person who gives the upper hand to monotheism and who requires that man subject himself with all his passions to an eternal principle of justice and righteousness which exists in and by itself, and which is absolute goodness and therefore unassailable.

And mankind, at least in Europe and in the USA, adopted monotheism in the form of Christianity. It became a monotheistic humanity but did not stifle the heathen within itself. It cannot. The heathen can only be conquered and bound. And this heathen, who lives on in the dungeons of the human soul, hates being bound and hates the one who has tied him down.

And who bound him? The Jew! Though not the Jew as he was originally, the Jew of Moses, of the patriarchs, or of the God who had rescued the nation from Egypt, but the Jew as he had developed himself *to enable* him to bind heathendom: Christ.

67

Developed or not developed, monotheism is the great spiritual achievement of the Jewish nation, an achievement through which it became, and has remained, a historic nation.

The heathen hates the Jew because the Christians pinion him. And there is not a nation and no period in history in and on which the heathen does not lie in wait to regain his former freedom. For this reason, anti-Semitism is eternal and has everywhere a chance – as eternal as Judaism itself.

This also explains why for centuries the Christian church has been the persecutor of the Jews. I am not suggesting for a moment that we are dealing here with the only reason, I am discussing here only the psychological causes. The church persecuted the Jew not because he is alleged to have crucified Christ. The church persecuted the Jew because the Jew had *given birth to* Christ. Christ's death is, in other words, a wishful thought of the heathen living among the Christians which he has shifted onto the Jew. The guilt that the Christian feels because his heathen soul rebels against Christ seeks to avenge itself on the one who placed him in the torment of ambivalence. That person is the Jew.

Do not tell me there have also been other monotheistic nations and ideas, I do not deny it. The civilised world, however, had hardly any contact with them. The monotheism of other nations may have been an interesting subject for scholarly research or the passions of poets, but nations at large came into contact only with Judaism. And how!

One could say: other nations, too, had their ethics. Indeed. But no nation has had such a profound influence on the human soul through its stories and legends, and through the fervour and force of its prophets, as the Jewish nation. For example, Greece may have been beauty and learning, Rome may have laid the foundation for our civil law, Juda was conscience for everyone; catechism, and what Juda had said, was a question of salvation or damnation, of heaven or hell. Does it follow from this that Jews are 'better' people than others? Not in the least. Jews are – and this should never be forgotten – heathens to the same extent as other nations. But their historical achievement was that they *knew* it. This 'knowing' is the revelation.

And when we say 'they' knew, it means only that a very small minority knew. But this minority has always existed.

The large majority of Jews adopted neither Judaism, Christianity, nor any other religion. It never wanted Judaism. It was always forced on them and all too often it resisted and a large part of the majority would fall away. There was always a 'remnant' that would return then! According to scholars, the God of Israel was at first not such a special god at all. The Jews themselves say that originally they were idolaters. It was only later that they embraced the God of Abraham, Isaac and Jacob, who distinguished himself at least from the gods of other nations of hoary antiquity in that he was the only tribal deity, and had to share this position with a number of other tribal deities. But that is not to say that he was the only god to exist. Just as Israel had its God, so did Egypt, and Moab likewise had a God, and Edom one, or more. At first, the task of Israel's God was also no different from that of those other gods. He had to wage war and win.

The God of Israel did wage those wars, but usually lost them. Then something remarkable would happen: when a nation had a god that had failed to win a national war, it proved that that god was weaker than other gods and therefore deserved to be dispensed with. And he did use to be dispensed with. The result was the disappearance of national culture and also of national identity. A levelling and assimilation. Defeated nations usually ceased to exist.

Among the Jews, a different process would take place. When the nation had lost a war, or was plagued by other disasters, it was not their god who was called to account and then abandoned: precisely the opposite occurred. Through his priests and prophets he called the nation to account, because He was the Good One, the Righteous One. It was not He who had neglected his duty, but the nation that had been remiss, and it acknowledged it. 'To You, oh Lord, righteousness, to us shame.'

Herein lies the seed then for the later development of the One and Only Universal God: in his inviolability, in his absolute righteousness. Gradually man learnt that 'what God does, is done

69

well', but that is merely a concept of global responsibility turned
into a cheap consolation that no one can escape from: over the world
and over our dealings reigns a principle. We are the sons, Thou art
the father, we are the slaves, Thou art the master, we are the subjects,
Thou art the King. This is not just the father principle, but the
voluntary surrender of individual right, the right of the fist, in which
strength is the principal truth.

And why could there always be a 'remnant that returned'?
Because there have always been Jews who turned to the bedrock of
their national history and knew that without the central concept of
a constantly probed monotheism the nation would perish. The Jews
were a small nation and in reality always – if not always in an
identical political form – formed a minority amid large majorities.
The universality and absoluteness of their god was the greatest
national recompense for the universality and absoluteness of their
misfortune. They appealed to justice, not to power, for they neither
possessed power nor were able to possess any, and because they did
not want to surrender to the majority in an act of unparalleled
historical courage either, they hoisted the standard of absolute
righteousness, to force others to respect them and to plant for themselves a star in the heavens to guide them in life. This is the Jewish
star. Lo, I called You out of anxiety and You answered me with
solace. The Lord speaks not through the sword but through the
Spirit.

Even now, now that the Jewish star has been forced upon us as
a mark of shame, it lights our path in this sombre life. Those who
persecute us are heathens and do not know how great the God of
Israel is. They hate us for our greatness and for our eternity, once
again they are resisting the voice that calls and calls, and will not
cease calling: 'Cain, Cain, where is your brother Abel?' And once
again there is a 'remnant that returns'. Again there rises in our
midst the voice of the prophets and in our heart the song of the
poet. Not for nothing do we sing on the Sabbath: 'Those who sow
with tears, will reap with joy.'

This joy exists in our eternal avowal. The more difficult our life and the more distressing our fate, the more clearly our thousand-year national programme manifests itself to us anew:

Hear O Israel: Jahveh our God, Jahveh is unity.

7 September It is only a few days since we started to notice the meaning of conviviality. Their lordships are getting nervous and seem to want to avenge themselves on us for the 'kleine Frontver-schiebung'.[59] This morning, the commandant himself came to select the men. He sent everyone to work. Men up to eighty years of age, sick people with thirty-nine and forty degrees of temperature; he sent for the hospital soldier, generally known here as the *Herr Sanitäter*, abused the Jewish doctor, and gave himself away completely. 'Ihr glaubt wohl wegen der kleinen Frontverschiebung könnt Ihr alle sabotieren! Ich schneide euch den Hals ab.'[60]

From which it may be deduced that the matter was choking him. He is beginning to understand something of the situation. Goebbels' propaganda is of no use any longer.

Except that the SS continue to cling to their job.

In the meantime the commandant has brought a surprise along. Three SS women, National Socialist bigots, for whose virginity the camp showed great concern.

Our future looks bleak. The mood is funereal. Eight days of the kind of work that now has to be done and again the British will arrive too late for a few more. Rain and wind. Beatings. A thirteen, fourteen, fifteen hours working day! Because it does not end at half past six in the evening. After the midday break we must carry on working from half past twelve till half past nine. The food is as meagre as ever. Today, instead of 1.1 litres of soup, there was only 0.6 of a litre.

The crematorium received only one victim today. A bargain. There were four roll-calls. At a quarter past six, at half past eight, at half past nine, and at half past twelve. Three of these were to

---

[59] Small shift of the front.
[60] You seem to think that because of the small shift of the front you can all start committing sabotage! I'll cut your throats.

report for duty. The *Judenälteste* is cursed, he curses the *Ältestenrat* and the latter curses the foreman, the foreman the people, and they each other. Everyone passes on the kick that he receives. It carries on from month to month and destroys morale. There is no time for a single constructive thought, no prospect, no application for it.

The biggest consolation is the news. How long will it last? Each day, each hour is unbearable. And what did the last few days bring us? The IPA says Brussels has fallen. Where is the king?

I still want to write about the hospital, the children, love – about the milk distribution.

At roll-call today, seven men collapsed. It is a lot. Usually, there are no more than two. But that is the least to be expected.

I believe that once I have written about the hospital, the children, love, and the milk distribution, I will have given quite a full picture of the world between two streams.

Today I saw a youngster walking with a bowl of milk. The SS woman told him not to spill any. The youngster got nervous and spilled half the bowl of milk. We shouted: 'What are you doing?' He started to cry and carried on walking.

We must carry the containers now. It is very heavy work. There will be many more huts. I believe the British will get here first. I shall take the dossier of legal cases away with me. If I can. It is very interesting.[61]

Hommage à vous, you courageous little grandmother, who remains the same in the old people's home, with your infinitely lovely face, your marvellous head of grey curls, your smiling mouth, your sound and still milk-white teeth, who helps wherever she can, nurses the sick, comforts the dying, helps the weak, gives this one a clean bedsheet, peels a potato for another, covers them, brings them a little warm water, offers a lump of sugar and keeps their faith alive. *Hommage à toi*, you little boy who cares for his lonely sister, combs her hair each day, and shares a little treat with her. *Hommage à toi*, you mother, who manages to look after her child, so that it stays

---

[61] (Author's note): Unfortunately it got lost.

clean and healthy as always. *Hommage* to all of you, who keep up your spirits and remain yourselves, who have not allowed things to get on top of you, who have not succumbed, who have stood your ground, in this indescribable misery.

A new life is on its way. It is coming. And you need that new life as human beings and as Jews.

7 September Last night B.'s appeal hearing. S. had presided. He had leant on his arms, had cross-examined while stooped forward as in the old days when he was a cantonal judge.[62] B. is a mystery to me. A sixteen-year-old with a bright intellect, whose responses are clear and fearless, continues without hesitation to deny his guilt in the face of every piece of incriminating evidence. If I had to predict his future, I would say: Sing Sing, electric chair, as state enemy number one. Well-mannered, even engaging. A handsome youth. I ask myself a hundred times: could we be wrong? To test myself, I formulate my doubt as strongly as possible and utter it aloud. But I am unable to change my opinion. The boy has to be guilty. He had stolen a suitcase at night, having first acquainted himself with its contents, had prised it open with a knife, had removed two and a half rations of bread and a one kilo tin of butter from it, had opened the tin and had eaten the bread and an ounce of butter. He had wrapped the tin in his leggings and hidden the lot behind a bed against the wall, where someone had accidentally found it. Could someone else have stolen B.'s leggings in which to hide the butter? Yet it had all been found in a blind passage that could only be reached by B. and a few others who are beyond suspicion. Moreover, he was seen in that passage shortly after six in the morning where, according to three eyewitnesses, he had lingered for ten to fifteen minutes without being able to explain what he had been doing there for such a long time. What is true is that he had gathered his luggage and had moved it to the top of the three-tier bunk bed. Why then had he not missed his leggings, which must have been in the blind passage? Why had

---

[62] Comparable to a county court judge.

he not reported them missing? Besides, during the night two other witnesses had heard him eating and rattling with a knife in a tin. Finally, he is also suspected of three other serious offences.

I delivered a long plea for the prosecution. Then the god of thieves came to B.'s aid: air-raid alert. Air-raid alert means the light is turned off. The case had to be adjourned. B. is unbelievably lucky. The crime was committed on the night of 1 and 2 July. His original sentence was on 5 July. Although as a rule the right of appeal is denied, by exception it was allowed in his case. He appealed. Immediately thereafter he falls ill and is admitted into hospital with pneumonia. One night, when he is a little better, bread is stolen on his ward, close to his bed. Everything points to B. being the perpetrator. It cannot be proved though. Meanwhile the appeal cannot take place because the commandant has forbidden the court to sit without his prior knowledge. Finally a means is found for the appeal to take place all the same. Then B. and the witnesses have to work overtime. When this obstacle, too, has been overcome, we have the intermezzo of the air-raid alert. B. gets another chance. When he is sentenced, the bunker will probably be full. Then the British will arrive. When are they coming? What will happen to us? Again and again these questions fill the air here. As for B., somehow or other I have a soft spot for him. He is an adventurer who carries out stunts, who tempts danger and tries to discover how far he can go. He is getting more adept at fooling us. I think an acquittal would be very dangerous for him. A hearing of this kind is a diversion for the camp, a veritable theatrical performance. Moreover, those who work here are not actors, but professionals, and everything is for real. These professionals all have their weaknesses, their conceit, their follies. Each in his own way is ugly and ridiculous. It makes the whole into an entertaining stage play.

As a matter of fact, everything one sees here fascinates, like brilliant film direction. Sometimes one thinks it is all unreal, everything is just a dream, just shadow, show, one is asleep, or has died, or is far away, or so absorbed in a film, or a book, that one can feel the pain being suffered.

It is all so senseless, so maddeningly senseless.

This morning, for example, they again sent an additional seventy men to work, despite enormous downpours. Three minutes outdoors was enough to be soaked to the skin. These seventy men comprise first the oldest who had remained behind, then the sick who had been left behind, and finally the hut leaders. Who cares if the sick or the elderly die? And what is supposed to happen in the huts without leaders or supervision? Who will see to the cleaning, making the beds, caring for the sick? Ensuring that the roll-call tallies? It is a deliberate attempt by the SS to disorganise everything and then to use that disorganisation for further measures. Because although the working day is long, between eleven and fifteen hours in fact, there is no work.

The huts are being unloaded next to our camp. Three hundred men are involved, though there is not enough work for even thirty. Intermittently two or three truckloads arrive. They can be unloaded by no more than thirty men. Several hundred men are now jostling each other, getting in each other's way and tripping over each other's legs. From time to time the SS dive among them with a plank or a truncheon. They have beaten a hole in my bunkmate's head so that he returned pouring with blood. The *Scharführer* who had beaten him had received a slight graze on his face. One of the Jews had offered him some iodine. That is slavery for you.

But that is an exception, of course. The others know very well what they must do. And they do it. They smash everything to smithereens. The huts were dismantled in Cracow, loaded onto trucks, unloaded again, brought here in rail wagons, unloaded here, loaded onto trucks again, and again unloaded here. A seven-fold operation. Seven times the load passed through Jewish hands and now it reminds one of apple sauce. Hardly a single plank has remained undamaged, there is not a door that is square, not a window that has not been pulled out of its joints, not a side-wall that has not had some of its planks kicked out, not a floor from which most of the joists are not missing, not a ceiling without large holes in it. In short, a jumble of useless splinters is all our old men have to hump away. Do you imagine that something like this would not drive the SS mad?

A regular soldier saw a Jew being beaten. He said, 'Es gebe Gott daß es noch mal eine Gerechtigkeit gibt.'[63] Since as far back as January we have known that three-quarters of the guards here are not to be trusted. The system relies on the NCO, the *Scharführer*, the subalterns. They manage all right though.

The work is really not heavy. And when – such as now while I am writing – the sky clears up, hope is revived. Many will perish. The majority will make it to the end.

And then? Start anew. There will be plenty of work.

There! At least it is raining again. It will carry on raining well into the evening. The men working outdoors will be pleased!

To save on overheads, roll-call was suddenly cut short this morning and held again in the afternoon. That is again four times today. I must count. Counting a hut is complicated work. In the three-tier bunk beds it is all too easy for someone who wants to be overlooked to be lying under the blankets, or a child whom you fail to notice to be hidden behind luggage, or some inadequate person who can no longer cope. And if he is missed, roll-call will not tally and everyone on the muster ground will be kept waiting for hours. Until it does tally. And the risk of roll-call being repeated is great.

The physics teacher at school told us that if we took a vessel filled with marbles or other bodies and placed it under pressure, the marbles or other bodies would not unite to form a counter-pressure, but instead each body would first seek a safe getaway. It would push and press against its neighbours, attempt to shatter them to gain space, and each of the bodies feeling this pressure would immediately pass it on till it reached the bodies closest to the walls of the vessel that no longer had a neighbour on one side, and which therefore would either try to push those walls in or escape through or along them. Man reacts in exactly the same way if, metaphorically speaking, he is suddenly put under pressure. At first there will

---

[63] Would to God that justice will return.

certainly be no question of a collective counter-pressure. Initially each will try to pass the pressure on, to escape and to keep his individuality intact. There is no point in complaining about it. Many a group, many a nation, many a social class owes its destruction to it, knowing that it should and could have been different. It is no use, that is how we are.

Here, too, we observe this phenomenon. The pity is that this is the phenomenon the children see before them and adopt as the correct principle of life.

They have never seen, let alone learned, that a social person should offer his seat to another when he is seated and the other is standing, especially if the other happens to be a lady or is older. For there are too few stools, and everyone is exhausted and happy with the place that he has managed to grab for himself. Whoever is seated remains seated, and the first to arrive is the first to be served, and to be first, you must run fast, push, shove and be cunning. When you go to collect your food you must not, as we were always taught, let another go first, because there is not enough room and not enough time, and anyone who lets another precede him must therefore be mad. On the contrary, you must do everything possible to be first, and the only question in this regard that might still remain open to debate is whether all means are permissible or whether there are some that are forbidden. It goes without saying that you must never leave the best of the food for another or offer him something extra, as is customary in society. Because in society there is sufficient, and even the person who receives the smallest piece of meat at table has too much, or will at least have his fill. Here, though, there is always too little of everything and everyone is hungry. So you must watch out that you get your fair share, and no one will blame you if you try to secure the largest piece.

Naturally, in society there is also combat, competition between individuals, contests between nations, war between classes, but in everyday social intercourse people nevertheless show consideration for each other and when – for example in business – people compete unfairly, social revenge always follows. Life mitigates itself and in times of peace it also mitigates the struggle between groups, classes and nations. Here everyday life is reduced to its simplest forms. I feel hungry and want to stuff myself. I feel sleepy and want the best bed. I need a coat, give! I want to get out of here alive. So you, my dear brother, can work in my place. Those are the ethics.

Naturally, there are numerous exceptions to this. It may even be a majority who remain themselves, though a majority that no longer set the tone. Among those exceptions there is one general one: the family unit remains indissoluble. It does not disintegrate, it remains intact and shines even more brightly in the wretchedness.

There is hardly a single Jew who does not accept that his wife is depriving herself, not a wife who does not save some of her rations for her husband, not a couple who do not deprive themselves to the utmost for their children, no children who are not filled with the utmost concern for their parents.

Naturally, there are exceptions to this too, quite noticeable ones even, but for the rest it is the rule.

And many times over an action may seem selfish that is carried out solely for the benefit of the family, without any personal gain. Indeed, it verges on exaggeration. Jews are sentimental, gushing, sweetly family sick. Go and sit at a table at mealtimes, it matters not which one, and you will hear veritable rows between husbands and wives over a potato or a piece of meat that the one wants to press on the other. Very indignant reproaches, because one of them took less than the other had shared out. People cheat to give the other an extra slice of bread without them noticing; one resigns oneself to one's own hunger if the other is satisfied.

And that is how parents feel about their children, children about their parents, often even brothers and sisters and other close relatives about each other.

And for this reason: everything goes to pieces here. Is the family at its strongest perhaps because family life here is reduced to a minimum? Possibly, but why do families become more united under oppression while every other community threatens to disintegrate? You should see how people fight here over a little skimmed milk.

Every day a little milk arrives in the camp for the sick, the children and the weak.

Responsibility for distributing the milk rests with the *Judenälteste*, who has delegated this task to his wife, Madame la Reine.

Madame la Reine, it is alleged, does not distribute fairly, but favours her pals.

I am convinced it is not true.

Madame la Reine is not dishonest. She is primitive and vain, and uses the milk distribution to give expression to her sentimentality and to show what a good heart she has. Naturally it gives rise to the grossest injustices. Goodness of heart happens to be a social vice. All kinds of people receive milk who are not entitled to it, or much less entitled than those who receive none.

The consequences will therefore be clear: intrigue and flattery on the one hand and gossip on the other, and during the daily milk distribution itself, indescribable noise, pushing, shoving, fighting with elbows, arms and legs. A little milk ...

And not only adults stand in the tangles of hungry, eager, pushing humans. There are also children, who learn here what life is.

Hommage à toi, you little girl, who stands aside, with tears in her great brown eyes, how you would love to have a little milk. But you cannot bring yourself to push. You will not do it. No one has ever told you, but you know how undignified all this is.

But what about tomorrow, when you go to collect the milk for Siegie, your sick little brother? What do you do then? Then you bite your lips and push and shove. You will learn for always: it really is possible to dishonour people.

8 September We have celebrated a birthday. Mrs L. was seventy. She sat all alone and received our congratulations. 'Naturally, I am pleased', she said, 'to have reached this age in good health, but it can never be a special day for me.' None of her children or grandchildren was with her.

And in the hut of the Albanians we celebrated a funeral. A man of eighty had died there. All the women, children and old men who are able to cry gather together and cry, wail and lament. It is a real lamentation party. There is no way of knowing whether these people are in sorrow, or create sorrow. They cry, they cry voluptuously, shed buckets of tears. There are two-year-old children among them, and small babies, also older children. Heavy tears roll down their dirty cheeks. Women come to pay their respects and cry and wail.

The visit should be imagined as follows. On a lower bunk, bent double in a twenty-centimetre wide passage, formed by two rows of nine beds each stacked three by three, something that is probably an elderly woman is sitting in the midst of a bunch of creatures in the midst of which I recognise something resembling a child and a few more women. Sobbing and wailing rises from their midst, other women force their way to and fro along the passage, the one crying louder than the other so that we, with our European eyes, see only the grotesqueness of the performance. It is like a performance: the Balkans in the world between two streams.

I was visiting the hut of the Albanians because of a theft. I have come to investigate. It is swarming with people, though the men are all at work. It is impossible to distinguish one from the other. An old man is reclining on a bed, smoking, for which he is reprimanded. Naturally he says it is not he who is smoking, but someone else who has just left. Were you to catch him with a lighted cigarette between his lips, he would swear that he has not been smoking but that you must be mistaking him for another.

The Albanians are far more unfortunate than we are. They find it even more difficult to cope, are treated even more roughly, have even greater hunger, suffer from malaria and receive almost no help from outside; they have nothing to wear, no shirt, no socks, no coat, no cardigan, no shoes, and must trade their last food for a few clothes. We held a collection for them which produced a great deal, but of course, not enough for five hundred half-naked men, women and children. We, too, are fast running out of supplies. Moreover, it is getting colder now and the poor people are walking about shivering. They pinch bread from each other to trade for clothes with other huts, and in the other huts people steal clothes to trade for bread from the hut of the Albanians. In this way a market was created in stolen bread for stolen clothes; we know about it and prohibit every kind of barter. For a while we were able to uphold this ban because transgressions were prosecuted and punished. However, now we no longer have a police force, no investigation team, no judge. Because everyone is working in the 'Abladekommando'.[64] Not a single ban can be enforced any longer.

The leadership will try to have a few of the men relieved from work ... in a few days' time. It is not the first time that our organisation has been destroyed. It happens repeatedly. We rebuild it. Slowly. One man at a time. We talk with the Germans, who – despite *all* their efforts – are tiring of us.

You cannot imagine how exhausting it is having to watch that reluctant, shuffling heap all the time, that simply *will not* work. One can shout, beat, punish, withhold bread, threaten with bunker, achieve a little impetus for a short while, but the lack of discipline, the indolence, the indifference, the aversion to work, the inability to work, all increase. It is one of the biggest stupidities of the Germans – and that is saying something for Germans – to believe they can make people work. It is a historical error of the first degree.

Unfortunately, we cannot fight because we have no weapons. We have another means of resistance. Inertia. Just look at how a Jewish working party pushes a cart along. It is like a softened mass of dripping tar. In the present circumstances, it is the most appropriate response. It drives the Germans to desperation. They cannot get them to budge.

The *Häftlinge* work quite differently. They probably work five times as hard as we do. I cannot understand why they do not emulate us.[65] We have no contact with them and cannot understand them. The Germans say we are lazy, indolent slouches, slow and incapable of work. Jews do not know how to work. They guess correctly. We

---

[64] Unloading working party.

[65] (Author's note): After publication of this account in *De Groene Amsterdammer*, a political prisoner from another camp informed me that relations there had been exactly the opposite.

cannot work under these circumstances and will not do it. They can drag us here, whip us and beat us, we will do it as slowly and as sluggishly as *we* want and not a fraction more than the minimum. Of all the methods of undermining a system, this is one of the best. To the Kraut it must seem as if he is chewing on a sticky mass, or walking through thick syrup. Let them rave and rant. In Westerbork they used to sing 'immer langsam'.[66] A means of warfare *par excellence*. I have the greatest admiration for the consistency of this attitude. It was adopted spontaneously, without prior agreement. Right from the outset everyone was of like mind. It is a united stance. For the Jewish *Kapo*, who would prefer things to be different, it was all too much.

It is just a pity that even *something* gets done. Inertia is one of the means. Continually restarting to organise ourselves is the second. Never to allow oneself to be beaten, that is the great art. Forty-five men turned out today. How that is achieved, nobody knows. Nevertheless, it is achieved. Granted, they also took seventy women, but they would have been taken in any event, and will probably get out of it later.

Those who remained behind were the men from the *Jugendbetreuung*. It was quite an achievement. First for the teachers, second for the youngsters.

Education is strictly forbidden in a camp for Jews. Also assemblies of youngsters. All that is allowed is *Jugendbetreuung*, that is to say, the Germans are made to believe that the youngsters are lawless and need disciplining. That they do understand. Everything else they do not understand, even though they may have an inkling of being hoodwinked. Naturally they are furious about it. The only question is who can hold out longest; and that is us. We are tough.

We have built up a school here under the guise of *Jugendbetreuung*. The school is far from ideal. For a start, there are no proper teachers. Because things work as follows: when permission has been granted for something like *Jugendbetreuung*, the leaders select the men and

---

[66] Always slowly.

women for the task and thereby withdraw them from the hated working parties. In doing so, they may take into account not just the greater or lesser suitability of the candidates, but also the greater or lesser need to get them out of the working parties. Those in the worst condition must come first. Naturally, this results in complaints about protection and these complaints are partly correct, of course; or can you imagine a community of people living in circumstances such as ours where there is no protection? There is that unconscious protection that flows naturally from having connections. At the same time, one has to be very careful that protection does not turn into corruption. In fact, that applies to all aspects of our life here.

The partly suitable teachers have scarcely any materials. There are no blackboards, no exercise books, no paper, no ink, no pens, no pencils, no books.

There are also no classrooms. When it is warm and dry, one can at least sit outdoors; when it rains one is committed to the huts, where everyone jostles about with the greatest noise and tumult. From these unsuitable teachers who have no materials or books, amidst the biggest quarrels and screaming, with schooling that is constantly interrupted, our half-starved children are learning reading, writing and arithmetic, French, German, English and Hebrew, singing and gymnastics, geography and history, and listen wide-eyed and open-mouthed to the stories being told them.

We could draw up a timetable, but who could keep to it? Whenever a time is fixed, roll-call intervenes, and if not roll-call, air-raid alerts and if not air-raid alerts, the teacher is commandeered to carry containers or for some other task. Yet no one abandons hope.

They will fall quite a lot behind their former friends in the normal world. But they learn that life is hard, and with this lesson they will have to catch up with others.

Once they are grown up they will be able to tell stories to their children. Of the days here when it was their birthday and they did not get a present yet still had fun, because there was always a light bulb or a piece of paper that one could put to use, or a piece of extra bread with a shape on top made with jam. Of how they used to play with the broken undercarriage of a perambulator, because there was nothing else to play with; how they used to fight over it and how they would then be told off.

How they would be admonished by their father or mother who was always in a bad mood, or by some other person. How they were beaten as if they were a rug being beaten. How they would creep into bed crying and fall asleep sobbing, and then have such wonderful dreams about St Nicholas[67] at school ... Doing without toys, though, was not the worst. Under the ruins of bombed towns in Holland, Poland, Russia and elsewhere one could also not play with one's doll, and the magic lantern would also fall to smithereens. The worst of it is that nothing is hidden from them, that they do not live in a room, do not know what it is, and that everything is displayed before them naked and shameless. I remember searching for stolen laundry when a small scrawny woman from Amsterdam was under suspicion. I interrogated her and noticed her getting nervous. I felt untold pity for her because I knew full well what was going on.

In the past, she told me, she would often visit the market and the Bijenkorf for her shopping, and it was one of her life's pleasures to touch materials, to look for them in a big heap, to scrabble for them, to buy a piece of silk, a woollen shawl, a flowered cloth, some haberdashery, a piece of lace, a child's dress, a pair of stockings, a slip or a towel. Each time it was a treat for her, she 'had to go shopping', would arrange to meet a friend and then they would first travel some distance on the tram, then go window shopping for a while before entering all kinds of shops where she would look for something that she knew in advance she would not find, and then in the midst of a large crowd of other people, impatiently crowding people, she would make her purchases, slowly and thoroughly enjoying the tactile quality of the goods and the price, which in any case was not very high. It was this 'indulging', this tactile acquisition, that she needed so badly. Thus she had walked past the clotheslines

---

[67] Dutch children are given presents on the feast day of St Nicholas, 6 December.

and had touched and felt the items hanging there and had taken a few, a pair of trousers, a towel, a child's dress.

All that I could understand very well, even when she was still denying it, but precisely because she was denying it, I had to search her bed. However, she also had a child, and that child was ill in the bed next to hers, and it had to be sent away while I conducted the search.

As it was being carried away, I saw how she hid something under the child's shirt. The child was startled. At seven years old, it did not know what was happening, but (something far worse than knowing) it suspected something, and began to cry.

Or when H. and his wife were caught stealing bread, their children of twelve and eight could not be driven away from the case. Whether you forbade them or chased them away, or asked them in a friendly manner or threatened them with punishment, they clung to their parents and would not let go of their hands. For a long time now they had known about the bunker and the shame of it. And their father and mother, who had definitely not done anything ...

Naturally everyone knows everything about everyone else here. It is not just a village of four thousand souls, but you also eat together, work together, sleep together, and people count the pieces of potato in each other's plate of soup and the traces of fleas on each other's shirts.

So, when your father or mother is sent to the bunker, all the children in the hut will say: 'Fine family!' After all, father and mother had sworn they were innocent.

Oh, children from a camp for Jews, considering all the bitterness bottled up inside you, how will we prevent you afterwards from hating mankind?

How shall we prevent you from cursing your nation, whom you must blame for all this? Because you are a Jew they dragged you out of your bed at night and brought you here; because you are a Jew, they starve you and have taken away your toys. What did Judaism offer you in its place then? Perhaps the philanthropy of the Jewish Council, which failed to boot? Come, come with us! I want to take you to a country which does *not* flow with milk and honey, where there is no gold to be found or any other ore and also no petroleum. Where no riches await, and perhaps not even rest. Where you must work with your hands under a hot sun for a piece of bread and a plate of vegetables!

But where, if you dig in the ground, you will find one thing that the Jew finds nowhere else in the world: that little bit of simple human dignity, without which you suffocate, without which you despise both yourself and your life, even though you may not realise it.

I do not want to make rich and great people of you, not profound and not prominent ones, but simple, natural people, without that eternal Jewish problem, that problem to which you owe the title of being one of God's favourites, and which in reality always brands you as the scapegoat, which causes you to hover between the pretence of having been chosen and the curse of being an outcast, and which robs you of the peace of the lad and the lass who laugh for joy and dance because the force of life inspires them thereto. Who thank and worship God with the labours of their hands and the kisses from their lips.

9 September It is Sabbath today. A storm is blowing over the muster ground and there is intermittent rain. The men outside will return soaked and many, I fear, will fall ill. It has also become cold and bleak and we fear the coming winter.

This afternoon I read from the Torah the portion which is read in the synagogues today. Deuteronomy 28. God's great curse on the people, the repetition of Leviticus 26. I also added one of those great consoling prophecies from Isaiah.

'Listen: and those of you who remain, I will drive fear into their hearts, in the land of your enemies, such that the sound of a wind-blown leaf will frighten them.

'They will stumble one over the other ... and the land of your enemies will consume you.

'And I will break the bread staff over you, so that ten women shall bake your bread in one oven ... and your bread will be brought to you by weight, you will eat, but will not be sated.

' ... And among these nations you will find no respite and for your feet there will be no resting place. God will make your heart tremble there, cause your eyes to droop with longing and make sorrowful your soul. Your life will hang before you, night and day you will be afraid and no longer be confident of your life. In the mornings you will say "if only it were evening" and in the evenings "if only it were morning".

'God will appoint a nation over you, come from afar, like a flying eagle, a nation whose language you do not know. A shameless nation, devoid of respect for the elderly or compassion for the young. God will strike you with madness, with blindness and bewilderment. In the middle of the day you will grope about like a blind person in the dark, and you will fail in your endeavours. You will experience nothing but oppression and be robbed day upon day without anyone coming to your aid. You will betroth a woman and another will lie with her, you will build a house, but not live in it, plant a garden but not enjoy its fruits. Your sons and daughters will be delivered unto another nation, your eyes will see it and pine for them all day, but you will have no power.'

God kept his promise to the nation he had chosen to receive his Torah.

I read on: 'Yet even then, when they are in their enemies' lands, I shall not reject them and be so disgusted with them that I destroy them entirely and break my covenant with them. For I am Jahveh, their God.'

This grim and cruel God, who leads them to the edge of destruction, and then has pity on them, who has brought about all His punishments, this God loved Israel. In essence, it never let go of Him, because Israel cannot let go of this idea, that is why, moreover, it recorded what is written here. That is why the great prophet comes and calls: 'Arise' (Isaiah 60: 1-22).

10 September The news from Holland has not been confirmed. On the contrary, parcels dispatched on 1 and 2 September have arrived from Amsterdam. Various people here are disappointed, but I am not sure we need be so sad about that. There will be many fewer victims now and the NSB[68] will climb down a peg or two. Here it has got very chilly now. We are already suffering from cold hands and feet. The mood is becoming more sombre; we are reminded of the coming winter. What an exhilarating atmosphere there used to be in Amsterdam in autumn. How we used to love to walk in Gooi when the leaves were turning yellow. The past year has brought us nothing. No spring, no summer, no autumn. Not a flower, no blossom, no fruit.

Hopefully, it will be better next year.

We have news: Belgium liberated. Aachen under attack. Three hundred kilometres away.

We are thrilled!

Here they are really trying to erect huts now. A few walls are already standing. But I still believe the British will be here before the roof is on.

For the rest it is said that the Polish women are Jews from Lodz who have come here via Auschwitz.

We hear about Bulgaria, Romania, Zevenbruggen. Everything retaken, liberated, peace ... It is happening really fast, but our distress here is becoming greater and greater. In the past few days the beatings have been very severe.

At the appeal hearing, B. was found guilty after all. I am *Einzel-richter*[69] now and also carry the investigations out. We have traced two coats and a basket full of laundry. Caught a cigarette thief. Sentenced a man for throwing wood shavings from his mattress into a tub. If the Germans were to see it, the entire camp would be punished with two days' *Brotentzug* and the perpetrator sent to the KZ. Now he must forfeit two rations of jam. He is a pitiful Italian, all alone here, who bursts into tears whenever one asks him anything.

---

[68] Initials of the Dutch National Socialist movement.
[69] Sole judge.

88

Apart from that, there is excitement today, Sunday: goulash!

Goulash is water smelling of gravy. For the rest, red cabbage and *Pellkartoffeln*.[70] Enough to serve as a topic of conversation for three days, yesterday, today and tomorrow.

12 September A few days ago the *Abladekommando* comprised three hundred and eighty-nine men. Today two hundred and eighty. Forty-four dropped out for *Jugendbetreuung, Barackenleitung*,[71] et cetera. The rest are ill, that is to say, other than ordinarily ill. At least two hundred are that. What I mean is, men whom it would be medically irresponsible to send out. Here 'ill' means 'ill' by the criteria of the *Herr Sanitäter*. And when the *Herr Sanitäter* thinks you are ill and gives you a sick note for it, you are finished. You have either pneumonia or TB or at least 39.5° fever or swollen legs or facial oedema, in short, something for which in the good old days a family would come together, pull serious faces and the solicitor would have ordered a taxi by now. Here families do not gather, because there are none, a serious face is a superfluous luxury, and wills can be drawn up even without a solicitor. Some do indeed do that. Wills are recognised. And – quite frankly – the work is killing. One cannot make old people get up at five every morning. At this time of the year it is dark and bitterly cold. Roll-call starts at a quarter past six. A damp mist hangs over the muster ground and a gloomy dawn starts to break. Aversion for the day, loathing for the work, for this entire life, fills the people. The Krauts arrive, shout and curse, and force people into working parties again.

And each morning there is the same hope: that they will stay away, that it has ended.

The work has become hard now for the men. Unloading lorries laden with joists, planks, walls, doors, windows and parts of huts for eleven to fifteen hours is no picnic. Time and again the men lapse into a kind of automatism, of indifference, time and again they are

---

[70] Jacket potatoes
[71] Hut leadership.

beaten. Once the lorries have departed, they crawl behind a pile of timber and hide. When the next convoy of lorries arrives, everyone crowds at the same time. There are beatings and abuse. The Jews form a tangle, tread on each other's toes, push with their arms and fists, and snap at each other. The one seizes a plank, another a joist, and in the general confusion there are naturally many accidents. Miraculously, it is not worse.

The older men have lighter work. They have to straighten bent, rusty nails extracted from the planks, because in the sixth year of the war the Third Reich has run out of nails. They do this sitting on the damp ground in the cold, in the rain. Whenever it gets warmer, they have to remove their scarves and vests.

The following day, the *Herr Sanitäter* can issue sick notes again.

Fortunately the women, apart from the large groups assigned to permanent working parties, do not have to work. Nevertheless, they all have something to do, such as sweeping, cleaning or caring for the children, *Jugendbetreuung*, kitchen work, et cetera. Today, a shudder suddenly went through the camp. All the women must fall in. What is it this time? All the women, irrespective of whether they have been assigned duties or not. All the women up to a hundred years of age!

A couple of hundred women present themselves on the muster ground. Nine women are selected as cleaners for the *Kommandantur*,[72] a sought-after job, because it opens the door to ... news, and also because they get extra food.

The rest of the women can return to their huts.

What is it all in aid of?

Do not ask. Nonsense, nonsense, nonsense governs Germany. Yes, nonsense governs. We overheard the commandant say to a *Scharführer*: 'Was für Köpfe wir haben! Wir ziehen zurück um dort Schlacht zu liefern, wo *wir* das wollen!'[73]

They believe it.

---

[72] Camp commandant's office.
[73] What brilliant leaders we have! We retreat so as to fight where *we* want to fight!

We, on the other hand, believe what the IPA is telling us: the British are in Aachen!

Is that also nonsense?

But if *they*, with their nonsense, extend the war, we, with ours, extend our lives.

In the meantime there are many victims. Whenever there is a westerly wind, all over the camp one can smell the bones smouldering in the crematorium. The bones of the Jews smell exactly like the bones of the Aryan *Häftlinge* when they are burned. What a wonderful smell the bones of the Heroic Teuton Warriors will spread when they are placed on the fire.

For eight months two of our lads have been living in isolation. Allegedly, their task is to work the crematorium. They speak to no one, have no contact with anyone, their food is deposited somewhere by a *Scharführer*, they collect it. All day they have but one task: they make besoms from twigs. They deposit them somewhere from where they are collected. For eight months they have not spoken to anyone, apart from to each other. They see no one apart from the distorted faces of the corpses.

Then there are the youngsters who are becoming increasingly lawless. At roll-call they fight, throw stones, run to and fro, create confusion, become abusive and are disobedient. They are disobedient not least because everyone thinks they can have their say, interfere with them and admonish them. Everyone who is grumpy, everyone who is overwrought from the work and the constant noise, snaps at them. And the parents? The parents are like all parents. Stupid and devoid of any pedagogic insight. Here you can see what that means. Man believes that for everything he does he must first have been trained. But apparently everyone knows how to rear children! No expertise and no training is needed for this until it is too late! And very soon it will be too late here.

People have come to me to ask for measures to be taken. I summoned a meeting of those who I thought were qualified to give an opinion. But among the Jews there was an important gentleman who felt he had been overlooked. He sabotaged the meeting. Nothing will happen now. Notwithstanding that we are prisoners here, we did not leave our touchiness at home. Man is a stereotype and also not very attractive.

13 September A day in B-B. Yesterday: roll-call 6.15 a.m. Roll-call 9.00 a.m. Roll-call does not tally. Kept standing till 11.00 a.m. Air-raid alert. Roll-call still does not tally. Roll-call adjourned. 12.30 p.m. duty roll-call. 1.30 p.m. roll-call for all the women. 3.00 p.m. roll-call. Roll-call does not tally. 5.00 p.m. roll-call tallies. Air-raid alert. 7.10 p.m. roll-call. It gets dark. Roll-call does not tally. 9.10 p.m. roll-call tallies. We stood for hours, hours and hours. The French women are diametrically opposed to Prussian discipline. They never forget their lipstick and speak Yiddish. Their parents fled Poland because of the Russians and the children were deported from Paris by the Germans and wherever they were, they were nationalists. What will happen to the grandchildren? They are remarkable women these Polish-French Jewesses. Returning from work on the fourteenth of July, they marched through the gate singing the Marseillaise. The Germans threatened collective punishment if they did it again.

14 September Today the *Doppelstaatler*[74] were summoned for registration. Once again their expectations are being roused with 'Austausch'. Who knows what might still happen in this lunatic asylum?

Mrs N. was missing two and a half rations of bread yesterday. The investigators suspected Mrs D., the wife of a lawyer. Slices of bread were found in her possession which exactly matched a piece that Mrs N. still had. She denies it. She says someone else had stolen the bread and substituted the stolen bread for *hers*. She had failed to notice it and that is how she happened to be cutting the stolen bread. As a result, she has become the victim of an ingenious trick. Anything is possible, but I do not believe it, though I must

---

[74] People with dual nationality.

admit that there was no reason for the woman to have stolen bread.

All week there has been no news. Today is the fourteenth. Our last news is from 8 September. One plague the Torah does not mention!

Life is barren here, barren, barren. The people are dried up. It seems as though the elixir of life has dried up and only hunger has remained. It is ugly here. It is so ugly here that even lewdness, that attendant of beauty and the longing for beauty, has disappeared. There is no love here. No Eros.

The men do not court the women, not the young ones either. Here and there one might detect something resembling eroticism, but it is declining more and more. There are no affairs, and those that do exist are confined to superficial admiration. There is also none of that spicy malicious gossip so characteristic of village life. Because where something like extra-marital love occurs infrequently, no one feels threatened by it. Besides, it cannot happen to him because he is dried up and his wife is dried out and there is no reason, therefore, to become worked up over the one or the other. After all, that 'other' is usually none other than the potential 'I'.

And because there is no Eros, the women no longer care about their appearance. Clothes exist for keeping warm, and those you put on, one on top of another, depending on how cold it is. A skirt on top of trousers, trousers on top of a skirt, three pairs of socks on top of each other, a green jumper on top of a purple one, a torn blouse beneath a dirty apron, a dirty piece of material around one's head – nothing matters any more. Everyone's shoes are gradually falling apart and are worn down.

A bunch of emaciated beggars in grubby cast-offs are dancing around here.

Where is there still shame?

The washrooms are assigned to men and women at different times. But it is quite natural for men to be washing themselves stark naked while directly in front of them women are doing the laundry. Men wander around in the women's huts while the women are changing; no one is particularly shocked, because no one is excited by it. How could the pitiful arms and legs, the protruding ribs and bones, possibly make any impression on skeletons covered only by a layer of skin?

The moon in the sky ponders: where are the languorous lovers who would stroll by my light with their arms wrapped around each other?

You will not find the tomfoolery of love anywhere either. Not a single dirty word on any wall; nowhere will you find those imbecile allusions to unfulfilled sexuality which infantile sensuality is wont to spread on every street corner. The children no longer understand that men and women might do something other than sleep in separate huts. They have forgotten their parents' bedroom. They hardly know what a house is any longer. Now and then when someone or other has to work in the village, on his return he will recount with excitement of having seen 'ordinary' people. All that remains for us, apart from tormented and persecuted Jews, are uniforms and jaded *Häftlinge*. We are prisoners.

In the beginning, one occasionally saw a *Chaluz*[75] lying in bed beside his *Chavera* (girl friend). Now they have jaundice or diarrhoea. Only the Greek foreman, who has shown himself receptive to presents, and the *Judenälteste*, whose greatest concern is his feeding trough, still pinch girls' bottoms.

Once in a while people still tell each other a dirty joke. But it requires visible effort to listen to it. Here and there someone still boasts of having dreamt of a woman.

Even so: men and women grow closer together. They rest their heads on each other's shoulders out of a dreaded fear of loneliness. 'Please, don't leave me alone,' they seem to say.

Life has become phantasmal. The fire burns, but it is cold, and the light casts no shadow. We seem to be made of glass, just as transparent, just as brittle. Love has abandoned us.

16 September And because love has abandoned us, we also hardly

---

[75] Male Palestine pioneer.

ever cry any more. Only the children cry; the adults have their stereotypical postures of sorrow.

There is no despair, though. These days it seems as if a flag is flying over our heads. It is eternal hope. The French women sing 'C'est la fin de notre misère.'[76]

Those who feel down are told to keep quiet. Something resembling a festive mood is fluttering over the camp. There is good news.

The news arrived yesterday. Liège taken, also Maastricht, Brabant, Aachen, Düren, Trier. That is less than three hundred kilometres away.

The news is confirmed by a transport from Westerbork that arrived here unexpectedly. Now, for the first time in months, there is also news from Holland. Except for a hundred persons, Westerbork is empty. The Barneveld group that I used to belong to went to Theresienstadt. Also the converts.

A false alarm, about Rotterdam allegedly having been taken by the British, had caused panic among the NSB. Six thousand members of the NSB are said to have arrived in Westerbork in a far worse condition than ever the Jews were in. They arrived in the pouring rain, some barefoot, some with missing dentures, having fled from their bed in their nightshirts.

Now they will say that the Jew is vengeful. Why? Because revenge is wreaking itself on them, without anyone lifting a finger. They will never realise or admit that it is they who are 'guilty'.

Things take their natural course. Rocks always fall downwards, yet when they strike someone's head, man forgets the laws of nature and shifts the blame for the calamity onto the wicked Jew. And the more he does this, the more the Jew points to the reason for what has happened and refuses to allow the dream, that tempting self-deception, to rise up so as to hide in mists what is true and to a lazy person unpleasant. The transport from Westerbork included thirty-five children under five with a sign around their necks saying 'Unbekanntes Kind'.[77]

---

[76] It is the end of our wretchedness.   [77] Unknown child.

There were sick people among them who were unable to walk.

The fat SS watched the unloading and we thought: are these men not ashamed to be the revolver-bearing guards of this pitiful 'Arbeits-einsatz'?[78] Were these children in contact with Roosevelt or did they make communist propaganda?

Now that the fatherland is facing its greatest peril ought healthy adult men remain behind the front so that they can shout at and scare sick women?

Why do they always say that the Jew 'sich drückt'[79] behind the front? One needs to have witnessed the loading and unloading of a transport of Jews to understand why they say that.

So as to shift the feeling of guilt for their own cowardice.

The transport took two days and three nights to travel from Westerbork to here, a distance of a couple of hundred kilometres, shut up in goods wagons, each moment exposed to the dangers of a bombing raid, without enough water.

Once here, they had to carry as much of their luggage as possible on their backs and walk for an hour and a half from the station to the camp. Only the little children and the sick were transported by truck.

When they arrived here, worn out and half dead from thirst, we were not allowed to give them water.

There is no bread for these 275 people. We must surrender some of our supply by making four days' rations last five days. Recently, the distribution of bread has been irregular. It repeatedly arrives a day late. To disguise this, the camp is punished with a day's *Brotentzug*!

Yesterday, the vegetable-cleaning working party from kitchen number 1 were searched. Two Albanian women were caught in possession of a couple of small onions. The working party had to stand against the fence from half past six till ten. Naturally, the two women will be punished with bunker, if not KZ.

A couple of children who had been sent outside the camp to

---

[78] Labour assignment.   [79] Skrimshanks.

collect some mattresses stole a couple of turnips from the heap next to the kitchen. The *Torwache*[80] is punished with fourteen days' bunker, another with one month's bunker. Being *Torwache* is a cushy number. The man had been given the job because he has a heart complaint.

The bunker is a dark cell with a wooden bed to which one may or may not bring a blanket and where one is given a beating.

Nevertheless, it is still a *Vorzugslager*. Unlike Vught,[81] there is no 'Prügelstrafe'[82] here. Our commandant is a 'good one'. Just like *Gemmeker* in Westerbork.

The latter had four men from the last transport shot as they tried to escape. One of them did not die immediately, but no one was allowed to intervene. Bleed to death ...

Yes, now you know why they are against the Jews. Man has to be 'hard'. Made of steel. Yet the Bible says one has to be righteous.

And it not merely says it: but its voice screams, screams in one's blood: 'Cain, Cain, where is your brother Abel!'

Oh quiet, quiet – damned feeble voice. You who feel guilty without murdering, let me murder without feeling guilt. Away with the Jews.

Commandant Gemmeker loads little children. Commandant Haas unloads little children.

Their parents in Poland no longer have tears.

Two hundred and seventy-five people; the camp is getting fuller and fuller.

The transport from Westerbork brought an entire hospital installation (operating theatre), medicines, sheets, instruments, et cetera. The Germans stole everything. We have *nothing* any more.

Boxing bouts in the reptile house.

Mr A., a man of sixty-five, highly regarded in his former home town, wants to enter the hut.

Mr B., a man of sixty-five, no less highly regarded in his former home town, suddenly has a fit of persecution mania, rants and raves and lashes out about him, and has to be led away.

---

[80] Gatekeeper.   [81] A concentration camp in Holland.   [82] Corporal punishment.

Mr C., a man of sixty-five, likewise a highly regarded man in his former home town, is instructed by the hut leader to stand guard at the entrance to the hut and to let no one enter for as long as the scene with B. continues.

Mr A., however, wants to collect his food bowl, and therefore must and shall enter the hut. Mr C. holds him back, Mr A. shoves, Mr C. shoves back, and soon Mr C. and A., together 130 years old and prominent people in their home town, are hitting and punching each other on the face, head and body.

A. says C. started it; C. says A. started it.

A criminal case for the magistrate. Each had to forgo a ration of bread.

Or Mr X. places his suitcase on the edge of IJ.'s bed and IJ. objects, because 'his bed is his castle' and X. is always doing that and is an unpleasant character.

You are selfish.

And you, Sir, are no gentleman.

Soon the distinguished Messrs X. and IJ. are rolling about on the floor fighting and biting. Or: Mr N. accuses Mr M., who happens to be distributing potatoes at that moment, of putting a potato in his pocket.

M. says N. is a liar and is always making accusations.

N. insists. M. adds a little extra.

It carries on for a while, a day, and then Mr N. offers his apologies to Mr M., and Mr N. to Mr M. Whereupon the path to future quarrels has been smoothed over.

Such is life from one day to the next in the *Altersheim*. I cannot enter it without getting that creepy sensation that used to possess me as a child when I entered the reptile house at Artis.[83]

Yes, when you get old …

When you get old and you have no house of your own, no attic, not even a cellar, no stove of your own on which to warm your hands, no chair on which to sit, no cooker, no book, no newspaper,

---

[83] Amsterdam's zoological gardens.

no pipe to smoke, when you get old and have no cup of tea, no mug of coffee ... no cupboard in which to tidy something away. Your socks are always getting lost, you cannot find your underwear ... And when you wake up in the night you do not even have a chamber-pot of your own. It is pitch dark then, and in front of the toilet there are three people ahead of you.

And the children are in Poland and the grandchildren – wonderful children – where are they?

And next to you sleeps a man with whom you cannot exchange two words. And behind you a man who prays all the time and throughout your life you have detested piety, because from the start you have belonged to the union of liberals ...

And on the other side lies someone who soils his bed. And below you, someone who for days now has been longing for death.

And farther along someone who in his ninety-second year has become senile. And over there, someone who spends the entire day admiring himself in a mirror and combing his beard. And another who is always nattering on about the war and knows nothing about it. And yet another who is always silent, silent ... to the point of driving you mad.

And another who is always jumping the queue when food is being distributed. When you get old – and all day you are hungry, and cannot tolerate the food. And you have a rich life behind you, but ahead only the setting sun and not even a grave. Pneumonia and on top of a refuse cart to the crematorium. No one at your bedside. Your wife is ill or dead – and you are so hopelessly alone – and not even crying helps. That is when you feel really angry. You would like it to be different, but you cannot manage it; you had imagined it differently: 'when you get old'.

The flag above your head has gone. Hope! You are so afraid.

As long as it is summer and the sun shines, it is still tolerable, but once autumn has arrived and it rains, like today ... Such a constant drizzling rain ... And gradually it gets dark.

Where in God's name can you go then with your lost soul?

17 September Today is my birthday, for the first time since 1933 or perhaps even since 1929 a birthday with prospects. Not only freedom, but also a better world is beaming out at us. Providing we are alive we will be able to live as free people and participate again in all those things that give meaning to life.

Today, though, there were many delights. T. had a bread cake baked and also a potato cake. We are sitting together on my bed, feasting. Tonight is Rosh Hashanah (Jewish New Year).

Good news has reached us from the front. The transport from Westerbork brought us newspapers. I read the *Deutsche Zeitung für die Niederlande*[84] of 8 and 9 September. It is a pleasure to read how courageously the Germans are falling in battle.

Here, too, we are gradually beginning to notice that the Third Reich is dying. A few days ago we heard there was a train with war-wounded at the station.

Last night a group of men were summoned to unload railway trucks. Apparently, Vught concentration camp has been cleared. The Third Reich robbed it of everything. Hundreds of parcels, Dutch books, underwear, footwear, everything new and bearing the 'Vught' address. Sender: Vroom en Dreesmann.[85] Shovels, rope, cutlery, live cows and pigs, clothes, bundles of them. 'Ludo', probably stolen from the children in the camp for Jews. Toilet paper, washing powder, washing powder and more washing powder, cigarettes and Dutch gin. We know where it is stored and are already rubbing our hands.

The work took till half past one at night. This morning at half past six they had to report for duty. Today – Sunday – the work continues.

Our minds are full of thoughts. *Tesjoewa*[86] – turnabout. Psychologically, one cannot imagine a more profound thought.

The transport includes sixty GIs (half-Jews) who had been *Juden-freundlich*[87] and who have naturally become anti-Semites now. They say that eighty per cent of the Dutch are anti-Semites. It is probably

---

[84] The German Journal for the Netherlands.
[85] Name of a Dutch department store.   [86] Salvation.   [87] Friendly to Jews.

exaggerated, but substantially true. Those who have suffered because of the Jews will avenge that suffering on the Jews. The 'Mischlinge'[88] in the first place.

We talk at length and often about what we must do. Naturally there are numerous assimilators here, but there is also a substantial movement for a national Jewish revival.

The reconstruction of Zion occupies much of our thinking. I had a splendid birthday. Two cigarettes and a couple of liquorice drops. It is brilliant weather. The IPA says Bentheim has been taken. It sounds highly unlikely. Yesterday the IPA said Düsseldorf, Cologne, Juliers, and in the east: Posnania.

A festive spirit is blowing through the air. Hope and faith. The year[89] has passed in a flash. A dream has passed by.

18 September In the past Rosh Hashanah (New Year) and Yom Kippur (Day of Atonement) were also central to Jewish life, but to understand what this means, one needs to have been in a camp for Jews. Last night everyone was absorbed in a solemn festive atmosphere. Despite everything, it had already begun in the afternoon; children were given clean dresses and the women baked cakes, decorated with shapes made with jam. How does one bake a cake? With bread, a little sugar, and some water. One or two people still have some milk powder, or a little oatmeal. Baking is done in the infants' kitchen. Some tables even had candles on them. After all, new groups arrive here all the time and bring fresh supplies of these riches.

And everyone knew that the war was reaching an end. Everyone believed there had been a definite turning point. Every half hour the IPA announced that yet another town had fallen. It began with Cologne and Düsseldorf, Posnania and Breslau, and soon we had occupied Bentheim, Karlsruhe, Stuttgart, Königslautern,[90] et cetera.

---

[88] People of mixed race.   [89] The year by the Jewish calendar.

[90] Germany has towns named Königslutter and Kaiserslautern, but apparently not one named Königslautern. Going by the other towns mentioned here, it is believed that the author meant Kaiserslautern.

Afterwards we will find out how much of it was true. This morning they announced an offensive in the Ruhr. Cologne and Düsseldorf are confirmed. Further advances in Holland. Towards dusk everyone began to wish each other good luck. A collective heartiness and a remarkable warmth sprang up into which everyone was drawn and everyone merged. I thought of the song of the *Chaluzim*: 'How wonderful when brothers sit together.'

All the mutual hatred and malice, and all the objections that people had raised against each other, were forgotten then. A collective perspective filled the air. The murmuring of an impending new happiness ...

Weeping for joy, women threw their arms around each other's necks.

People from the last transport are horrified by the death-roll from the world between two streams.

We live in hope; but know that large numbers will not return from Poland. There were many, many crematoria ...

We know that difficult days may still lie ahead and know the dangers. Who knows if the SS have not already loaded their rifles for us ... ? They had promised us twice as much work for today and ... gave us double rations. They are mad. For the first time in more than eight months we had enough to eat. Potatoes, gravy, meat and cabbage. In honour of the Jewish New Year. And this evening we are having porridge. The SS are crazy.

For the rest, they are building at a stupendous rate. The two muster grounds are already partly occupied by new huts. Four out of the forty-four are already standing. Whether they are watertight is another question. We are going to move, we are told. It is not clear to us who will move into our huts. Probably the *Häftlinge*.

Are they planning to expand the camp? With whom?

Four days after Yom Kippur is Sukkut (Feast of Tabernacles).

We will cover the roofs with the green from the nearby pine trees.

We will go for a stroll in the woods. Our longing for freedom is infinite ...

Rabbi S. is not going to cut off his beard. The Third Reich hates

Jews and among the Jews, rabbis in particular. Rabbis have to do extra work here.

And everyone with a beard is called 'rabbi'.

Consequently, beards must be shaven off, but R.S. refuses.

Surprisingly, the SS relent. R.S., however, complete *with* beard, is assigned to a hard labour working party. Rabbi S. laughs and triumphs.

But the outdoor working party is stronger than R.S., and one evening, when he has to stand against the fence for punishment, he collapses.

They carry him to his bed and everyone advises him: shave your beard off. The next morning R.S. gets up at five, goes to his work, combs his beard and grins. It is not a very pleasing beard. On the contrary. It is a short woolly beard, greying black, which gives R.S. the appearance of a typical Polish Jew, conspicuous in this camp and the object of derision of the entire SS. Rabbi S. is also not in the least an important man; he is neither learned, handsome, nor intelligent. He is a pious man and does not deviate in the slightest from the Laws of Moses and of Israel. R.S. does not shave his beard off. The SS can order what it likes – a Jew like him wears a beard.

R.S. loses his strength. For a long time now, the *Ältestenrat* has offered him an easy job, but demands that he shave off his beard. It *has* to demand this because if a *Scharführer* were to see this beard *inside* the camp, he would get wild and mete out harsh punishment. Not only to R.S., who in the meantime is assigned, moreover, to a hard labour working party again, but also to the *Vorarbeiter* and others.

R.S. remains silent. He does not shave. The *Ältestenrat* cannot understand that he is attacking an entire world. If R.S.'s beard were to fall, part of that world would fall, a bastion.

The bastion does not fall.

Germany falls, the Third Reich falls, R.S.'s beard does not fall. I dare you to say again that Jews cannot organise themselves. That, gentlemen of the myth, that is how a nation makes history.

And it is highly debatable who does more for the survival of the nation. The chairman of the Jewish Council, or R.S. who obstinately and at the risk of his life refuses to shave off his beard. An ugly woolly beard, an absurdity to do something like that for a beard.

No one knows if he has not made a vow: to serve God in *his* way. He does not shave and will not allow anyone else to shave it either. R.S. entered the war with a beard and intends to win the war. His beard remains beard.

19 September The crematorium will have a good laugh today. 'Der Herr Sanitäter' has died. What is more, he died by his own hand. He used to threaten it: 'Wenn die Sache schief geht ... '[91] Despite this threat, *die Sache ist nicht recht gegangen.*[92] *Der Herr Sanitäter* had drunk a large bottle of rum, and with the courage of melancholy drunkenness, had pressed his revolver to his head.

When he has arrived at the throne of eternal accountability, they will call a number of witnesses. Material witnesses. Jews from Bergen-Belsen, who had stood before him trembling with fever, whom he had refused to make *Dienstfrei.*[93] Jews who had been sent out to work last winter when they had longed for a little warmth and rest.

In heaven they will stand before the throne of justice. All that the *Herr Sanitäter* can do then is to hope for God's mercy. Woe betide him on his day of judgment.

20 September The SS are angels. For Rosh Hashanah they gave us enough to eat. Yesterday it was red cabbage, so rancid that it was uneatable. But probably it was not their fault. For however much we may condemn them after the war, they always tried to prepare tasty food. Indeed, the food was usually most palatable. Nowadays we get turnips to eat, Sunday turnips, Monday turnips, Tuesday and Wednesday turnips, Thursday and Friday turnips and for a change, more turnips on Saturday. The turnips are as woody as our mattresses, but apart from that, they are excellent. True, there are never enough.

---

[91] If things take a bad turn ...   [92] Things did not go well.
[93] Exempt from work.

Last winter we had swedes every day, seven times a week. Not until the beginning of spring were we occasionally given pea soup, or carrots or unpalatable spinach. Apart from that, swedes for four whole months. Because monotony is one of the tortures they thought up for the Jews. The work is monotonous, the surroundings are monotonous, and the food is monotonous. Only the punishment, and the way we are treated, has variety. Although the methods of torture employed thereby are also becoming more than familiar, and hence quite boring in fact. If we remain here much longer they may even give us *Prügel*.[94] Though there will probably not be enough time for that. This morning I fainted from hunger. Another new experience. The IPA speaks of Osnabrück, Hanover, and more such unbelievable things. Holland is said to be free. Since 15 September we have not received any reliable news.

21 September The dying continues ...

Every day.

Today, there are two for the furnace. S., a bank director from Hamburg, an aesthete and distinguished figure. On 9 May he received his visa for England where his wife lives. Now she is waiting ... the final days of the war.

De W.; day by day we saw him starve to death here. He used to sell oranges on the corner of Kloveniersburgwal and Hoogstraat in Amsterdam. The most decent and obliging person in the world. I can see him repeatedly toppling over. I had given him plenty of warning.

Others who died here are the lawyer M.J.P. and G., to whom I used to offer my arm because he had difficulty in walking. The British are taking their time.

Though the guards did tell us that Holland is free now. The guards are men of almost sixty. They tell us the 'young ones' are pulling out of here, by which they mean all those under fifty. They will take over guard duties then and reassure us. We have nothing to

---

[94] Thrashing.

fear from them. They promise aid, and something that makes more of an impression, cigarettes.

Hundreds of thousands of cigarettes have arrived in the camp from Vught. Furniture, machines, also from Vittel.[95] Everything points to Germany's retreat. The SS gave us splendid clothes from Vittel; enough for at least one man and two women. Tomorrow we will get cheese from Vittel. Though, for the past two days there has been no bread. All sorts of reasons are given for this. Lack of transport, a dispute with the baker, but that is all IPA. The fact is, that we are hungry and have no bread.

On the muster ground, there are already four huts standing. Not until one looks more closely at them does one realise what they consist of. Gaps and holes, partly decayed and partly broken planks nailed together, where the lice make merry. Not a single pane has remained unbroken. They are unfit for people to live in. Apart from that, there is much stealing again. Now it is the ladies' turn. A slip, gloves, wool, all by people who are totally confused. A man who stole four cigarettes ...

How much longer will this war last? Ought we still to prosecute? Is it still worth the effort?

There are also many thefts of bread again. Not a trace can be found of the perpetrators.

The bread has just arrived. Pieces of crust and entire chunks have been broken off fifty-eight loaves. The carriers will have to answer for that. X. got very worked up.

The Germans know about it. Naturally X. is dead scared again. 'Harsh punishment!' he sighs, 'harsh punishment.'

I acknowledge that it is a sordid business. When a search was made chunks of bread were found in the carriers' pockets. It is a serious offence against the community. Yet I can no longer get so worked up over it.

I look at the sky. Are they not coming yet ... ?

The Albanian's wife and daughter-in-law, who made such a

---

[95] An internment camp in France.

hullabaloo over his death a few days ago, came to see me, quarrelling and arguing with their hands and feet. I need an interpreter who explains to me that it concerns the inheritance.

The inheritance consists of a bundle of clothes. If the wife were to receive the overcoat, she would be satisfied. So the wife gets the overcoat. Again I look at the sky then. Where are they … ?

Yesterday, delousing shower for fleas and lice; they kept us standing for four hours. When we returned at half past five, there was roll-call till half past seven. Give me fleas and lice any time, especially as even without them we will die from the itch.

I am homesick. It is taking too long.

De W. was a jewel of a man. An example. Poor wretch.

22 *September* Mrs S. looks terrible. She has suddenly become thinner today. Her head has grown small and gaunt, her cheeks are sunken, her mouth and teeth are disproportionately large, her nose juts out, her eyes are veiled by a grey shadow and grimy wrinkles show in the corners of her mouth and across her chin. Her clothes bag on her body, her stockings are too big, and her shoes have become too large for her.

Yet still she smiles, but her smile makes her look ugly.

What has happened?

The transport from Westerbork had not brought a letter or parcel for her. However, her husband is in Westerbork, and although we try to inspire her with courage and tell her that nothing could have happened, her disappointment and fear, of which she may not even be conscious, are so great that she cannot surmount them.

Besides, what has happened to the rest of us?

Sometimes, holding your head in your hands, you ask yourself full of dismay: what has happened to my life? How old am I? It has gone. It is destroyed.

It has passed by so quickly that in retrospect it seems as if time has not existed, as if everything has happened simultaneously, and 'one-after-another' had just been an illusion.

From the moment you are born, you begin to die, you marry, you beget children, they leave you, you build up your world, and it collapses.

It seems as if suddenly you see your entire life reflected in a drop of crystal. Time does not exist.

There is only war. From the beginning of the world until now was just a twinkling of an eye, a sigh; but from now till the evening meal will be ages still. 'Yesterday' lies in front of me, as tangible as this sheet of paper, 'tomorrow' lies somewhere in the unreachable distance.

Besides war there is also all-consuming nostalgia such as the eyes of a little child that you recall, her sweet posture when she presses herself closely against you and asks you something: 'Dad!'

Then there is roll-call, of course, roll-call, roll-call!

23 September The longer it lasts, the more difficult it gets. The mood is getting worse and worse. Impatience is mounting by the hour. One day we are abuzz with optimistic IPAs and the next the reaction is that much greater.

The day started with news of fighting near Amsterdam. The fierce interest in what is happening in Holland has subsided.

Five people were sent away. No one knows where to, not even they. What kind of new cruelty is this? Are they destined for Palestine or KZ? Opinions are divided.

S. died suddenly. Inventor by profession. Once, I also caught him stealing cigarettes. It stopped at an attempt. The crematorium will probably forgive him.

The crematorium here stands in the background of our entire existence. And just as we do not know where the five went to, so none of us knows whether it will be liberation by the British or by the crematorium.

The beatings are getting increasingly vicious. They have resorted to using their rifle butts. Some of the prisoners can no longer move from the pain.

On the other hand, we hear that the SS are leaving and are being replaced by elderly soldiers.

After the war these young SS men, who order women and children about, will have the most to say about the front.

We know nothing.

Yesterday there was cheese. From Vught. A delicacy, and more nourishing than anything else. At the same time, the bread ration was cut by ten per cent. We are now getting about 300 grams a day. It used to be 375.

Our cooked meals have also been reduced. Yesterday there was less than the day before; today, again less than yesterday.

It is so-called punishment. But the truth is probably quite different. Either is possible.

Soon we must move to the shanties that are currently being built on the muster ground. They are really lousy shanties, aside from the cracks and holes in them.

Heaven help us.

The remarkable thing in this war is that one keeps thinking it cannot get worse, and then conditions get worse all the same.

The ultimate is never reached. The only ultimate is the 'crematorium'. That is where the world ends. That is where infinity ends.

Two men operate the crematorium. Now, after eight months of loneliness, they have become unreal characters. Mysterious creatures, who would not surprise us if they were suddenly to acquire wings and fly, or were to propel themselves on flaming wheels. Dream characters, come alive.

Across the barbed wire news is also getting through about the adjoining camps. Groups of Jewish women – besides others – live there, that is certain. They are separated from their husbands and children. They are from Lodz. They wear uniform dresses and walk about with short hair.

They are like animals. Completely dishevelled and shattered. When food arrives, they behave like animals. It is far worse than here.

I know that all those who want to escape from Judaism will use it as a pretext. Those who behaved most selfishly, who pushed themselves most vigorously to the fore, who obtained the greatest advantages for themselves, who stole and deprived others, who have a bad conscience, will be the first to revile the Jews so that they might abandon Judaism.

I also know that every anti-Semite will turn the life of the Jews in this misery into an inexhaustible mine of accusations. I shall not ask how they themselves would become in circumstances like ours. One need look only at the bestialities and foul deeds committed against us by the Third Reich.

The crimes they have committed against us, daily, we have not committed in all these years.

But to justify their inhumanity they reproach us with bestiality.

I am not prepared to gloss over the conduct of the Jews or to forgive them their failings to which they succumbed here. Even so, it is important to know how a person's soul and spirit can be destroyed by the pressure that he is put under. There is nothing that can help to withstand that.

It is ugly here. A camp for Jews is ugly, more ugly than anything else, outside and inside. None the less ... None the less, sometimes you notice the finely curved outline of a sweet profile which tells you that all the world's suffering need not attach itself like fungus to the human soul but can also raise to sublime heights something solid and heavy lying partly hidden in marshy ground. None the less, sometimes you are greeted by eyes that shine, in which the miracle of love has remained untainted, or a face so fresh, so happy, so young, so full of trust and hope, that it seems as if the dew of happiness has settled there for ever. None the less, sometimes you hear a single word reverberating with the magic sound of people living in brotherhood.

None the less, occasionally you see someone helping another, a doctor applying a bandage, a woman cooking for a sick person, another doing her washing, or quietly giving a warm coat away, a mother who has adopted one or more orphans and assumed full responsibility for them with the courage that nature sometimes gives its creatures.

None the less, it restores your basic faith in the existence of civilising, constructive forces that will persevere in the community of mankind so as to regulate relationships according to reason, to ideas, to spirit, and not according to force. If you now tell me that these are none the less very small, insignificant and isolated moments in the gruesome life from the world between two streams, I will take from my pocket the book from which people better than you and I have drawn so much wisdom.

24 September And it becomes evening and it becomes morning, the days are getting shorter, autumn has arrived, it is cold and wet. We had a beautiful September, but now the rains have set in.

When we get up in the mornings it is still night; in the evenings it already starts to get dark while we are having our meal and once again the full melancholy of winter threatens in the background.

Do you know what winter is like in a camp for Jews?

There is no light, a single light bulb in the hut casts a faltering shadow over the people crouching closely together.

We spent the evenings apart from each other. The women in the women's camp, the men in the men's camp, divided by a wall of barbed wire and another wall of barbed wire and a gate of barbed wire, which would be shut at 7.00 p.m.

That closing was yet another ceremony in itself. It was the source of all kinds of vexations and pettifoggery, as was everything to do with the 'Dienst',[96] beginning with hounding people, waiting for the *Scharführer*, and inspection of the huts for the presence of forbidden sexes. Heinz or Fritz or one of those other sadists would enter, closely followed by the *Judenälteste*. Everyone jumps to attention, caps doffed. Those who are busy stop whatever they are doing.

'Blockältester Block 13 meldet sich. Keine Frauen mehr anwesend.'[97]

The hut leader recites his lesson.

What next?

Pettifoggery: because a piece of paper is lying on the floor, or a table has not been cleaned yet, or despite it being forbidden, someone

---

[96] Duties.   [97] Hut leader 13 reporting. No more women present.

is smoking (we all do that when we have something to smoke, but do not always succeed in spiriting the cigarette away), or the stools are not set out neatly enough for their lordships, or … there is always something. There is shouting and punishment; withholding of bread.

I recall an occasion when a Jew from Eastern Europe had tied a belt around his coat according to the custom there. The sight of it irritated the *Herr Scharführer*. *Herr Scharführer* wrenched the belt off and belted the poor Pollack around the ears with it. Then he snorted out of the hut, but returned again!

'Und das will *uns* Kultur lehren. Je mehr man Euch kennen lernt, je mehr hasst man Euch.'[98]

Nevertheless, it sounded like an apology. No doubt it was meant differently. That is how they inspire themselves with courage.

Sometimes the *Scharführer* walks through the sleeping area of the hut, returns, says something meant as a joke to the *Judenälteste*, who then laughs in a most obsequious manner – and then departs to another hut where the same game commences.

Once inspection is over, we can breathe again.

We gather together and try to converse then.

It is not very successful, though. We try to maintain a certain intellectual level.

After eleven hours of work, after having been hounded all day, the men retire early. Besides, they are getting hungrier and hungrier. The culture programme is a failure.

It is not easy to overcome the feelings of dejection, or to struggle against the sombre mood of dusk. Some of the men remain seated, a few old ones, a few others, too lazy to go to bed. They try to push each other aside to obtain some warmth from the stove.

The stove, though, emits hardly any heat for there is no coal and insufficient wood. The top is nevertheless covered with mugs and pots in which their owners try to heat something. People fight and quarrel for a place.

---

[98] And that wants to teach *us* culture. The more one gets to know you, the more one hates you.

Around the stove is a length of wire from which water bottles are hanging. Everyone wants a little hot water for a hot water bottle or a hot drink. This one still has a few tea leaves, another a stock cube.

Very occasionally someone sings.

Those who went to bed to sleep, complain.

In any case, the singing is not very good. No one enjoys it. It is no use.

'How can we sing on foreign, foreign, foreign soil?'

We tried to give one or two lectures. The interest is minimal. It is doggedly repeated a few times. Then it, too, comes to an end.

Only the *Chaluzim* continue to find a little strength in each other. They meet regularly at least once a week and keep alive the dream of working in the land of Israel.

The others are lonely and try in vain to forget their sorrow.

The devout had their God to whom they flee endlessly with a doubling of prayers now that fulfilment of every commandment has become impossible for them. They had to eat from the unclean animal, eat food that had been prepared contrary to the law of the fathers, violate the holy Sabbath, and forgo the prescribed rest on the feast day. With a hundredfold devotion they now threw themselves into prayer to prove to the Lord of hosts that they were not acting like that out of disloyalty to Him, but that they still loved Him as always, 'with all their heart, with all their soul, and with all their intellect' ...

25 *September* The men are refusing flatly to work. Fewer and fewer report for roll-call. The Germans rage, it is no use. They punish with *Brotentzug*, it is no use. The entire camp will be punished now. It will be of even less use.

Why are they refusing to go? Because they cannot go on any longer. They are worn out. There are some who are assigned work in the morning, and by the afternoon are already hiding themselves. This afternoon, there were twenty-two.

The only question is, how long this wretchedness will last.

Again we have had no news. The last reliable news was from the fifteenth. That means that we are nearly two weeks behind. It depresses our spirits. The food is abominable. Filthy spinach soup. The bread is getting less.

This afternoon three cases: theft of four cigarettes and a fag-end, theft of two and a half rations of bread, and the famous theft of bread while it was being transported.

I am damned if I know what punishment to demand. I would prefer to acquit all of them, notwithstanding that the culprits are some of the most extreme egotists and that the theft is most disgraceful.

The Third Reich has come to observe, and the thieves are certainly not such out-and-out scoundrels as they are.

P. has stolen cigarettes from V.'s bed; four days. Mrs D. has stolen bread from her neighbour's bed. She denies it, but is simple-minded. We will have her examined. Sentence? Four days? The transport thieves deserve at least fourteen days. I have the interests of the camp in mind. Four days' bread and water. Perhaps the British will arrive in the meantime ... I wagered that by 1 October they would be in Berlin ...

Oh, that wretched stench from the toilet when one sits on one's bed here. They say that the SS are also no longer receiving newspapers. It is more likely, though, that they are put off by the endless reports of disasters, that they have had enough of it of their own accord, just as we often used to have enough of reading the newspapers or listening to the news ...

The IPA says Posen, the IPA stands by Osnabrück.

H., poor devil, has stolen a fountain pen. The boy is as lonely as can be here. He ought to get some help and guidance.

28 September Thursday morning. No one who has not experienced Yom Kippur in his childhood and grown up with it from year to year will ever understand the enormous significance of this feast of feasts. A feast that is celebrated by a complete and continuous fasting for more than twenty-four hours, a long day of unbroken concentrated prayer, which ultimately brings about such a deep and spiritualised joy, such a clarity about the sense and purpose of life, that people do indeed draw strength from it with which to endure every imaginable tribulation. And what tribulations has the Jewish nation not experienced over the thousands of years of its existence! ...

The ideas to which the Day of Atonement is dedicated, pursued with an intensity and obstinacy that characterises Jewish ritual, make the Jew into a free and sovereign person in his relationship to others. The total submission to the idea of the Oneness of God, the acknowledgement that every passion, every wish and every desire, without reservation, must be subjected to this idea, make him unassailable to debasement. By doing penance, by making a collective avowal of guilt, insight is acquired into the primacy of the spirit of which the Jew becomes so much a part that it truly raises him above every act of violence committed against him, and it achieves this despite every pain. At the end of Yom Hakippurim (the day of atonement), imbued with an unshakeable sense of the crucial value of this insight, the Jew returns from the synagogue to everyday life with the worthiness and self-consciousness of a man who, come what may, sees himself capable of mastering this life.

The Jew is not a hero in the sense of the sagas or in the spirit of the knight, but if you want to learn something of the power of a considered and responsible profession of the Jewish religion, take an objective look (if you are still able to) at the pride and the sublime joy with which, after a tiring day of fasting and prayer, he commences that same evening on building his tabernacle, that most meaningful symbol of the courage to live. See how he needs to clothe himself with humility so that he might experience the worthiness of his optimism.

All religious observance in an SS camp for Jews is forbidden, the celebration of Yom Kippur above all. The result of this ban was that religious observance took place in *every* hut, despite the work that still had to be done that day, despite three roll-calls, despite the air-raid alerts, despite the pouring rain. We can meet before work, before six in the morning. Those who remain inside the camp also meet between roll-calls, and after half past six in the evening, when the working parties have returned, there is an opportunity for the final prayer, that poetic mystical web of verses and avowals which, in the evening twilight, creates a mood all its own. With their *talliths* over their wet working clothes, the men stood in the falling darkness full of nostalgia for their God, Whose praise they declare and Whose help they implore. Not everyone understands all that He utters, but everyone understands the hidden meaning of the melody.

And then there occurs that remarkable phenomenon that Jews so willingly repudiate: a unity among them, which is a unity of brothers, a love between souls. It is neither general nor lasting, but wherever it exists, and for as long as it exists, it is close.

The Jewish nation is an apolitical nation. Much to its cost it has not managed to form a national political unity, but a religious unity keeps growing from within, spontaneously, like palms near water, its roots striking ever deeper the larger the groups affected by the suffering of the Jews. Granted, at first sight the Dutch Jew appears to have nothing in common with the natives from North Africa or the poor Albanian shopkeeper. And even in their devotions there are differences in form and appearance. But when they stand before their God you can exchange the one for the other, for they are characterised by the same willingness of heart, the same courage with which to face life, the same subjection to a task prescribed for life. Judaism flows apart and then merges again and always issues into a single thought that makes the religion into a world religion of universal and eternal character: God is unity.

Judaism is much scorned, and often the Jew himself mingles willingly with the choir of scorners. For although religious unity among the Jews may be extensive, those who out of self-interest seek their community elsewhere naturally need justification for their – otherwise futile – flight, and seek it not within themselves but in the nation and its religious culture. The feelings of the Jew towards this are comparable only with the feelings of an artist driven by his genius, whose work is ridiculed when subjected to the criticism of his contemporaries. Neither criticism nor ridicule can shake in him the proud knowledge that he is eternal.

And in this way the Jew knows (he does not feel, he knows) that by discovering and each year rediscovering his truth, he is eternal. And it is like new, even though he may discover it a thousand times.

Now, the annual reawakening of Jewish immortality belongs to the riches of the Day of Atonement, and clearly, a day that possesses such power must have an atmosphere all its own. There is not a Jew who would not want to belong to this atmosphere for as long as he wants to be considered a Jew. The numerous individuals – and they have always been numerous – who are unable to fathom the concept of this day of atonement nevertheless know that an eternal thought is being expressed, and out of a secret respect for it, they understand that this thought cannot be abandoned with impunity. Almost all join in 'a little'. People fast, people fast for half a day, people fast and go to synagogue, people fast and do not go, or people go but do not fast, or people fast a little and go a lot, or fast a lot and go a little – in short, an infinite number of variations exists. But hardly anyone relinquishes everything. These thousands (and they are the large mass of the mediocre) are like a page in love, who, though not chosen to be the bridegroom, at least wants to carry the bridal train.

That is how, at the bottom of this ocean of misery, we celebrated the Day of Atonement here. A motley group of people, driven and held here by the enemy's revolver, greatly astonished at the wonder flower[99] flowering from its heart. For just one moment, a flame of unity flared up, warmed every soul and melted them into an eternal alloy. Sorrow and tears, sorrow and tears and the longing for life and the will to live, trust, the positive and heroic acceptance of life sounded from the general wish with which they greeted each other on this and subsequent days: a long life.

This has been the sound over many centuries, and for many centuries to come it will sound no different.

---

[99] Marvel of Peru – *Mirabilis jalapa*.

And every enemy, including the SS, exists for us as if they were yesterday, as if they were last year's snow. They are worthless. They lead to emptiness and vanity and we will survive. Next year in Jerusalem. With these words the Day of Atonement ends too.

29 September The mood among the Jews in Bergen-Belsen camp is bad.

The mood can be good only when there are prospects of an early release. But the news that has reached us precludes such a prospect.

Apparently Arnhem has been retaken and there is also talk of Eindhoven. The dark prospect of another winter in this camp is already looming in the background. In any event, the illusion of a very rapid end has evaporated.

We have little news. The waiting is an unbearable torment. We all have relatives in Holland. Our children are there. We fear, we hope ...

Oh dear, oh dear, what has this world come to?

It seems as if people are living under a curse that is driving them mad. This, too, we have noticed again in the last few days. The SS are raging. Yesterday the commandant dismissed the Dutch members of the *Ältestenrat* because of sabotage by the 'Holländer'.[100] We are accused of sabotage. After the war, it will be an honour. Now, it is far from pleasant. To be accused of sabotage is extremely dangerous, because the punishment is at least KZ. KZ means the end. The end means the crematorium.

Moreover, who in the *Ältestenrat* will look after our interests? And they exist. Again we can only wait wearily. In the meantime we can amuse ourselves by contemplating the corrupting influence of slavery on the human spirit. For example, consider the verdict of M. and his cronies.

M. went as foreman with a group of ten men to collect bread from the bakery. On their return, 127 of the four thousand loaves were found to be damaged, in so far as large pieces of crust had

---

[100] Dutch nationals.

been broken off. The driver called the *Scharführer*, and naturally the fat was in the fire then.

The first of the German measures is to search every member of the working party. Pieces of bread crust are found on M. and his brother. Every name, in particular those of the M.s, is noted down. That can cost four weeks' bunker. Alternatively, even KZ. And KZ means crematorium.

M. claims that many of the loaves had got 'scalped' during the loading, that is to say, the crust had fallen off. The bread had been very fresh. Besides, after the truck had been loaded, the working party had been ordered to load an extra twelve hundred loaves, in the process of which they had to walk with their shoes on the loaves that had already been loaded. This had caused further damage. He claims that during loading he had drawn the *Scharführer*'s attention to the damage to numerous loaves. As for the bread found in his pocket, he claims they were crumbs that had fallen off which he had found on the floor of the truck.

One need have only a superficial knowledge of the mentality of the SS to know that such resistance – like all resistance in fact – incites them only to harsher punishment.

To 'prevent worse', the *Judenälteste* stepped in and punished the entire working party with forfeiture of three rations of bread, although there was not the slightest evidence that *all* of them had broken off pieces of bread, and before anything of the kind had been established.

For the rest, the matter was referred to the judicial commission.

Immediately there are two currents of opinion. The first says 'administer justice'. Administer blind justice, independently of the SS.

The second says 'play judicial politics'. Punish with an eye on the Germans. Punish so that they will be satisfied.

Against this, the first maintain: you do not know what will satisfy them. Besides, as a matter of principle, justice is not politics.

Neither of the two currents manages to win.

The investigators begin a preliminary investigation. It yields serious suspicions against the foreman, and yields *nothing* against the others.

Several members of the working party report that during the loading there had been talk of eating bread, that one of them had given a firm warning against breaking off crusts, that the M.s had done this before and that it had caused serious difficulties. There is great fear of collective punishment if it is discovered that one of them has broken off pieces of bread. Of course, bread that had *fallen off* which would otherwise be thrown away, can be eaten. And indeed, it seems that most, if not all, did eat bread. Some of the witnesses also report that on the way back, the foreman M. had placed himself somewhere on top of the truck where he could grab with his hand under the cover that had been thrown over the bread, and that he had indeed grabbed. Both he and his brother had eaten during the journey, and a couple of youngsters from the working party had said to each other that they found that mean and unsociable. Naturally the bread that was broken off is all at the expense of the community. M. denies his guilt and sticks to his story.

The dispute between the two currents naturally grows in intensity in this situation. The one says punish M. and no one else. The other, by way of all kinds of detours, decides on collective punishment. They argue that it is inconceivable that one man could have nibbled from 127 loaves. Hence the Germans will not be satisfied if he alone is sentenced.

Viewed objectively, it is indeed highly probable that more than one person had broken off pieces from the loaves and eaten the broken pieces.

However, on the strength of the witnesses' statements it is impossible to establish *who* is or are guilty, and to what extent they are guilty.

Acquit, shout some. Convict, shout the others. Suddenly the independence of our jurisdiction is at stake. The intrinsic independence of the judiciary. Finally, it is decided to summon both the brothers M., to subpoena the other members of the working party, and that it will depend on the cross-examination by the bench whether further prosecution takes place against all or some of them.

The cross-examination shows that despite his denial, foreman M. is guilty. Again no evidence can be found against the others. We were no further than the original well-founded suspicion that more than one man had done the breaking and eating.

The majority on the bench vote for a collective conviction.

The opposition resists with utmost force.

Then judgment is given: M. is sentenced to fourteen days' bunker; bread and water for the first three days, then every other day. As for the rest, withholding of three rations of bread by the *Judenälteste* is judicially confirmed. It is assumed that most of them had eaten, and that on those grounds all of them can be punished. And then something remarkable happens; the *Ältestenrat* does *not* accept the court's judgment.

However, the bread remains forfeited as an administrative measure, which has indeed something to commend it. Besides, a group sent out to collect bread is in a certain sense responsible for ensuring that the bread arrives undamaged. The administrative measure is felt to be a kind of compensation.

As a measure of punishment, however, it is *not* carried out, and the requested public announcement – except for the one against the brothers M. (the charges against the second M. – though insufficient for a conviction – were unanimously felt to be quite well-founded), is rejected.

Thus, the odium of theft does not fall on the group as a whole. They were not punished. People will say this is only of moral significance. Anyone who has lived in a camp such as this will know the practical significance of morality.

Those are more or less our concerns. Concerns for our purity.

30 September Late last night a new transport of twenty people arrived from Theresienstadt. They are mainly people with South American papers and appear to have been sent here as a kind of 'favour'. They tell us all kinds of things, but little that we do not already know.

Theresienstadt is a Jewish town under Jewish self-government. Out of the forty-five thousand people, twenty-five thousand are still there. The rest were gradually sent to Poland and, most recently, to Germany for *Arbeitseinsatz*. As a result, men of from fifteen to fifty-five years were separated from wives and children.

The transport felt quite low and extremely tired. They had been on the move for fifty hours. We heard that the transport from Westerbork, consisting of *Barnevelders* (those previously interned in Barneveld), converts and others, had arrived there. The *Barnevelders* and the converts were not yet included in *Arbeitseinsatz*. The promise made at the time relating to the possibility of Dutch reprisals, since realised, still appears to be holding good. Krauts always renege on their word in stages. Never entirely and never not entirely, but always by degrees. Just as they also intensify a persecution by degrees. A very deliberate policy – see *Mein Kampf*.

The transport brought no other news. Theresienstadt has the advantage and disadvantage of Jewish self-government. The advantages of this exceed the disadvantages by far, something that we, who have experienced Westerbork and Bergen-Belsen, are qualified to judge.

The disadvantages are: thoroughly corrupt relations. The advantages: Jewish control over work assignment, supervision, administration, maintenance of public order, organisation, et cetera.

It is not difficult to tell where corruption originates. The strain of persecution creates an atmosphere in which corruption flowers. First, under German administration the first to spring to mind are the so-called 'bruisers', that is to say, those who have the least scruples. All those who used to live a responsible life tend to keep themselves in the background. Those elements who have the least to lose are liked best by the SS. A kind of mutual congruity exists between them. The SS need the active, the energetic type, the person of action who does not think too much but acts and is not troubled by all kinds of reflection. Above all, he must also not show too much 'character', be their lordships' most humble servant, read their wishes off their lips, understand their mentality, and be capable of that remarkable love-hatred which determines the relationship of the 'good' and 'loyal' slave to his master. This man, who by way of thanks may carry around with him the feeling of being first among the persecuted, will collect with a certain naturalness all sorts of advantages that escape others. He believes he is entitled to them. Soon, the favours that are offered to him are met with counter favours. Criticism of his conduct does not exist – and may not exist. Public opinion is out of the question. The only judgement that he allows, and that may be allowed by his masters, is praise. For in relation to the multitude his position is that of leader of his nation. Every semblance of democracy is stifled, as a matter of principle. Conceit does the rest. Praise stimulates the need for more praise. The flatterer is given his opportunity, the one knows something about the other, like seeks like, and before one knows it, corruption has infested the entire leadership, matched only by intrigue.

That is how it was in Westerbork. From what we hear, that is how it is in Theresienstadt. It is impossible for the Germans not to know this. Rather, there is every reason to believe that they foster it and gain big advantages from it for themselves.

Conditions here are a model compared with elsewhere.

Besides, one should never forget that the calamities brought about by corruption exist in the present case only, or mainly, not in the bestowal of privilege, but in mitigating injustice. Even those who reach a very privileged position are still far from where their most basic rights begin. For example, hard though it may be for someone who is sent to Poland to see another remaining behind, the one who remains behind is also affected by the general calamity.

And surely it is something else that there are degrees of advantages rather than of disadvantages, something else when one person enjoys and another suffers, or when one person suffers more and another less.

And perhaps this, too, is different. I am busy writing, but am distracted by a terrible row. Someone from another hut has used our toilet, in broad daylight. As a result, a sick child has had to wait.

Here there was no corruption for a change, but just try to apply the theory ... of the degrees of advantage and disadvantage. I am unable to work it out.

The transport from Theresienstadt brought a few messages for individuals: a mother has passed away ... a brother ...

That is more or less the unknown tragedy. The wretchedness behind the shutters.

2 October A new month with the old misery. Construction of the huts is continuing. The poor *Häftlinge* work on it every day and do it much better than we do. The entire muster ground is already filled with huts; they are even fixing the roofing. There are no window panes yet but they, too, will soon be arriving. Granted, the panes in our hut are never renewed, but replaced with cardboard. How they intend to do that later with this new ramshackle heap remains a mystery for now. What is certain is that they are infested with lice. We are afraid of the impending move.

The British have not arrived though, and there is also no news.

A new month. The previous one disappointed us. Although we ask what this one will bring, we know we will not get an answer. Waiting. It takes rather a long time – waiting.

That is how I come to be writing between a civil and a criminal hearing. Herewith three civil cases.

We have organised a *Nähecke* (sewing corner) here to carry out repairs for men who have no wives here. Now Z. had given his worn-out overall to the hut leader to pass on to the *Nähecke* for mending. The *Nähecke* had accepted the overall for mending, and during the midday pause had placed it on top of a cupboard, in a box, where such goods are always kept. That day there was complete disorder in the hut because the two-tier beds were being replaced by three-tier beds. In the confusion, the overall was stolen, or at least got lost.

Now the question is whether the owner is entitled to damages, and if so, from whom, and how the loss ought to be made good.

There are no spare overalls. No one is allowed to possess money, which in any case is worthless here. The only time money is of any use is when parcels arrive on which import duty has to be paid.

Without money, the parcel is not handed over. All money must be handed in and is controlled centrally. Purchases from the canteen are paid for collectively from the deposit accounts. From time to time, the canteen distributes a few trifles via the hut leaders: a tube of lighter fuel, shaving soap, boxes consisting of ruined packing materials, chalk for cleaning one's teeth, some kind of ghastly hair pomade, and more of such trifles that one hardly knows what to do with. These items are distributed by drawing lots. From time to time the canteen buys mussels, which are distributed like normal rations but are paid for by the owners of the accounts. So what use is money here?

When we are allowed to write (which is once a month) we are given a postcard. There is no need for a stamp. The postcard, which may contain thirty-five words, will not arrive with or without a stamp.

The pencil I write with, I beg from the office. I still have some paper. I have no shoelaces any more and will have to see, therefore, if I can get some from the W. The W is the *Fürsorge*. In Westerbork it meant 'welfare'. The name W was brought from there. The W collects whatever is found and not reclaimed, and whatever is left behind by those who die intestate. Occasionally we also impound things, for example goods that are offered for sale without permission. The W has only very little here. In Westerbork it was a wealthy institution, because many of those sent to Poland used to leave much behind. Here there is no such source, of course.

I shared my comb with someone who had lost his own. Afterwards I lost my share. For months now I have been asking the W for a comb, but have not received anything yet. Now I must manage with a small stub with only a few teeth. Naturally, someone or other here has a comb for sale ... for one or two rations of bread. But paying with bread is a luxury I cannot afford.

How should a case such as that of the overall be settled?

Second case: someone has deposited his bread in the bread safe of the hut. The hut leader, who controls the bread safe, appoints someone to perform this task. A bag, containing a few rations of bread, disappears under mysterious circumstances. Is there a liability to compensate for the loss, and if so by whom, and how?

Someone has lent another a rucksack in which to carry laundry for the hut. The laundry belongs to single men and will be washed by women who have been appointed thereto by the leadership of the camp. The lender stipulates expressly that the rucksack is not to be lent to anyone else. However, the laundry women want to keep the rucksack a day longer and promise to return it the following day. This they do, but in the bustle, the rucksack goes missing. Again, is there a duty to compensate?

Under the influence of the German-trained jurists in particular, we quickly assume responsibility on behalf of the entire camp. Who and what is 'the camp'? A legal body, not a statutory entity. We accept it all as fiction. Something will have to be issued then from the available supplies.

For example, if the W happens to have an overall, the camp will have to give it to M. After all, the *Nähecke* is an organ of the camp, appointed by the camp, and the overall went missing as a result of its negligence or carelessness.

Similarly, the camp is occasionally ordered to hand over bread. Each individual case is given the most serious consideration. Many an established court does not face legal problems as difficult as those we face here.

And resolving such cases is useful ... for us to while away time.

By way of a supplement, here are some more civil cases. A couple with a baby had to leave a perambulator behind in Westerbork as there was no space for it on the train. On a subsequent transport another couple arrive, also with a baby, which is pushed around in the lost perambulator. The first couple demand that the second couple return the perambulator. The second couple plead that they had received the perambulator in Westerbork from the W in full accordance with the rules (see above). Naturally, the importance of a perambulator in Bergen-Belsen is inestimably great. The bench managed to come to an arrangement in this matter.

There was even a case concerning a 'rate of exchange'. Someone had sold a pair of shoes to another person for six daily rations of bread, to be paid in six instalments at the rate of one ration per bread distribution. After the first ration is paid, the daily bread ration is reduced. A loaf[101] which was originally distributed for five days now has to last for six days. The seller demands a ration of the same thickness as applied at the time of purchase, therefore a fifth of a loaf. The purchaser believes he need give only a ration of the thickness applying at the time of payment, therefore a sixth of a loaf. Alternatively, the seller was prepared to accept payment of the total amount of bread bargained for not in five but in six instalments. A loaf was from twenty to twenty-four centimetres in length and a centimetre more or less of bread was important. The bench found for the purchaser.

Meanwhile, there is an enormous increase in theft again. In the past three days we have received seventy complaints. These include insults, losses, and undoubtedly also mistakes. But the majority concern theft. It is getting cold and clothing is much sought after. Most of it seems to be disappearing from the hut of the Albanians.

Hunger, too, is an evil companion. Very exceptionally, there was barley gruel cooked with 'Kürbis' (pumpkin) for lunch yesterday. And, as happens more often, the food tasted simply delicious. One can starve here, but never because the food is unpalatable. Rather, because it stimulates the appetite.

A hungry person who gets only three-quarters of a litre of barley gruel with *Kürbis* in a day will not have enough. Even three times that quantity will hardly be enough for him.

It can happen that once you have eaten, you simply crave for a second helping. It dominates you completely. I have known people who were unable to sleep because of it, who got worked up and lost their temper, because another had received something extra. The other was entitled to that extra, but a wild, uncontrollable jealousy can overcome a person for a spoonful of soup. Apparently the best among us.

---

[101] Army bread (a Tommy).

Who is honest – who is selfish – who has social understanding – is something one learns only when hunger reigns.

And now I will make for the courtroom again.

I will depict this courtroom for you – tomorrow.

3 October Today the magistrate heard the case against a man from the old people's hut who had accused the leadership of unfair food distribution. Having been reported for this, he stuck to his accusations and was granted leave to offer supporting evidence. This afternoon he turned up with several mumbling, querulous old men as witnesses who one after the other began to pour out their bile about the woman who had distributed the food.

The poor soul was as innocent as could be, had done everything possible to give each his due, and was now sitting in a corner getting annoyed at all the virulence that one reptile after another was pouring out.

The ugly skeletal old men were all starving with hunger. And as none of them was under sixty-five, and most had passed seventy, and as it was also cold and draughty in the huts, each of them could already see the refuse cart waiting to take him to Hitler's silent ally standing in the background: the crematorium.

All of them had counted on a quiet retirement, and hardly a single one will not have had a life insurance policy or a pension. They all had children and grandchildren in Poland about whom they knew only that they, too, were working in camps for Jews, which were still worse than theirs, and where in any case there was also a crematorium standing in the background.

They were embittered, disappointed, felt hatred. They were jealous of all those whose lives were a little better, and surely they had to be somewhere. They longed for a piece of meat the size of a nutshell in their soup. That had become the substance of their life. Their topic of conversation.

They lay in bed and dreamt of hot potatoes, of brown beans. They chatted with their friends about tasty food. Rice with butter and sugar, duck with stewed fruit, prune tart and pancakes – and their only reality was a broken denture.

They quarrelled when another was given that piece of meat, and abused the hut leaders, because they 'had not seen anything for months'.

Their white lips trembled. Their dry hands trembled. They leant on their sticks and their eyes spewed hatred. That is how man is – when he grows old. Such a sitting amid the ear-splitting noise of a hut is indeed a most remarkable contribution to the evolution and history of justice. Sometimes the sittings are also held in the evenings, sometimes on Sunday evenings. In the hut of the Greeks they play music on Sunday evenings. First-rate singers and world-class violin virtuosos can be heard. Albanian, Finnish, Serbian, Greek and other girls also go there to perform their folk-songs and then you will see how similar the Jews are.

Part of the hut serves as a dormitory. That is the largest part. Sick people lie there, and women who go to bed early. Next, separated by a row of cupboards, is a section for eating where there are always five times as many people seeking a place as there is room for, even if the area is chock-full. Then follows another row of cupboards. And then comes the 'office'. In the evenings, the office serves as a courtroom. *Palais de Justice*, the French women call it. However, the various branches of the *Ältestenrat* also hold meetings there at the same time.

Someone is sitting there taking down details for the card index, or for an application to the commandant, or to compile a list. For the Germans from the 'Politische Abteilung'[102] are forever asking for lists. Lists of people with Palestine certificates, lists of particular nationalities, or of all the internees classified by nationality, or of people with more than one nationality, or of internees ranked by family, et cetera, et cetera.

Each time a summons spreads through the camp concerning the compilation of a new list, it is immediately accompanied by IPAs.

---

[102] Political Department.

'Have you heard, the *Doppelstaatler* are moving into 21.'[103] 'The *Doppelstaatler* are being exchanged.' 'The *Doppelstaatler* are going to the *Schneebaumlager*.'

The *Schneebaumlager* is the camp next to ours, so named after the *Judenälteste* who officiates there. The *Schneebaumlager* is better off than we are. They are not required to work.

In another corner of the office there is an exhibition of lost property. Twenty, thirty people are crowded there.

It can also happen that at the next table shoes are being accepted for repair – or rather, not taken in. But shoe repairing forms a chapter of its own. Anyway, it is a source of quarrels and noise.

On the right, the office is partitioned off by a couple of linen screens. Behind it, the Greeks sleep, some thirty men. By means of cupboards and planks, part of the space has been turned into a separate room, commonly known as 'Albala's Puff', in plain English, Albala's brothel.

That is where the *Judenälteste* lives with his wife and child. It contains two beds, a couple of chairs, and a small table. The windows even have curtains hanging in front of them. The table is covered with a cloth, the beds with multi-coloured spreads. Everything is gaudy, glaring tastelessness, yet an attempt at maintaining a semblance of human culture. And as such, the *Judenälteste* is not a little proud of it. Every visiting SS man is obliged to see Albala's Puff.

All sorts of things rise up from the Puff. The wonderful smell of fried butter and onions. Or the tremendous spectacle the queen makes when she quarrels, which happens daily, of course. Or did you imagine she would let herself be deprived of her right to be nervous?

Has she not also her father and mother in the camp, who visit her endlessly, smoke cigarettes from an apparently inexhaustible supply, and for the rest, gossip and make trouble, and spoil the almost two-year-old crown prince?

The crown prince is a monster with long hair combed every day into ringlets with the aid of a kind of perfume. The perfume has a

---

[103] Hut no. 21.

stench which is both sweet and acrid. The family exudes a nauseat-
ingly unpleasant odour of musk, which in certain circles enhances
their esteem not a little.

Naturally, the crown prince – who is about two years old and who
for some two years and nine months has insisted on being the centre
of attention – is an insufferable worm.

Whoever wants to ingratiate himself with the *Judenälteste*, or is
afraid of quarrelling with the queen, kisses the crown prince or
fondles him at least.

The crown prince is fully conscious of his special worth and his
irresistible attraction. Now and then he deigns to play with other
children and they, too, have already learned to treat him with esteem.
He walks about in a conceited and provocative manner, placing his
feet exactly as his father does, and amidst general laughter shouts:
'Appell, Appell' or 'Achtung, Achtung'.[104]

Every so often, even a crown prince has to piddle. The queen
then dashes through the room to look for the pot. And when she
places the pot in front of the crown prince, the crown prince no
longer needs to piddle. However, when the crown prince does not
need to piddle, the pot is put away again. No sooner has the pot
been put away, than the crown prince decides he does need to piddle.
And to prove it, he piddles his piddle all over the floor.

Hereupon the queen starts to educate, but a queen, particularly
a Greek queen in a Jewish camp, cannot educate without screaming
and shouting. And the mother of the queen, must she stand aside in
such a situation? And should the father of the queen not also interfere in the education process? A few moments – then all hell seems
to have broken loose. In a fit of despair hands are raised aloft, an
assortment of French, Greek and Spanish invectives are poured over
the crown prince. The mother of the queen interferes in the scandal,
takes sides with the crown prince, and turns against the queen. That
is enough for her father to say to her mother that she ought not to
interfere in such a highly political matter as the piddle of the crown

---

[104] Roll-call, roll-call, attention, attention.

prince, whereupon queen and queen mother launch an attack on him with the batteries of their tongues. Meanwhile the crown prince squeals like a pig being cooked alive. The entire family throws itself into a state of agitation, and at least ten minutes elapse before the crown prince is kissed better and given clean trousers.

It may happen that the king's father-in-law, with his eternal cigarette dangling from his mouth and his cap askew on his head, walks through the courtroom and that one of the dozens of people who crowd there accidentally treads on his toes. He will open his mouth then, roar, and disappear into the Puff of the great king. Immediately thereafter His Majesty appears with a ruddy complexion and starts booming. There is nothing the king is more sensitive about than his family. He reckons he owes it to his dignity.

The poor judges! They try so hard to show the injustice of collective punishment, and now they themselves become its victims. Are they perhaps some kind of plaster for the corns of the fathers-in-law of kings? They have but one consolation: the anger will soon pass, the punishment will not be carried out, and the king's prestige will have suffered once more.

For all that, it contributes to the special atmosphere in which justice is administered here. In an atmosphere of shouting and snoring, of music and applause, of a deafening noise of people simultaneously talking, bawling and roaring, an atmosphere in which people can scarcely hear each other, amidst a continually pressing throng fighting over every corner of a bench, over every stool, surrounded by odours of musk, people and food, we seek with exactly the same earnestness as reigns in the Court of Appeal of a civilised European power, with the same sovereign calm, with the academic thoroughness of a university, the rules of law by which the *Lagerwache* must conduct itself, or the liability of camp internees is determined for their mutual property, or the limits within which everyone's honour and dignity must be defended.

This community, bad, poor and hungry, seeks justice.

And if it lasts long enough, a system of law will evolve whose principles will be unassailable.

5 October The accused have an ally: Canadian airmen. In the evening – an island of tranquillity in a sea of noise – while we are deciding whether someone or other is guilty and what kind of punishment to impose, the Canadian airmen arrive and the light is turned off right under our noses from within the *Blockführerstube*.[105] The camp is plunged into darkness and the sitting has to be suspended!

Air-raid alert! The one joy in this joyless existence!

They used not to sound the air-raid siren here. The Third Reich had assumed that being allies, the Jews would not be fired at or bombed, and their stay in a camp for Jews would be safer than in the safest shelter.

But then one day a couple of stray Canadians arrived and began to fire at us. They were really angry and their machine-guns crackled lustily. We had two casualties, the *Schneebaumlager* one, and the poor *Häftlinge* eight. The crematorium had a feast.

Since then, whenever the 'enemy' approaches, the air-raid siren is also sounded in the camp for Jews. At such times we are not allowed to leave the huts and must not have any light at night.

Despite the attack, our one fear is that the 'enemy' might miss a day. Lately he has been coming three, sometimes four times a day, and we are already dissatisfied if he limits himself to two.

Very occasionally we can see Hanover or some other place burning in the distance. We are almost satisfied then.

The roaring aircraft overhead are a greeting from distant freedom, and distant happiness.

Last night there was again an air-raid alert. We had sixty-nine accused. They were the men who had not reported for duty.

Lately, the Germans have been complaining more and more about the slackening of 'discipline'. From their point of view, they are right. The Jews no longer come to work regularly.

As a result, the entire camp had its bread withheld for three days this week. A catastrophe. Nothing less. We could not even imagine

---

[105] The office of the SS officer responsible for the huts.

how terrible the actual consequences of such a measure would be.

At the last moment, we managed to get the measure rescinded.

The *Ältestenrat* and *Judenälteste* draw their strength from this. They consider their right to exist to have been proven with such 'successes'. In the meantime, it is a matter for conjecture whether the entire punishment had not been cooked up for the sake of the success.

There is doubt about whether the punishment had indeed been imposed.

Perhaps the commandant had threatened with something like that. Perhaps even that is not true. What is true, is that the *Judenälteste* got a two-hour dressing-down.

And that is working now. It is marvellous to be able to say: I have achieved this and that for you. Such things must go hand in hand with disciplinary measures of one's own. One has to assert oneself and orders *everyone* to report for duty. That is no small matter. Because on 1 October, we had changed back to wintertime. Our people were already rejoicing. Work finishes at six in the evening instead of at a quarter to seven.

However, the rejoicing had been premature. The start was brought forward from half past six to half past five. That means roll-call at five and reveille at four. At five in the morning it is still dark, and at this time of the year, bitterly cold. Roll-call can last a quarter of an hour, but if it works out that way, it can also last two hours.

For all that, the order was understandable. Measures had to be taken that could be shown to the Germans as evidence of goodwill. Such measures must also be upheld. And upholding them is again conceivable only with punishment.

That is how we, the judicial commission and two magistrates, sat sentencing people yesterday as if on an assembly line.

Never before have I been so glad to greet the Canadians as I was last night. Because the work palls on me.

There were two movements. The one says: prevent worse, protect the camp from punishment and thus preventively punish ourselves. The other says: it is no use because 'preventing worse' does not work. Besides, we must do everything possible to avoid becoming accomplices of the Germans. We must stand by our principles. It is not *we* who should punish when Jews fail to go to roll-call.

Both points of view, if administered consistently, are wrong according to others. And in practice, the champions of each point of view are probably not so far apart. It is more a difference in attitude that expresses itself here. Some of them are particularly keen on prosecution. In all sincerity they consider non-appearance at roll-call socially reprehensible. Consequently, they go much further than others in administering punishment.

The Canadian airmen decide the conflict. It gets dark and the sitting has to end. However, the arguments become more heated. We return to our hut. We search the sky for searchlights and the flickering of exploding shells. In the collective joy, the conflict becomes less heated. Besides, the IPAs about the theatre of war take priority.

'They say Emden, north-east Holland,' one whispers to another, and is answered with: 'Grossmaul.'[106]

'The *Wehrmacht*[107] is on our side; they are going to protect us.' German soldiers had indeed promised us that. From the very beginning. We hate the SS. Though no one hates the SS as fiercely as the German nation that created this institution, fed it, and let it grow so large that it can no longer rid itself of it.

Tonight, we will resume the sentencing. However, I am not taking part any longer.

From the moment one opens one's eyes here, one finds oneself in an atmosphere of sweet hatred.

This morning my downstairs neighbour asked my upstairs neighbour what time it was. But my upstairs neighbour thought it a stupid question. What does it matter, what time it is? And he was right. It does not matter now. Because the entire day is lived according to a set schedule, determined by the Kraut. However, my downstairs neighbour thought that it did matter, and that my upstairs neighbour was being unfriendly. And he too, was right.

---

[106] Loudmouth.   [107] The German army.

And there, between five and six in the morning a quarrel erupts between two intelligent and decent men, because one of them had asked what time it was. And not just an ordinary quarrel, but an intellectual one, ending wonderfully in an apotheosis of oaths and insults. And when it had ended my downstairs neighbour still did not know what time it was, and in his fury, my upstairs neighbour told him.

When will we laugh about it? Certainly not today. It is cold, and all day we have cold hands and feet. Tonight it will prevent us from sleeping, and tomorrow it will be the same again ... Oh God, do not let it become winter!

Diarrhoea is on the increase, likewise influenza, and pneumonia is threatening.

8 October Winter is probably on its way. After a long, long time we have news again. It is extremely disappointing. Not a word about the liberation of Holland north of the Maas was found to be true; Arnhem destroyed. Fighting on the Eindhoven–Nijmegen axis. Breakthrough thwarted on the Emden–Munster axis. In the east, no change. And so it goes on.

The IPA will not allow itself to be defeated, though. It returns with redoubled strength. It announces landings east of Emden, breakthrough east of Aachen, and so on. The IPA's influence is unbelievable. Although people ought to know better, they live for it. And no one escapes from this influence.

The day before yesterday, delousing shower. Fall in at half past seven. Waiting till half past nine. Ten minutes later, the bathhouse. Waiting till eleven. About half an hour for showering. Waiting till two. Standing on two legs for six and a half successive hours.

Today, they are suddenly composing a departing transport here. The *Kallmeyer*,[108] the *Doppelstaatler*. Nobody knows where they are

---

[108] A list of people with outstanding claims that they were not (full) Jews. So named after a German-born lawyer, Dr Hans Georg Calmeyer, head of the department that investigated such claims.

going. Again 120 people, men, women and children, are leaving
without knowing where they are going.

Every day, air-raid alert. They last for two or three hours. The
outdoor working parties are not allowed to return then because of
the danger, yet they do have to carry on working normally by the
roadside. Yesterday, the working parties returned for their midday
meal at 3.00 p.m. A working morning from half past five till three
makes eight and a half hours! They know no shame.

This morning, two deaths. A baby of eight months and an adult.
While the corpses were being collected the Germans just carried on
shouting. M., too, is leaving tomorrow. Last night, he and another
were brought back by *Scharführer* Hammer. Report! They had stolen
onions.

They had not stolen onions. However, because they were denying
it, they were hit in the face. And how!

Five others have stolen overalls. They are sending them to the
KZ. Here, there is an alarming amount of thieving again. Over a
ten-day period, sixty thefts of bread and forty-five thefts of laundry
were reported. How is that possible? The huts are more disorderly
than ever, new transports have arrived. Among the Mischlinge, there
are highly unsavoury characters. The air-raid alerts cause us to be
thrown into darkness quite early in the evenings. Nothing is equal to
coping with the crime. The hunger, too, is getting increasingly worse.

Lately, we have been eating *Kürbis*, pumpkins. Unpalatable. Day
in, day out. They turn my stomach. The stuff is difficult to digest
and tastes floury.

It is assumed there will be more transports ... We too perhaps?

Business: someone had given an acquaintance a watch to sell. The
watch is stolen from the acquaintance. An action for damages follows.
Dismissed, as there was no evidence of blame.

Someone discovers another person with a pocket torch on which
he claims to have written his name and which he says is his. Despite
misgivings, it was allowed. The defendant (H.) is a shady character.
The plaintiff was instructed to take the oath, which he did.

We are constantly getting new cases. A child's stolen overalls, supposedly brought from W.[109] via Theresienstadt. Implausible, as the overalls had not been manufactured in W. until after the accused had left there.

A lady, the wife of a well-known and highly respected civil servant, had offered glycerine of phenol in exchange for four rations of bread. The medication was intended for a child with an ear infection. The father had said he needed only ten drops. She had answered: 'You might as well sell the rest then.' We will definitely punish this. Bunker or bread.

I am sitting on my bed. I am hungry. It is midday. I have not had a crumb to eat since six last night.

Facts: the commandant, railing and abusing, is walking through the camp together with the *Judenälteste*. The *Judenälteste* is trying to persuade him to rescind the punishment of three days' bread stoppage for the entire camp. They reach the exit to the camp where men are carrying timber. Three men are standing around doing nothing, see the commandant, are startled, and do the wrong thing; simultaneously they grab hold of a plank and start to walk away with it. A ridiculous sight, and the commandant is irritated by it. Understandably so. One of the three gets his ears boxed. A moment later the other two men are walking with a plank; the *Judenälteste* wants to show his goodwill, and before the commandant can utter a word, starts shouting abuse. The commandant carries on walking. One of the two men, annoyed by the attack on them instead of the expected defence (the normal tactic 'to prevent worse'), says to the *Judenälteste*: 'Trage es dann selber.'[110] The *Judenälteste* fails to hear it but has his attention drawn to it by a *Rottenführer* (corporal), who taunts him: 'Schöner *Judenältester* sind Sie, wenn Ihnen die Leute so was zu sagen wagen.'[111] Immediately the prestige of the *Judenälteste* and the entire system, such as it exists, is at stake. It is most important to remember, though, that everyone is living on the edge of his nerves. A few blows are handed out. A trial.

---

[109] Westerbork.   [110] Carry it yourself then.
[111] A fine leader you are, when your people dare say something like that to you.

The accused is a fifty-year-old engineer from Zagreb. A cultured and upright man, quiet and steady, who understands the situation fully despite having received two resounding cuffs around the ears. He gives a precise explanation for his improper remark, but realises how dangerous it had been.

The bench finds itself in a major impasse. I suggest a compromise to the *Judenälteste* who, weak and sentimental as he is, agrees to it. Shake hands. We sigh a sigh of relief.

The magistrate has exceeded his powers. An accused who had been acquitted, 'despite there being suspicions about him', objected to this qualification while judgment was being pronounced. The magistrate ordered him to remain silent. The accused refused to obey. Shouting ensued. The magistrate withheld two rations of jam. In a free society, this is fully permitted. Here it is unwise because it leaves the accused with a feeling of bitterness. Another crease to be ironed out.

The departure of the transport tomorrow has brought much disquiet to the camp. Again we find ourselves in the atmosphere of Tuesdays in Westerbork,[112] again in that of the evenings in Amsterdam, waiting for the police. Again Jews are tossed to and fro, families wrenched asunder. Again we do not know where we are going, again farther from home, from family; again an unknown fate, a gloomy future.

And in this mood, peace seems to be further away than ever.

Not a comforting thought brings comfort. It is all too familiar: you never know what it is good for ...

Yet hope remains. The IPA is working feverishly, just as it always did in W. when a transport was about to leave.

The fact, though, that this camp offers no stability either, has a gloomy effect.

To think we had feared moving to another hut! Now we will be content with it.

---

[112] Every Tuesday a transport used to depart from Westerbork taking prisoners to the east, i.e. the extermination camps.

That is what always happens in this war! One hopes things will improve and then they deteriorate.

9 October Sometimes one wonders if the poets who wrote and sang about the bitterness of life had also experienced something like a camp for Jews in Germany, and if not, with what right they had spoken. Did they suffer only from a vague languishing world sorrow, that had crept from their hearts and was unrelated to external circumstances? Or is what we are now experiencing the realisation of such a world sorrow, the reaction to it, caused and dominated by it?

What is it with this unfortunate humanity? And what is the purpose of this constant cruelty, which never seems to bore yet never satisfies either?

One will hardly know life if one has not experienced what we have experienced this morning: the transportation of 120 Jews from this misery to another misery, a misery of which nothing is known except that it is greater than ours.

Like all people, out of an intuitive urge for self-preservation we are ready to deceive ourselves, but we are not completely mad yet. And our self-deception is not so advanced that we are unaware of what is hanging over their (and all our) heads: the men are separated from the women, the children from the mothers, and like slaves, each is put to some kind of annihilating work. Life hangs on a thread. The thread is called luck. Not one person here conceals the truth from himself.

One will also hardly know man if one has not experienced what we have experienced here: the persecution of the Jews.

Terrible things are happening in Holland at the moment and we must not weigh our wretchedness against the wretchedness of Holland because we must not weigh types and quantities of human wretchedness against each other.

But the wretchedness of Holland, is it not mine? Do my three children not live in that sorely stricken country at present? And what I am experiencing here, is that not a supplement to what every father in Europe is experiencing? As Dutch subjects we bear all the wretchedness of Holland, and not until we have felt its full burden can we start on the wretchedness of the Jews.

Bombed by the same bombs, afflicted by the same hunger, our property and life threatened by the same war, we must also suffer expulsion and slavery, shame and humiliation, the knocks and blows of Israel.

Here we see this man, face to face, in his true light. We – and I believe this to be our historical, our eternal, experience – encounter him in his nakedness, far away from the path of civilisation, there where he feels no embarrassment. He gives rein to his passions. He does what his heart desires, he pursues the lust of his soul, and we are his spoils and his sacrifice. We Jews see man in the crevices and depths of his true nature. We see him as the fly sees the spider, as a roe deer sees the panther.

And we even managed not to hate him. Instead, out of a most profound love for mankind and out of a vital urge and a philosophy of life, that could not be surpassed or tempered, we gave him a rule of life. Out of an all too great mercy for mankind we gave him the principle of accountability and retribution so that he might control himself.

However, it was made into a kind of 'love' and 'mercy' which, from a psychological point of view, meant the enfeebling of account-ability – and therefore became acceptable to him.

And when one sees here how men, big strong men, send women and children on transport, shouting, cursing, raging, or when one has seen just once how the SS man transports corpses with a cigar-ette in his snout, unmoved as if he is transporting manure – no, worse – as if he is transporting bricks, then one knows: this is man. *Ecce homo!* [113]

And even more than unmoved, the SS man is pleased with him-self, precisely because he is unmoved. That he has succeeded in attaining this state in the face of the most extreme human suffering,

---

[113] Behold the man! (*John XIX, 5*).

that and that alone he calls victory and power. It is the victory over
the principle, which he senses to be a Jewish principle: the principle
of the omnipresent Spirit, as God is called by the Jew. *Ha makom*.[114]

This morning they said their farewells. The people departed with
the same composure and with the same pride as in Westerbork.

The women kissed each other, the men wished each other good
luck. Everyone helped with packing the luggage and dragging it to
the muster ground. Perhaps a superfluous last help. Perhaps they
will never receive their luggage.

The SS offer consolation: they are going to an *Ilag* in Bavaria.
Ilag means *Internierungslager*.[115] No one believes them.

Just before her departure, Mrs X., the wife of the once so wealthy
manufacturer, divided her surplus riches among her friends. I was
there and heard one of them say to another: 'Here Eef, take this
dress. It still has a little salt in it.'

And man is what he is.

Recently some bombs fell nearby. The window panes rattled. We
rocked from side to side in our beds. I went to the old people's home
and asked a lady if she had been very scared. 'Scared?' she said. 'I
am far more scared of a mouse than of a bomb.' And not a word of
it was exaggerated.

10 October It has rained, it rains, it will rain.

Streams, streams, streams of water, leaking roofs, the roads are
almost inundated. And the rain continues. The clouds are hanging
low.

The IPA says the offensive has begun on all fronts. For the time
being, all we can see is water. Churchill and Eden in Moscow. Lubbe
was almost human yesterday – towards the departing transport. Just
now, a transport has also arrived. Hungarians. The Hungarians who
were here were sent away yesterday. Try and make sense of that.

Rain. The final days of the Jewish month of feasts. Last night,
Rejoicing of the Law.[116] We visited the North Africans and saw them

---

[114] The one who is omnipresent.   [115] Internment camp.   [116] Simchat Torah.

dance with the Torah in one hand and a small candle in the other. Even here one could detect something of the religious excitement, the rapture, with which these people reached an artificial joy. They fall into a trance, into a stupor.

The annual cycle of reading the Torah has ended. The last chapter has been read, the first word started on. The moving story of the death of Moses has not yet faded away before that of the creation of the world is already begun! Everyone has read it dozens of times. They know it by heart, word for word. But every word has remained so new and so alive for them, as if they were hearing it for the first time.

Rejoicing of the Law has always been a big feast, particularly in Eastern Europe and among the mystic-religious groups of the Jews, who are unknown in Holland and were never understood.

The soul is inflamed on the fire of the Torah. The nation, proud beyond measure of its eternal law, experiences anew the feeling of belonging to the chosen.

I shall never forget how they danced in the much too small space of hut 15. In the hut of the North Africans they are all devout, hence everyone joins in. The religion they practise is very primitive. They really still believe in every letter, every minor point of the law. The Balkan Jews are quite different. Some of them are as much assimilated as we are, naturally to *their* environment. A considerable number of them are converts, Greek Orthodox, to be exact. A Dutch Jew, who has lived in Yugoslavia for decades, had also converted to the Greek Orthodox Church and was just as active a thief as many of the others. In a Jewish sense, not much happens there. There is a group of very devout individuals among them. Some remind one of Arabs. Especially the Albanians. Others, with their majestic bearing, seem to be absorbed in cabbala.[117] Wonderful people.

We also went to hut 13, where the *Chaluzim* celebrated the feast. The same prayers, the same songs, but the religion practised entirely in a nationalist light and aimed at the reality of Palestine.

---

[117] Jewish mysticism.

Tunefully and passionately and with an indomitable rhythm they sang prayers for the reconstruction of Jerusalem. Once again, as happens constantly in Jewish history, religion and nationalism are inseparably interwoven. The idea bound to politics, the principle of eternity to the opportunity of the moment.

The *Chaluzim* form the only group in a Jewish camp that lives at a certain level, knows community and has unity. The only group with a will, a programme, a responsibility. The only one with Jewish and human value.

11 October What do they sing?

> Save us, save us!
> How good our share,
> How pleasant our fate,
> How beautiful, how beautiful our inheritance.

Had it been gallows humour, it could not have been said better. It is not gallows humour, though. It is the honest opinion of every Jew. With which he maintains himself, and with which he proudly imagined, and with all his strength continues to imagine himself, to be above the Third Reich. That is how he has always resisted power and fate, and aroused the wild anger of his persecutors. He is so powerful, that no one who does not know what spiritual strength is, can imagine it. Anti-Semitism does not know it. In essence, anti-Semitism is despair of the spirit. For the Jew, the downfall of the Third Reich is self-evident. What he does not understand is why it has not already happened. And in this he will remain consistent with himself till the moment he dies.

P. has just died, twenty-nine, married last year, only son of his mother and dying father, who are also here. Cause of death: physical exhaustion and dysentery.

We know that if our present conditions continue, it will be the fate of all of us. None of us has any illusions. But in the fever of death there appears before us the glowing vision of eternity in which the Third Reich is completely consumed. They know it, those pagans. That is why they hate us so. They shout and boast about their power: from a feeling of powerlessness.

And now I shall make my way again to the Palais de Justice.

13 October Friday the thirteenth, a difficult day for superstitious people, particularly at a time when each day there is one misfortune after another. Superstitious people will therefore have the satisfaction of being able to say: 'You see?'

You see? For a change, Rau has been in a huff again. Rau is the *Arbeitsdienstführer*, with the rank of *Scharführer*, that is to say: SS lance-sergeant.

The problem? The *Stabsarzt*, *Obersturmführer* in rank, or SS lieutenant in British terms, has a human vein in his body. He has been here a short while, and his human vein consists in being a professional. He is a doctor, a medical man through and through – one of those medics who are dedicated to their profession. Muscles, nerves, tendons, ribs, bones, intestines and lungs, ears, noses and membranes, lumps and ulcers, inflammations, pimples and pus, wounds and mucus, fractures, fever and dysentery, pneumonia and consumption, oedema and exhaustion, disturbance of equilibrium and rheumatism, diarrhoea and sciatica, in short, more or less everything that presents itself here is an eternal source of joy to him. He treats people for what ails them, and if he were not an SS man and therefore still had a heart, one could say that he had a heart not for his patients but at least for their illnesses. The art of curing something seems to have its attractions, especially as nature usually does it by itself without the intervention of a doctor, and the latter can delude himself by believing that he is intervening. He can always keep the illness and its progression under observation, and as a means of amusement, that too is worth something in an essentially boring camp for Jews.

The *Stabsarzt* indulges himself in that amusement. His patients are given light work, *Bettruhe*,[118] and whatever else one prescribes a sick person. In the huts, twenty per cent of the people are sick at

---

[118] Bedrest.

present. It is 13 October and still far from cold, in the last few days it has even been splendid weather again.

This twenty per cent and death from total exhaustion augur something for the coming winter, therefore!

Rau is after the twenty per cent. He cannot have that, so many sick. He is only a very small *Scharführer* but with a large mouth and tremendous power. Everything and everyone here was bent to his will. Perhaps he has special connections, this serpent ...

The *Stabsarzt*, *Obersturmführer*, a bigwig, shall pay for this.

Thus: all men up to sixty-five must report for roll-call. And all those who have been prescribed 'leichte Arbeit'[119] must join the *Abladekommando*.

'Bei uns gibt es keine schwere Arbeit.'[120]

Of course, lugging timber for eleven hours a day is 'keine schwere Arbeit'. It is not worth bothering about when you are giddy from hunger, exhaustion and wretchedness. A conflict of prestige between the small creep of a junior officer and an experienced senior officer placed much higher in his profession. The junior officer wins. In Germany, he always wins. Germany is governed – and this is Hitler's secret – by the *Feldwebel*.[121] He gives the soldier good fodder, and the officer a leg up. He earns a good salary, pulls on his boots, and with his unbelievable insolence and unsparing coarseness walks through the land: the taskmaster, the slave driver, who will 'niederschlagen',[122] 'ausradieren'[123] everything, the servant as 'Herr'.[124] The ruffian as the chosen one, the depraved in the role of the man of noble blood. The unworthy, who is fooled into thinking that because of his muscles, he has been called upon to form the ruling race and will, therefore, 'in die Fresse hauen'[125] 'im Arsch treten'.[126] The lazy good-for-nothing who finds everything 'Scheisse'[127] except getting others to work for him. Others, whom he envies and hates for their achievements and talent.

---

[119] Light work. [120] We don't have any hard labour.
[121] Sergeant in German; (company) sergeant-major in British military.
[122] To smash down. [123] To eradicate. [124] Master.
[125] Smash their faces in. [126] Kick them in the arse. [127] Shit.

And as everyone has a rotten or worthless spot in his soul, there are many, many National Socialists and many, many men in the SS. They will be sorry enough, but regret is also one of the begetters of the incurable disease that Germany suffers from: *Deutschtum*.[128]

For some time now, the *Häftlinge* have been working inside our camp. Some of them are tradesmen, apparently brought here for that reason. They are building a new kitchen, installing the cauldrons, and erecting the huts.

Under the *Lagerverordnung*,[129] the Jews are strictly forbidden to make contact with them. But in circumstances such as have arisen here, not even the death penalty can fully enforce such a ban.

However, that contact is of the greatest danger to all of us. Its discovery would result in collective punishment and new restrictions in our already very limited freedom of action.

We try to prevent it, therefore, especially as there is also nothing to be gained from this contact. The trading that results from it must not take place.

Consequently, newly accused have been appearing before the bench lately: people who were caught having contact with *Häftlinge*.

And once again we get a special insight into man's sophisticated nature.

The Jews want bread, but the *Häftlinge* have none. They offer cigarettes, which we hardly ever receive and they apparently do. Cigarettes are very valuable here. With six cigarettes one can get a ration of bread. Moreover, as trading bread for cigarettes has been forbidden by the Germans, the risk makes the cigarettes even more valuable. Numerous men here seem to be addicted to cigarettes. Though with some women this is even stronger. In exchange for cigarettes, they would even be willing to offer more than bread.

As a result, people try to buy cigarettes from the *Häftlinge*, partly to exchange for bread, partly to smoke. Often they do not try to do this themselves, but make use of middlemen.

---

[128] Germanity.   [129] Camp regulations.

These middlemen have gradually become known to us. Intermediaries are kept under constant observation here.

They were caught inside new and still empty huts. Apparently, ten, twenty, fifty marks are being paid for a couple of cigarettes. We are not allowed to have that money; everything had to be handed over, and any money that is still around, is illegal. I believe not one person does not have illegal money, sometimes even substantial sums.

Our accused are complaining now: the *Häftlinge* had taken a large sum of money for a box of cigarettes which, when opened ... was found to contain straw. Someone had given a middleman money with which to buy cigarettes. While he was negotiating with a *Kapo*, a *Scharführer* appeared in the distance. The Jew throws away the wallet with money. The *Kapo* picks it up. The Jew takes flight.

The next day he comes for his cigarettes. 'Ich niks weten, ich niks weten.'[130]

Homo homini lupus![131]

Once he has returned to his country, the *Kapo* will no doubt become an anti-Semitic agitator.

Today's harvest: F. is dead: exhaustion. Mrs R. is dead: camp fever, pulmonary infection. R. is dead: exhaustion, dysentery.

And if my fears are true, we will even be envied in Amsterdam. Bombing raid upon bombing raid, famine and terror. Fear, shock and blood.

We have absolutely no news about Holland. For weeks now we have had to content ourselves with guesses, and at present we base those on military reports of 5 and 6 October. Defeat near Arnhem. Fighting for the bridgehead at Wageningen. For the rest, Holland is said to have gone off the air.

Are the transmitters broken? Or are the British in Hilversum?

The sick shuffle past my bed on their way to the toilet. They can hardly move their legs any more.

Soon there will be duty roll-call again. All the men under sixty-five.

---

[130] I know nothing, I know nothing (said in a mixture of German and Dutch).
[131] Man is wolf to man.

The political discussions, and the question of when it will end, are unbearable.

The IPAs are unbearable. Next Monday a transport of holders of Palestine Certificates[132] is leaving.

14 October The only real question is how the war is progressing, and when there is no news about that, hope and mood tend to plummet here. When the news is bad, though, people feel as if their hearts are being pounded on; they become dismayed and are wrenched out of their few remaining joints. At such times it is difficult to keep their blood flowing and their expectations alive until better tidings arrive.

Today the news was not good. It is still only IPA, but enough to cause people's heads to droop. For a few days optimistic news circulated about a breakthrough at Aachen. Today it seems that Aachen and even part of the Belgian coast are still in German hands.

And many a person sighs 'God be with us'.

And he sighs it not so much because he means anything by it, but to vent his heart and to come to terms with his utter powerlessness.

What would E. say about it, if he were still able to say something? He cannot say anything any more, because he is dead. He died this morning, suddenly and unexpectedly. He had been suffering from angina pectoris, but that was not the cause. A man of sixty-five cannot live with impunity in a hut such as this, on this food, in this cold. A man of sixty-five contracts pulmonary oedema and dies.

It is God's will. And if people should find this hard, who gives them the right to reproach God with it? E. certainly would not have confronted God. He was His humble servant and saw what God did as being well done.

Each day he waited, like every religious Jew, for the arrival of the Anointed One. And though he did not know the day of his arrival, every hour he looked out for him longingly. E. was devout, more devout than any man in Holland, in all his being and humility, in

---

[132] Usually Zionists with certificates that allowed them to enter Palestine.

goodness and in purity, unpretentious and upright, modest and distinguished. If a person may be said to be made of pure gold, then one may say it about him.

Everyone had loved him for his modesty and goodness. He had no enemies, for he had not given anyone a problem. Thus, it came about that when he died, this person who until recently had none the less been a stranger to most people here was seen off by everyone. The Albanians were there, the Greeks, the North Africans, and not only us, whose friend and companion he had been for many, many years. Apparently, one can still mean something to others here.

We had belonged to the same Palestine transport. We had been sent back together. I had never seen a man bear misfortune more nobly.

He had hoped to see the country and his children there again. 'But if it is not to be, God must have willed it otherwise.'

He was no fighter, nor a tremendous doer; but someone who waited, who endured and who was sensitive. Right up to his death he lived and flowered here in silence.

Today – Sabbath – he was cremated.

It was the first time in his life that he had transgressed the Sabbath.

Is it not time for our deliverance, now that the virtuous have become transgressors?

17 October Last Saturday evening, a service of mourning was held in memory of E. Everyone attended. The service was held in 27, where the *Altersheim* and *Invalidenheim* are located. It was crammed to capacity and stank there as always, because there is always someone who has soiled his trousers. The Chief Rabbi gave a speech, beginning with a reading from the portion for the week, followed by an inconsequential series of platitudes, and ending with a *Kaddish*.[133] All of it was performed with the requisite hand gestures, and made not the slightest impression. Notwithstanding, everyone was satisfied;

---

[133] A doxology ending with prayers for the welfare of the Jewish State and for peace.

it would have been improper to have been disgruntled at the service of mourning in honour of E. Everyone said the same about E. He was virtuous, good, noble and modest. As I have said already, he had always made it easy for everyone and had never caused anyone a problem. He had always reacted as was expected of him, and more one cannot ask of anyone.

The Chief Rabbi had tried to put warmth into his words, and he probably succeeded in it, but the entire business reminded one far too much of the dreadful vanity of our earlier life for an intelligent person to have been taken in by it.

Even the reminder that with E.'s departure part of 'old Jewish Amsterdam' had gone too did not really move anyone, because for a long time now everyone had resigned himself to the destruction of old Jewish Amsterdam. Everyone knows that the old has gone for ever, never to return, and there is still so much at stake that the past no longer evokes sadness. The old will be more than happy if they just manage to save their lives. For the present, though, fellow sufferers are dying all about them. From one hour to the next there is additional food for the crematorium, and dying in Bergen-Belsen is not exactly pleasant.

When someone dies who has children here, or a husband or a wife, they are at least not entirely alone, but many lonely people die here. And when a lonely person dies, like vultures they immediately prey on the corpse. The one needs trousers, the other a pair of spectacles. A third reflects on the ration of bread left behind and a fourth on an overcoat. The commission for inheritances comes to seize the unattended estate; wallets are searched, old letters read, portraits of grandchildren and other beloved relatives looked at ... and then everything goes to the W. The W shares it out. Those who are closest to the fire receive the greatest warmth. Razorblades, a rucksack, shoes, everything has tremendous value here in the camp. We have nothing any more. Our clothes are worn threadbare, our shoes rotten, our spectacles broken, half our underwear has been stolen, and our socks are more holes than wool.

We receive *nothing* new. Only condemned wooden shoes, too heavy to wear, are sometimes 'loaned'. To mislay them means sabotage, and sabotage is punished with KZ.

Yesterday afternoon the bench dealt with another 'serious' case. Again a Dutch Jew, accused of having stolen a jumper, gloves, cigarettes, tobacco from a parcel from Amsterdam, matches, bread, et cetera, et cetera. The jumper and gloves were found inside his mattress. He claimed that someone else had hidden them there. A Gillette razor had also been stolen. Its case was recognised, though not the blade. By chance it transpired that he had 'borrowed' another blade and had swapped it for the stolen one ...

To convince the investigators of how badly they searched, he had said. He was sentenced to eighteen days, six on bread and water. I had asked for four weeks, with three days on bread and water. I care little for the latter. The formerly wealthy wife of a manufacturer has stolen a pair of gloves from someone ... Lack of evidence. I am certain of it, though.

Hunger is a rotten feeling. It is our vital urge that requires us to eat. Eat. Eat. For a moment I had thought that at least the family unit was immune to it. But after having heard an engineer quarrelling with his wife over potatoes and bread, and after having heard people cursing on multiple occasions because of the way things were shared out among their wives and their children, I know better.

A horror here is the marriage problems. People who thought they had an ideal marriage now see how big the rifts are that divide them. They face unknown, unexpected problems, and their reactions are completely different. They do not understand each other, and hate each other, because they are not understood.

People who have had enough of each other, without knowing it or without wanting to admit it, can no longer avoid the problem. People whose own pain is too great to bear simply cannot bear the other's pain as well; they are *incapable* of offering consolation. They have enough problems of their own.

People who have always been sure of themselves, people who have been relied on like beacons, are all at sea now and lose respect and prestige.

People who had followed their spouse's advice and now regret it, hate, hate, and are choking with bitterness.

People who once knew how to rear their children, now discover they are powerless in the circumstances. The child rebels, becomes lazy or disobedient, insolent and wild – and the mothers see the fathers and the fathers see the mothers who are failing in their duty and are not giving any guidance, yet expect it from each other and have always expected it, and in the past they were never disappointed in each other. Men, who think of their children in Poland, from whom they have not received any news, who must talk about it, talk, and talk. Wives, who want to repress it all, who do not know what to reply, who can also not stand the talking – and the other way round.

Men who chatter endlessly about the war, boastfully and with the expertise of the pub bar.

Women who are scared and sombre and cannot suppress their repugnance for this braying optimism.

Men who start to believe in God, and women who make fun of it, or men who curse God, and women who despairingly reach out for support from religion.

Men who care nothing for their families any longer, who have preserved only a presumptuous insistence to be recognised as bearers of authority, authority which serves no purpose and gives hardly any direction.

Women who grow old, who get lines in their faces and grow hairs on their upper lip and chin, women whose signs of grief become ever more distinct, who start to look like witches, and men who notice with irrepressible aversion how ugly they are becoming.

Women who worry about relatives or children, men who would rather court a young face, being not entirely numbed and frozen yet in the broad field of love.

People whose children are ill and dying, who reproach each other for not offering their butter or jam.

People who suddenly recognise each other's stupidity, each other's cowardice, each other's weaknesses. Every veil falls away. For the first time they discover each other's disgusting ugly nakedness.

And all these people are hungry. All these spouses, all these parents, all these children.

Hunger – hunger.

And there is no separate room where one can be alone in the evenings, no household that binds, no chairs, tables, paintings, tea-cups, that demand respect, no activities that impose obligations. Nothing remains that would cause pain if abandoned, nor is there a bed any longer for a little reconciliation – to feel each other's bodily warmth, that bodily warmth which is the only remedy for sorrow.

18 October The IPA says, Hungary has capitulated, but who cares? We are getting less bread. We started with 375 grams a day, went down to 360, and have now gone down to three hundred grams. And the end is not in sight.

When you lie awake at night, for hours on end, and you listen to the howling of the wind between the huts, to the patter of the pouring rain, to the tapping of the raindrops through the leaking roof, when you hear how on one side someone is snoring and on the other a child is coughing, and farther away a man wakes up with a start, moaning with fear, how men are constantly shuffling past your bed on their way to the toilet in the corner, when you then think of the past and of life today, of everything that has been lost, never to return again, when you ask where those who are dearest to you in all the world have gone, and you cannot sleep from worry, from fear, from hunger and from an uncontrollable itch on your arm, back, chest and stomach, to your astonishment you suddenly notice that you do not even mind so much, that you still have hope, still make plans. How can one live like this? How could all this have happened – to us in our safe middle-class homes in the south,[134] with our pleasant rooms, with those wonderful evenings, with visitors and tea and biscuits and chocolates, which all of us nevertheless used to have; of different quality for sure, but nevertheless we all had them. We had cigars and cigarettes. We had enough to

---

[134] Amsterdam south.

eat. Now, when we fall asleep, we dream of a slice of bread with butter. And where, where are the children? Are they alive still? Are they ill? And still you make plans and say: when the war is over ... Oh, once the war *is* over, the wretchedness will begin. Whom will we never see again?

'T. is ill, sciatica. Autumn is well advanced now. Rain, wind, cold, and early darkness. The working day is being shortened a little. It will be ten hours in winter instead of eleven. Men are dying at the fronts.

By God, I can find nothing attractive about such a war. Yet in fifteen years' time, filled with a great fervour, man will start another war again. And the Jews will be the first to suffer.

And everyone who now says that it is finally over now, is deceiving himself.

Peace does not exist.

Just look at the past. What have we not experienced over the past fifty years? Will it not repeat itself? Jews will continue to be persecuted. The *Mischlinge* predict it. And they ought to know.

21 October There is no news. There is only endless bullying, provoking and tormenting by the SS, and every day anew it amazes us that a body of perfectly fit, well-fed men, at the peak of their lives, tall, muscled, strong men, who in fact could be the flower of the nation, actually have no other work and no other worry than daily to harass this wretched heap of wrecks formed by us men, women and children. Daily, now that the German fatherland is in great danger and the German nation finds itself in a historic crisis, in which lasting decisions are made about its fate, its happiness, indeed its life or death. One would like to shout at them: gentlemen, have you nothing better to do now? But naturally we do not shout it, because that would mean KZ. Moreover, we all want to make it to the end, which means holding your tongue and more than that: compromising and wriggling, and living a repulsive life. We not only do not shout it, we not only refrain from protest, we also cooperate and know of no limit to it. Thus, the question arose in the judicial commission of whether we ought to prosecute fellow camp internees who do not go to roll-call or do not go to work.

Everyone agreed that we must first warn them, attempt to persuade them with suitable words and subsequently with threats. But must we also go beyond that?

For example, there are women (the French women in particular are inclined to do this), who simply refuse to report for duty or go to work.

The Germans require 190 women for the 'shoes'. The Jewish leadership must supply the 190 women. There are two points of view. The one says that for every woman who refuses to go, another has to suffer in consequence, and that if the required number are not supplied there is the threat of collective punishment. Transgressions must therefore be dealt with and punished for the sake of maintaining order and discipline and the rules laid down by the leadership.

But another opinion is voiced, too, albeit by a small minority. It says that much as the organisational motives may seem just, it is nevertheless an unacceptable anomaly that Jews should punish Jews because they do not want to work for the Germans. It almost means the recognition of individual rights. This view will probably be defeated. And unless at the last moment a way out is found, it will mark the end of my work.

Its champions could be reproached with inconsistency perhaps. Because once a system of cooperation (a more agreeable word for voluntary slavery) has been adopted, gradually one also arrives at a judicial commission that pronounces judgments against people who do not want to subject themselves. And not without justification one could add that these people are not even led by considerations of principle, but rather by the opportunistic one of letting others work in their place. But none of this alters the fact that somewhere there ought nevertheless be a limit to our own subjection, to surrendering our dignity – and that not quite *everything* is conceivable. A bench of Jews, delivering justice as an extension to the German arm.

If all this makes any practical difference? Indeed it does. But irrespective of that, a certain degree of self-preservation is none the less indispensable.

But who still has feeling for it with the boundless demoralisation that the German measures bring about?

Because if pleading your principles cannot get you exempted from work, a couple of cigarettes have a better effect. There are only a few with whom this does not work; but at least they exist, and that is a miracle in itself.

For the rest, the bullying continues as it has always done.

This morning at six o'clock the office staff had to fall in for duty roll-call. In itself it is sheer nonsense, because which office starts work at six, even in times such as these, even in a camp? However, during roll-call this morning, the office staff had laughed.

The *Hauptscharführer*[135] had cracked a joke. The *Scharführer* had not found it funny. The office staff had sided with the *Hauptscharführer*, had laughed and hence were punished by the *Scharführer* with the loss of three days' bread ration.

A similar punishment is being threatened for the entire camp. A lamp is missing, and as no one is willing to own up to it, it is laid at the door of the Jews. The Jews have stolen the lamp.

What a Jew should want here with a large electric lamp is indeed a mystery, but if the lamp is not returned by tomorrow, the entire camp, without exception, will go without bread for three days ...

In the 'shoes' they are presently working fourteen hours a day, that is to say, till half past seven in the evening. Women *never* see their children any more.

Mrs W. is working in the *Kommandantur-Reinigung*,[136] finds a piece of bread there, and takes it to the kitchen. The *Scharführer* enters and asks for his bread. 'I took it to the kitchen,' she says. The bread, which has been touched by Jewish women, cannot be eaten. Mrs W. is accused of theft!

30 October For a number of days I have not written anything. The

---

[135] Senior SS sergeant.   [136] Cleaning of the camp commandant's office.

fact is, it has become too dangerous to sit here writing on the bed. Once again they have appointed an SS woman to inspect the huts, and she does indeed inspect them a few times a day. The beds must be made according to regulations, and Auntie Bitch walks around in high dudgeon making trouble. In every hut ten to twenty beds are stripped, that is to say ten to twenty rations of bread are withheld. And that is just one of the latest provocations.

We, too, had to sacrifice two rations of bread. Why? We had fallen in and no one had told us that we were meant to walk to the gate. But because we had not walked to the gate, we were punished with stoppage of a ration of bread. Because we were guilty of sabotage. And when the day of the bread distribution arrived (three rations of bread were to be distributed at the same time on this occasion), instead of one, each person had two rations of bread withheld. That is not sabotage. Carry on starving.

It is filthy weather. It does nothing but rain and there is a biting, penetrating cold. There are stoves, but no coal. It had been promised for 1 November. Today is 30 October, but there is no coal to be seen. The British will probably be here before the coal.

Our shoes are broken. They are beyond repair and the price for those that can still be repaired is two or three rations of bread. For the material, so-called. Our socks are in shreds. Most of the people walk about in rags. The work – outdoor work – lasts from half past six to half past five. In the 'shoes', two hours longer.

The men return soaked. Everyone has to go. The sick, the old, and whoever can be found. Twenty-five per cent of the people are ill at present. Six hundred are in bed, four hundred in the home for the elderly and the disabled. Every day people are dying there. In the documents they leave behind we read ...

Today I saw a family tree. Great grandfather: 1761 farmer in Saxony ... not every German can say that. I also get to see private correspondence. A bank, informing that nine hundred thousand German marks have been confiscated by the state. That, too, cannot be written to every German. The wife of this man, who had apparently been a millionaire many times over, is now begging for a pair of shoes or a crust of bread. The SS are in a foul mood. They fume and rage like madmen or drunks. We get to hear about it when one of them has had his home and family bombed. Naturally, it is our fault.

In the meantime we have dealt with many cases.

M. has stolen tobacco and cigarettes from a friend. Another has loaned a camp blanket in exchange for two mugs of food a week.

A young man of twenty, placed with great difficulty as an orderly in the *Invalidenheim*, has stolen seven slices of bread from a blind person and two cigarettes from a colleague.

A Yugoslav has stolen a loaf.

An Albanian woman, who seems to be simple-minded, steals repeatedly.

What shall we do here with the many psychopaths? We have them examined, but what is the point?

It is wretched here. I am thinking of the wretchedness in Holland. Let us not compare wretchedness. It is all equally dreadful.

Last night there was a cabaret here. It goes with the wretchedness.

Air-raid alert, any moment now. We wait and we wait.

On Saturday, it is J.'s birthday. She will be ten years old.

Two women have given each other a beating. A man had 'shirked'.

The entire working party of 167 men were punished. They got no food and had to stand all day in the pouring rain. They also had two rations of bread withheld.

Mrs A. had sworn at the guilty person. Mrs B., the wife of the latter, had attacked Mrs A. Mrs A. had hit back.

Scratches – black eye ... Both punished.

A man is punished for having put his hands in someone else's mattress.

And that is how it is every day. Rain, rain, air-raid alert. *Brot-entzug*, cold, death, darkness. When you have worked fourteen hours in the 'shoes' and then return in pitch darkness. The food can no longer be distributed. It rains, it is cold, there is no heating, not a spark of heat.

Not in the hospital either.

That is when you begin to understand what B-B is.

Yesterday we saw E. off. She had died of exhaustion.

8 November A couple of days ago, three thousand women arrived here. They went to the women's camp. We have no contact with them but were able to establish that there are also Dutch women among them. They even include a few who, not so long ago, had been sent away from here.

As far as we could find out, all these women have come from Auschwitz; they have been separated from their husbands. Their children, too, were taken from them. The most horrifying stories are being told. The children and all those not eligible for work are said to have been gassed. It is impossible to believe such an atrocity.

In any case, there are only women here, and only women who are fit for work. One of them told us that she and ten others were the only survivors of an s-transport[137] of eight hundred people from Westerbork! Everything had been taken away from them. Literally everything. They have nothing, therefore, apart from the underwear they are wearing.

They live here in tents and sleep on the ground, on straw. Meanwhile, though, the weather here has become terrible. The November storms have arrived bringing rain, hail, snow, and penetrating cold. Yesterday afternoon, the storm tore the tents to pieces and left the women standing in the pouring rain and dreadful weather without any protection at all. In great haste they were allocated the shed, where the shoe working party normally sits, and a large kitchen tent. However, the floor of this tent became inundated. The water is ten centimetres deep.

Besides, it is impossible to imagine the effect that the terrible weather is having here. The ground is almost completely inundated, which signifies a catastrophe as no one has whole shoes any longer and possibilities of having them repaired are almost non-existent. Furthermore, the roofs of the huts are leaking and inside them there

---

[137] Probably: *straf* (punishment) or *sonder* (special) transport.

is a terrible draught. Consequently, we are very afraid of the winter.

Despite the foul weather, outdoor work and roll-calls continue normally. When people re-enter the camp they are chilled to the bone and soaked from the rain. The SS derive a satanic pleasure from it.

The food is getting significantly worse. The bread ration was reduced long ago. The midday meal contains hardly any potatoes any longer. Our daily food consists of swedes. Seven days a week. I have stomach ache. Diarrhoea and jaundice are rife.

A medical orderly who has jaundice has been refused bedrest. 'Ein Sanitäter soll nicht krank sein.'[138] Latest order from the Third Reich.

The current procedure for reporting sick is that in the evening one must first report to a Jewish doctor. By means of a preliminary medical, the latter determines who shall appear before the *Sanitäter* the next morning. Naturally, he is extremely cautious and declares everyone fit. He, too, fears for his job and not without reason. Were he to declare too many sick, he would lose his job, which would benefit no one.

The following morning the provisionally sick must report to the *Sanitäter*. All those with less than 38.5° fever are rejected, or rather are declared medically fit. Such people are then sent to duty roll-call, beaten, and put to work.

There is no work, though. There is only bullying, rain, and more bullying. Apart from a few duties such as working in the kitchen, et cetera, there is no work.

The kitchen workers – also the women – usually work from three at night till six the following evening. Sometimes even later.

Unlike before, they no longer get extra food, apart from a mug of soup.

As for us, we are giddy with hunger.

At every roll-call, people collapse.

To make room for the women who are living in the tents, an

---

[138] A medical orderly must not be ill.

order has suddenly arrived that the hospital hut and the old people's home must move.

Everything must start within the hour.

It is raining, it is pouring. I visited the old men's home. Everyone is jostling, luggage goes astray, a woman collapses. Several others drag her away, but are too weak for it. In a state of dying, she is placed on a bed. Help from a doctor is out of the question in this tumult.

The new huts have no light, no water, no toilet, nor heating. It can always get worse.

9 November The move from the *Altersheim* became one of the biggest scandals ever to occur here. At ten in the morning we were told that the two huts of the *Altersheim* and *Invalidenheim*, in all 325 unfortunate, helpless individuals, had to move immediately to one of the new huts. No beds had been erected yet in these new huts.

We went all-out and managed to assemble the bedframes. There were no bedboards, though.

By now it had got to two in the afternoon and the actual move began. Meanwhile, it had been announced that the hospital (huts 14 and 16) also had to move to the two new huts.

Furthermore, women's huts 25 and 26 had to move to the former hospital huts. The chaos that ensued is impossible to imagine, even for someone who had experienced it.

For a start, although there were beds in the *Altersheim*, there were no bedboards. Everyone went to work, went to help the sick and the aged. There was no direction and so everyone got in each other's way. The beds are spaced forty centimetres apart. The crowding in the resultant narrow passage caused bottle-necks, made worse by the rolled-up blankets, suitcases, baskets and trunks that had been hauled across.

The inside of the new hut had just been painted. Everyone got covered in white paint. Various people arrived with boards ... They turned out to be too short for the beds. The bedframes were too high for old people. The old men and women were quite unable to reach the second tier.

A terrible, uncontrollable shouting rose up from all sides. There had been no time to allocate the beds so that everyone took whatever bed he could. The helpless, who had to be carried, arrived last, were unable to enter the hut, and did not get a bed.

The beds that had been made up, collapsed. Suitcases and luggage fell down onto the lower beds. Women screamed that their luggage, the last of their possessions, was being stolen.

People pushed, jostled, and trampled on each other. This hell lasted a couple of hours. Then it got dark. There was no light.

The new *Altersheim* contained not a single chair or table. The food had to be distributed in the dark. Loaf after loaf was stolen – six days' bread ration.

And that is how it was in hut 14 and also in 16.

It started to rain, to pour. Part of the luggage and blankets was lying outdoors and got wet from the rain.

That night, dozens of people had to sit or lie on the floor.

It is not true that hell is fire. It can also be hell without fire and flames.

'Time' no longer exists here. The days pass by but sometimes it seems as if they do not follow one another but coincide, and that what happens today occurs simultaneously with that of yesterday and tomorrow. This imprisonment is like a book that is handed to us, of which all the days are pages. One need only turn the pages; the time is up to us, things happen and all simultaneously, except that we cannot read and absorb everything at once. We last – the war does not last. We are like a barrel with too narrow an opening through which we are filled much too slowly. The torture is inconceivable: no news from home, no news from the children. Inconceivable, too, is the torture of the nightmares and the terrible visions that torment us and about which I can or may speak to no one, no one.

Again I am alarmed this morning. The Germans have pierced all the dykes.

The stories about the liberation of Holland are a lie, a swindle. It is becoming terrible.

11 November Armistice Day, L.'s birthday. Wedding anniversary of my deceased parents. A festive day in the past. Bright and full of joy. The days remain full of worry and sorrow for Holland. For the children. And L.? I am hoping for you.

T. is very kind. I cannot stand it when she is irritable and turns away.

I read *Verdi* by Werfel – 603 pages. *Gone with the Wind* – nine hundred pages. Fifteen hundred pages read. It could have been fifteen hundred days. It only makes one grow older. Pages of our life which are turned over. And most of the pages are not even being written. Between chapter and chapter lie years; tired are the eyes of the writer when he has completed his manuscript. Tired are the eyes of the reader who closes the book.

Yesterday afternoon, mother L. rested her head against my shoulder and cried. A woman there had swallowed something. There is little hope. She was thinking of M.

It is dusk. She is waiting in the queue for jam. She is even more dear to me now. The lovely dear woman. What a strange relationship. I go there every day. A woman of seventy.

At times, the distress is so great that one's heart seems full of tears.

All such 'romantic' feelings are reality.

They are bad people who rule over the world.

13 November Since yesterday, a great commotion. Lists are being compiled of South Americans and of people with relatives in North, South or Central America. There is talk of an exchange transport in the offing. Optimists ... pessimists ... Conditions here are terrible, unbearable.

It is wet and cold. The roll-calls are awful. T. has a low temperature. Each day the food is equally disastrous. The news gives no hope. There is no relief either. Have people ever had it as bad as this?

14 November Today Hans L. died. Laryngeal tuberculosis. That, too, we had never expected. Father in Poland, brother in Barneveld, now in Theresienstadt or who knows where? The first frost has arrived. It is better than constant dampness. There is no heating, though. The mood is very bad.

It is H.'s birthday. Mrs L. gave me a piece of bread with synthetic honey. Food for the gods.

15 November Of course it can get worse. It is snowing. I believe no place on earth has a worse climate than B-B. There is no heating, the food is bad, our shoes are broken, our feet are swollen, and our hands are sore from injuries. Outdoor work continues.

In the *Altersheim* lonely people are dying every day.

17 November In a few days there have been many changes here. The *Doppelstaatler* went on transport. The British too. Firstly the North Africans. It deprives the camp of much colour. Many acquaintances are leaving. Where to? People are optimistic. But why? Maybe they are going to Auschwitz

The orphanage, too, is leaving. Children who have resurfaced, where are they going, these poor creatures? God protect them from Auschwitz. God have mercy on all of us.

Forty women from the women's camp have left. At the station they met some of our men and shouted: 'Chin up!'

Today, the sun broke through. The mood immediately changed. Yesterday it was terribly gloomy here.

The news is better.

Harry W. has died. One of Berlin's top lawyers. G. died, thirty-seven years old. And another, the third one today. The South Americans, too, have been summoned. They are very nervous. What will happen to us?

18 November They are beating terribly and concentration camp manners are the order of the day. Poor lonely and neglected J., who had not shaved for a long time and was walking about with stubble, had his beard singed off. Z. got a terrible beating. The

Stubbenkommando[139] is having a hard time of it. People are nervous and are frightened of joining it.

Result: commotion during duty roll-call. Today there was kicking and beating there. A man fell to the ground. The ground was flooded from the rain. They carried on kicking him but still he had to go. All this takes place in the dark of the morning. It is unbearable to watch.

Red Cross parcels are arriving. The tins are being confiscated. Yesterday, Friday, a dull day. Unmentionable sombreness. Today, all-day rain. I have diarrhoea. It is incredible how few people lose hope.

23 November I am sitting in the passage of hut 14 as roll-call inspector. The bitch has just been here. She has forbidden laundry to be hung out to dry in the huts, 'aus hygienischen Gründen'.[140] The women are desperate. Where is one meant to hang the nappies and the children's laundry, now that it is winter and it pours with rain every day?

And most of them have diarrhoea and keep soiling themselves. Oh, the gloom, the darkness, the intolerable filth in the huts. People lying the whole day in a dark hovel where one would not leave a dog. And the clothes, the blankets, the sheets, have become rags. Oh, this hideous poverty, this constant hunger that gets worse and worse.

Our daily food consists of swedes boiled in water with hardly a single potato.

The butter repeatedly fails to arrive.

And punishment is meted out all round. Yesterday more than two hundred people had their bread withheld for two or three days.

Work continues. Occasionally some news trickles through. There were Red Cross parcels. Whatever could not be delivered, was divided up. It caused much dissatisfaction again for it was claimed to have been done unfairly.

Apart from that, there are more removals. Hut 21 is moving. The

---

[139] Tree stump working party. Prisoners had to dig up tree stumps in the surrounding woods; these were used as fuel for the cauldrons in the kitchen.

[140] For reasons of hygiene.

new hut we are moving into is better, but right next to the *Block-führerstube*. We are living in a glass house.

It is better not to speak of the lice. We are crawling with them and they itch.

25 November How many things are there not in the world that we do not have ... For example: marinated herring, calf's liver with macaroni, a croissant with butter, pea soup with sausage and knuckle of pork, broad beans with ham, a cup of coffee with a lump of sugar, a cigar or a pipe full of tobacco.

They all exist. But not *here*.

Here it is cold. Here the rain comes down daily in torrents, here there are sick people and broken shoes. Removals, senseless removals from one hut to another – right through the rain.

Mrs L. is ill, traumatic fever. I am beginning to worry a little.

27 November Fans of Victor Hugo and Jean Valjean can have their fill here. Here, too, we have such types.

Jacqui S., an Anglo-Dutchman, and like all *Doppelstaatler* already suspected here on those grounds alone, ended up in the bunker.

Together with a couple of others he had eaten from the containers of the SS. After all, we are all starving to death here and take food from wherever we find it. Jacqui and five others had to serve time and suffer hunger for eight days for it. Three days' bread and water, the fourth day normal *Verpflegung*.[141] It is no small matter in this pervasive cold.

Jacqui had also stolen three large swedes and had given them for safekeeping to his 'friend' R. so that he would have something to gobble on his release. However, on his release, aching with hunger, it emerged that R. had gobbled the swedes himself. The temptation had really been too great. No one could tell him what had happened to the swedes.

Furthermore, all Jacqui's other possessions had been stolen. His towel, his shirt and the few pairs of socks that he still had.

---

[141] Treatment.

Jacqui snivelled. His trousers consist of a couple of legs without a middle. On top of these he wears a second pair of legs.

'Rags' is a euphemism for these clothes. His shirt hangs out at the front and at the back, at his stomach and his buttocks. Frayed underneath, patches on top.

Jacqui cries, 'Just look at me, I look like a tramp.' Jacqui S. is a well-known thief. Thus, no one comes to his aid. He himself is a degenerate, his wife a poor wretch who does not, or cannot, look after anything.

Jacqui comes to seek my help. And I promise to help him.

Jacqui's only possession is a good overcoat; he has no outer or under garments, socks or shoes any longer. On his feet he wears a couple of rags and broken clog shoes.

I refer Jacqui to the *Fürsorge* and manage to persuade the people there to help him. Jacqui is called to the office, questioned, and asked to return in the afternoon. In the meantime they will see what is available and sort something out for him. But while Jacqui is in the office, he behaves as he usually does, that is to say: he uses the opportunity to steal a jacket. He is caught, gets a kick, and no clothes.

That is what he comes to tell me: 'I don't know what to do, I don't know what to do!' He really is at his wits' end. He wants a pair of trousers and does not have any trousers. Once more, people are willing to help him, but then it appears ... that he had also stolen a pair of shoes from someone. Jacqui gets nothing. The world war will end and Jacqui will have no trousers.

Meanwhile he carries on stealing. In the end these people live better than we do. They grab, and what they cannot grab, they steal. And they steal a lot.

H. H., who was once a prominent businessman, was caught for the third time committing a burglary at night.

The Germans got to hear of it and have promised him KZ. It is a promise they intend to keep.

A similar promise was made to H., who has twenty-five to thirty crimes on his conscience. He has a way of talking everyone out of valuable objects (especially watches) and bartering them for bread. He promises them a high price, and people believe him; but instead it is he who guzzles all the bread. His plea is always the same: trade with *Häftlinge, Arische Vorarbeiter,*[142] et cetera and the impossibility of contacting them. Sentence of sixty days' bunker, a third of his bread withheld as compensation for damages, and once every six days' bread and water. You try to live on that. No sooner had he been sentenced than he stole a coat, an overall, a pair of shoes, bread and more. What can happen to him?

Yesterday – Sunday – T. volunteered to work in the kitchen to get some food. For a cup of broth and half a cup of soup, and otherwise eating surreptitiously from the raw swedes, one spends an entire day peeling in the cold. No heating, a damp, cold cellar, a blocked toilet, which may not be used ... Result: diarrhoea.

We get to hear about other camps. This must be one of the worst and worst managed. The organisation is miserable. The commandant does nothing for us.

The women in the tent camp next to ours have it even worse. They do not even have any underwear, not even a coat. And there is no end in sight.

What have we got from the canteen? Perfume! I dare you to say again that the world has *not* gone mad. Also shampoo and similar rubbish. Naturally paid for out of our own scarce resources. We are forced to buy it.

And when your canteen money is used up and you receive a parcel, the parcel is confiscated because you are unable to pay the import duty.

28 November When the Germans catch someone in the act of stealing, he has to stand against the fence with a notice in front of him saying: 'Ich bin ein Dieb, ich habe euch bestohlen.'[143]

For criminologists: apart from whether this can be justified under criminal law, it makes not the slightest impression. The intended

---

[142] Aryan foremen.   [143] I am a thief, I have robbed you.

humiliation is not achieved. The measure is a measure from an enemy and already condemned on those grounds alone.

But even if the measure did not come from the enemy, but from us for example, it would still not make any impression. It is too barbaric for that, and too unpopular with the public. And does the delinquent feel it? He feels the standing and the cold, not much else.

It is an old barbarian image to see such a man standing there. Is that what we used to practise criminal law for, what we had centuries of development of criminal law for?

Everything has fallen apart.

Every day there are deaths from exhaustion and hunger.

This morning I saw a woman crying for her husband. Their son was fetched from work.

'Oh, Gustav, lass mich nicht allein, ich habe so wahnsinnige Angst!'[144]

All these people are just ordinary people, afraid and not much advanced from when they were little children.

29 November The women who work in the kitchen are given a mug of soup nowadays. They also surreptitiously eat raw swedes there. The rush to work in the kitchen is so great now that the Germans are at their wits' end. Hundreds of women report for duty roll-call. A large horde presses forward not only in violation of the sanctified 'Fünferreihe', but in complete chaos. They jostle each other, kick and dig with their elbows, pull each other back, shove forward, push past the German *Scharführer*, defy blows, threats with revolvers and guns, ignore kicks and thumps, are dragged across the ground, get up again, and continue pushing to the front. No honour, no reflection, no dignity, nothing exists any longer. All that exists is a mug of soup.

Most of them do it for their husbands and children. In this way they manage to save a piece of bread. Class and position have been swept aside, all for a mug of soup, a mug of soup.

---

[144] Oh, Gustav, don't leave me alone, I am so terribly afraid.

The Germans are at a loss and prove that *if we wanted*, there is little they could do. All they could do would be to wreak revenge.

30 November Every day people die of hunger and exhaustion. It is unbearable. Oedema, furuncles, et cetera.

Further news: as a result of the move we now have one washroom with twelve taps for four thousand people, men and women together.

The two men from the crematorium may be 'written off'. They 'sind abgereist'.[145] One more matter that will have to be investigated after the war.

The IPA says the commandant is leaving.

1 December Day of reckoning. Fifty-one deaths in November! To-day C., twenty-two years old, tuberculosis. Rushing, rushing, rushing from one roll-call to the next. Constantly seeking people for work. A new working party: plaiting cellophane. We have to supply a thousand women. They are mad.

2 December Today P. died in the *Altersheim*, the man with the handsome beard. Chief clerk at a bank. Lately, completely confused. He stole slices of bread from other patients.

The IPA was right. A new commandant has arrived.[146] No doubt we will get to hear about it.

More Red Cross parcels have arrived; nothing for us.

Van L. died, also L., forty-eight and thirty.

4 December K. died, twenty-two. His mother a few weeks ago, his father in the *Altersheim*. Cause: exhaustion, hunger. I have diarrhoea and feel dizzy. Today we are having the leaves of sugar beet. For the rest swedes, swedes, and no potatoes.

First they become moral and spiritual; then they keel over and die. For months now L. has been begging from everyone. L. had committed theft and burglary here.

---

[145] Have departed.   [146] Josef Kramer.

I feel so dizzy that I can hardly write.

At night, in front of the toilet, continual fighting over priority. It is repulsive, it prevents us from sleeping. I have stomach cramp.

We had been hoping for good news about transports and did indeed get news about a transport.

At 10.00 a.m. the order came that at half past twelve 164 men from the diamond industry had to go on transport *without* their wives and children. That is how a list *platzt*.[147] There had been plans to set up a diamond industry here. Calculations had been made for it, a hut built, everything had been prepared. Today the men suddenly had to leave. Many were at work. They returned at half past eleven and heard the news. There was not even time to wash their hands.

The parting was of the kind that is called heartrending. Many women and children cried, yet the majority controlled themselves very well. No one knows the destination of the transport.

A few of the sick were kept behind. The majority must go.

A heavy shadow lies over everything. We are dominated by the question of whether this is how the camp will be evacuated. Historically, what does it matter if the war lasts a few months longer? If one wants to call the fate of thousands of people 'historic', it matters a great deal historically. It gives them time to carry out an entire programme. The seventeen hundred Hungarians from the camp next to ours are also leaving now. Throughout the day they have been clearing the camp. Probably we will be moving there. We have not much hope left. If reports about the war do not change fundamentally we are in a bad way.

I have terrible stomach ache.

We had thought: however wretched it may be here, at least we do

---

[147] Collapses (German *platzen*, to burst). During the war people sought to have their names included on lists which they thought would delay, or exempt them from, deportation. There were lists of *Mischlinge*, prominent people in the Dutch Jewish community, Jews who had become converts, et cetera, and in this instance, of people who belonged to the diamond industry. In time all these lists collapsed, that is to say, the protection they had given was suddenly removed.

not have the wretchedness of the transports from Westerbork. But we do have that wretchedness, and worse than in Westerbork.

The *Stabsarzt* rejected twelve of the sick and declared them not 'transportfähig'.[148] In their place they have now taken twelve boys aged fifteen and sixteen, who were also on the diamond list. Our spirits are sinking lower and lower.

The men are standing outside the gate and must unload their luggage. It is lying by the side of the road now. The *Hauptscharführer* walks past with a stick and beats.

> St Nicholas
>
> See the moon shines through the tree tops
> Fellows stop your wild cavorting
> The wonderful evening is upon us
> The Eve of St Nicholas

Can you imagine worse or more senseless doggerel? Nevertheless, it is a verse full of atmosphere and more popular than any other. Incomparably more than the most beautiful chorus by Vondel.[149] There is not a Dutch person who does not feel a quiver in his heart when he hears this song.

We, here in this wretchedness, no less. What is beauty, what is poetry?

I am ill in bed with stomach trouble and fever. For the first time since being imprisoned. I thought I was immune. I have become scared now.

St Nicholas. The first item of news this morning was: the death of the lawyer L. It is getting tedious. Much good will his elegant flat do him now! Forty-seven years old.

And apart from that?

Yesterday, when the lads arrived to replace the sick (from thirteen years upwards) the order came that the sick had to leave after all. See, that is Jew-baiting. That is mastery of the art. And this morning

---

[148] Fit to go on transport.
[149] One of Holland's greatest poets and dramatists, born 1587.

the news came that the wives and children of the men from the diamond industry were leaving. They have no provisions with them.

Will they be staying in the women's camp? And what will happen to the children? This is persecution! The refinement is unsurpassed. *Einmalig!* [150]

St Nicholas, Tuesday 5 December 1944.[151] How much longer?

In the evening We have just heard that the children have remained behind. Separated from their mothers.

The children are huddled together in the garage outside the main gate of the camp. They gave them white bread. How kind! A few older children are looking after them. Just now they came to fetch camp blankets for the children. Poor H. with your sweet little face, six years old! The children are unaware of anything. We know what will happen. I am not writing it down. After the war perhaps.

6 December We know more or less what happened yesterday. The women and children were taken outside the gate where the women were informed, near the garage, that they were being separated from the children. The luggage had to be divided up immediately. Then the women were led away. They were each given a whole loaf, butter, and three small cheeses. The children were given white bread, butter, and sugar. But apparently there were not enough blankets for the children. Those were fetched later from here.

For the rest, things are going badly for us. For weeks we have had no news again and each day our condition gets more critical. It reminds me of an old-fashioned horror film, about people sitting in a cellar, and the water rising higher and higher. By nature, I tend not to rely on happy endings.

7 December Four men have been sent to the KZ. Two of them had stolen overalls.

Conversations: (a) R. also received a parcel. J., too. They need it

---

[150] Unique!   [151] The feast day of St Nicholas is 6 December; presents are exchanged on the eve or on the day itself.

badly; (b) This morning, during container collection, Trenke was beating again. Fifty litres were spilled; (c) Did you hear them flying last night? What use is it to us? There is no end to it.

Will it or will it not end?

T. is a strong, quiet, level-headed and courageous person.

She says: 'Don't worry if you can't do anything'; (d) Are there any deaths today? Not one. Hm. My pyjama trousers have been stolen.

Twelve hundred new Jews have arrived. From Hungary, from Romania, some say. They file past the whole day, men, women, children, with bag and baggage, covered in mud and dirt, worn out. Almost not human any more. But men, women and children have remained together. I see them filing past and think: it could turn one into a Zionist.

They end up in the camp to the right of us. For the time being, we will not have any contact with them.

What is the point of this senseless organisation of wretchedness? I have conducted an investigation. Several months ago, ninety three Hungarians arrived here. They are tradesmen for building the huts. A band of unrecognisable, indescribable creatures dressed in rags. There was a large gang of thieves among them, but also great aristocrats. Devout Catholics and superstitious *Chassidim*.[152] The riff-raff were spread through both groups, irrespective of race or belief.

They would remain for only a few days and then return to Vienna from where they had come. They waited and naturally did not return. But ... the transport which arrived today included their wives and children.

Our people from the diamond industry are leaving by themselves. The women separately and the children separately.

These Hungarians are being reunited. Where – where – where is the rule in all this? The sense? The reason? The intention? The objective?

Many of the new arrivals collapsed on the road; and many never got up again.

---

[152] Jewish mystics.

8 December I have visited the new hospital hut. It is certainly a significant improvement, but only in part. The ward for 'the infirm' is like a chest of drawers. It is all quite unbelievable really, boxes stacked three high.

The sick – just as in the *Altersheim* – worn-out, starved people, oh, oh, oh, thin is not the word for it any longer. Emaciated down to the bone. One spoon of soup and they would live for dozens more years. One egg, one or two extra potatoes a day.

But there is none; I see them fading away.

H., S., J. and so many others, who would get better if they had a mug of broth.

We must not reproach anyone with anything because we have no information, but the Dutch government, why do we not hear *anything* from them? Is it not *our* government? Why do so many people *never* receive a parcel? Why not ten times as many? It is needed so desperately.

Why is everyone forsaking us? Why do we receive nothing, nothing, nothing? Even Palestine, even the Agency[153] is failing us.

We are starving.

10 December Today, S. died. His brother H. is at death's door, his wife has taken leave of her senses. His son is lying in hospital with chronic diarrhoea. H.'s son has wasted away and is lying in bed. Only one person remains calm, is indefatigable, works and cares, cares and works, drudges, toils and hurries: Aunt M., the oldest and toughest. In September we celebrated her seventieth birthday. She is still as lively and agile as a young girl and has kept her charm.

She attends to the burial, the inheritance, she cooks and heats food for her dying brother, tidies the documents left behind, arranges the property left behind, worth many loaves of bread, and which may therefore be the salvation of the son he left behind. 'Life takes

---

[153] Probably the Jewish Agency for Palestine in Jerusalem, 'the Zionist body which had been set up twenty years earlier by the British government as its liaison with the Jews of Palestine' (Sir Martin Gilbert, *Auschwitz and the Allies*, Michael Joseph/Rainbird, London 1981).

its course here,' she says, 'and I won't let myself be dragged down.'

And she battles and remains herself, upright and indefatigable.

And that is how one day after another passes by ... people waste away, life vanishes and there is no news, no change.

And whatever there is, is bad. That angry little member of the bench who should have been a model of composure and stead-fastness, runs about and screeches out his pessimism about him like a black crow. His prognosis is always sombre.

Unfortunately, he is right, but not very cheerful. Today he was talking about the *Stubbenkommando* which has now been placed under the supervision of one of the *Häftlinge Kapos*. Naturally he says that this characterises our conditions in the camp ... And unfortunately, it is true. The *Stubbenkommando* is now the personal working party of the new commandant. Apparently he is making it into a kind of personal hunting ground. The other day he supervised the work. He is said to be 'streng aber gerecht'.[154] Yes, that well-known reputation.

This afternoon there is *General Appell*.[155] It will probably bring changes along. It is almost impossible to continue with the legal cases. People are being refused leave of absence from work. And without the accused and the witnesses, what can one do?

Yesterday a *Zivilsache*.[156] For some time now the containers have had to be dragged across the road from the kitchen to a gate approximately two hundred metres away, and from there to the huts. As each container holds fifty litres and the container itself often weighs ten to twenty kilos, the total weight is one that two people can barely carry, people who also happen to be starving. Moreover, the containers are fitted with two handles which make them awkward to carry.

Someone then hit on the idea of converting perambulators into container carts. The Jewish *Dienstleiter* of *Dienstbereich* 3[157] (food distribution) ordered two perambulators, which he reckoned were

---

[154] Strict but just.   [155] General roll-call.   [156] Civil case.
[157] Leader of service unit 3.

unusable, to be dismantled and a cart to be made with the wheels. No sooner had the container carriers learnt about this than they all pounced on the perambulators, dismantled them, ruined them, and every hut tried in the shortest possible time to secure a cart for themselves for collecting *their* containers.

Within a day every perambulator had been dismantled and reduced to a heap of scrap. What that means for the owners is known only by someone who experienced the sudden transportations of families who were desperate because they were at a loss how to carry their babies and baby clothes. And the other day there was the diamond transport, when mothers walked about crying with sorrow and wretchedness.

An owner of a perambulator has now brought an action for damages against the camp for having dismantled his perambulator. To be precise, because the leader of DB 3 is supposed to have ordered *all* the perambulators to be dismantled, which he denies.

We will see though. Anyway, it is an interesting case.

H. has just died. Three burglaries, thirty days' bunker, fifteen days' bunker. He still had to be sentenced for the third offence. Once a respectable businessman; here a dangerous thief. Cause of death: *Herzschwäche*.[158]

They all become corrupted – then they die. For many the destruction starts in the brain.

Hunger is a disease of the brain.

12 December From a report by DB 1 (*Arbeitseinteilung*)[159] to the *Judenälteste*: Conditions during *Arbeitseinteilung* are becoming more acute by the day. The difficulties are due to two factors:

1. reduction in the number of camp inhabitants;
2. deterioration in the state of health and an increase in the number of sick.

Ad 1. The number of prisoners has decreased from 4,350 to

---

[158] Heart failure.   [159] Labour assignment.

3,587; a reduction of approximately eighteen per cent. When the number was 4,350 persons we had to supply 950 to 1,050 persons daily. Now, however, 1,200 persons, an increase of twenty per cent.

Ad 2. Not only is illness on the increase, but also its average duration. This has risen from approximately one to three days, to from three days up to two or three weeks.

The number of sick comprising the *Altersheim*, the *Invalidenheim*, and the permanently disabled, now amounts to 563 men and 529 women, altogether 1,092 persons, an increase of fifty per cent in the past few months.

For the rest, children 684, pregnant women and nursing mothers 100, persons from the year 1928/1929, respectively 1885–1888, who are excluded from Arbeitseinsatz 290,[160] hospital staff, doctors et cetera 150, hut leaders, food distribution, camp cleaning, et cetera 170, total 1,392. Therefore, 'Arbeitsfähige'[161] persons: 1,100.

Now the illnesses.

Naturally, those who fall ill most often are the outdoor working parties: *Bahnhof-*, *Transport-*, *Stubben-*, *Reisigkommando.*[162] These people become ill. They are the manpower aged between eighteen and thirty-five years. There are no substitutes. Sick, exhausted, old people must now join the outdoor working parties. People are dying.

The food situation is unbearable.

Likewise the hygiene conditions. Sometimes dirty laundry has to be kept in beds for weeks, laundry from diarrhoea patients.

One washroom for thirty-five hundred people. They have one hour in which to wash themselves: men and women together. At the same time, the women must do the laundry. Half of the taps are broken. Everything is blocked up. The floor is ten centimetres deep in water. People must go to work with soaking wet feet.

Conditions in the latrines are indescribable. In the mornings there is never any light. One can imagine the consequences. Every, every morning: deaths, victims.

---

[160] What is meant is that people born after 1928–1929, or before 1885–1888 were not required to work; 85–88 may be a misprint for 85–86.   [161] People fit for work.
[162] Railway, transport, tree-stump and wood-gathering working parties.

Yesterday afternoon the office staff were assigned to the *Stubben-kommando*.

It freezes, it snows, it hails. Then it thaws again. The mud is indescribable.

No heating anywhere unless one can find a piece of wood. It is unbearable.

T. has diarrhoea. I try to boil some water. It gets warm, but there is not enough wood to bring it to the boil. Till now, there has at least been some form of organisation. Each of us had a bed and therefore also a fixed place in a particular hut. Some even had a share of a cupboard in which they could store their rucksack, their bread, and their suitcase. The rucksack and the bread went into the bed, the suitcase underneath it. At least one had a place to sleep at night and in general one slept well.

The night before yesterday the *Scharführer* arrived: 'Albala!' Albala appeared.

By ten o'clock tomorrow morning the *Altersheim* (350 men and women) and three other huts containing women and children must be vacated and moved to the existing huts.

The catastrophe is indescribable. Thirteen hundred and fifty-six people must suddenly move now to eight crammed huts. The instructions said: if necessary, men and women in the same hut. Apart from that, place two persons in one bed. We are not given any additional beds.

The *Ältestenrat* convened and deliberated. A detailed memorandum was drawn up to prove that the order could not be fulfilled.

The following day, after a night's work, the memorandum was ready.

Albala gave it to the *Oberscharführer*.[163] He put it in his trouser pocket and announced that the move was to be completed by eight o'clock. And that is how the chaos and the greatest possible wretchedness came to engulf us.

We no longer have a bed and must lie two to a bed at night. The

---

[163] SS sergeant.

advantage is, it is warm. That is all one can say for it. The beds are forty centimetres wide. We are not given any extra mattresses, either. Where are we meant to leave the luggage, the rucksacks, the blankets?

How are we meant to sleep?

During the day, slave-work, beatings, and no food. At night, no rest. An unimaginable filth never seen before.

The people from the *Altersheim*, many of them invalids, the rest sick, infirm and exhausted, must all move into three-tier beds.

One hundred and fifty beds are being cleared in the hut of the Albanians. The elderly women are going there. A hundred and fifty beds in my hut. Those are for the men.

There they lie in the mire then, among the lice, groaning, shouting and dying. A few are unable to endure the tension and die.

Every day people are dying, every day ... On some days five or six at a time.

You should have seen aunt M. Yesterday afternoon (Friday) – the Sabbath had just come in – I went to tell her that her sister-in-law had died. I thought she already knew, but she did not. She had just returned from the funeral of her second brother.

Nevertheless, she jumped up: 'I must keep my wits about me now,' she said. 'I must go and help that boy now. He is so alone.'

M. – that is the best of humanity to exist.

For what she is and does, that is what counts.

Perhaps there is one still better. M. asked someone to thank T. for the mattress that arrived last night. T. had not mentioned a word to me about it. And it is not easy to obtain a mattress here. Only one thing counts. Do something for another.

To avoid any misunderstanding; the people from the *Altersheim* each have a bed to themselves. That had been decided by the Jews. The wretchedness is enough to turn one's stomach.

In all situations, though, a privileged circle immediately develops. Even here. A number of people are sleeping by themselves again. They are the selfsame who receive extra food.

And that is how we carry on living – if one can call it living. To add to our troubles, it has started to freeze. There is no heating anywhere. There are six to seven degrees of frost.

The women in the kitchen worked till ten last night and this morning they had to fall in at half past two. By way of thanks, they were all suddenly dismissed this morning, without a word of explanation, and replaced by Polish women.

The food will get worse, of course.

The men are also being dismissed.

A sudden announcement this morning: fifty-eight *Mischlinge* are to go on transport.

They are lucky. Worse than here is unimaginable for them. A few months ago they arrived here in good spirits, looking down on the Jews 'who did not know how to work'. And as worn out, crumpled, and to a large extent totally depraved sick slaves they are leaving, exhausted and emaciated. When they arrived here they were already anti-Semites, now well and truly so. Van T. had complained of rheumatoid arthritis, lack of food, lack of sleep, lack of clothing. How someone can make himself generally unpopular in no time at all! I do not understand why.

Nobody knows where the transport is going, but they are happy to be leaving here.

The transport left accompanied by kicks and blows. A very bad prognosis. Many of them are sick. We live here as if on a dunghill now. The people, for whom there are not enough toilets, are using the floor. There is no embarrassment any longer, not a single reserve. The stench is unbearable.

19 December Yet another transport is leaving today. The remaining wives of the men from the diamond industry are leaving with their children. Again sorrow and wretchedness.

In the camp next to ours there is a constant coming and going of large transports of women. What we learn from them amounts to tears, grief and wretchedness. They are more hopeful than we are, though. Perhaps they have already got used to the worst that is still threatening here: transport, separation of husbands and wives.

Separation of parents and children. The mood here is hardly bearable any longer.

The absence of hopeful political news, disillusionment over the duration of the war, the prospect of a still indefinitely long imprisonment, the more aggressive attitude of the Germans, the constant worsening of the food, the bestial sanitary conditions, the stable in which we live, the lack of beds – there are still people who have no place to sleep – the very bad weather at times, it all makes our life into an inferno and worse.

The hunger is growing. The work continues and increases. Their hatred of us expresses itself daily through new and harsh pettifoggery; stopping of bread, taking food away, punishing with bunker for every minor matter, kicking and beating.

My God, my God, how much longer?

Many have given up hope.

Every day deaths. Every day cremations.

The cart driver a *Häftling* speaks Flemish!

He is Belgian.

Yesterday there was post. Perhaps afterwards people will say: They got post in Bergen-Belsen. The truth is: in Bergen-Belsen *someone else* got a postcard once a year, that was five or six months old. Oh, a few hundred people receive something. The majority, three thousand five hundred, receive nothing and long for a word from those who are dearest to them in all the world.

Will anyone reading this afterwards ever understand it?

This is intended as a note to be expanded on later. Perhaps it will become a testament ... which no one, no one will ever open.

Oh, how abandoned we are in this place which is nothing but a grave. Death does not mean something frightening. It means only that all hope is in vain.

Dying is a transition from death to death, no longer a transition from life to death. People lie dying here in their filth and their lice. Have human beings ever had it as bad as this?

They are robbing the corpses.

A grave, a grave – at night and in the mornings I lie awake

mournfully in my coffin, which we have not even to ourselves, but must share.

And suddenly the world looks different. Yesterday parcels arrived for H., who is not here. A name is a name. They were distributed to us. I have eaten a piece of bacon and a little sugar. And the world has perspective – happiness. I no longer feel hungry. I have faith again. Is it humiliating? Is it just fact? It has lasted almost a year now.

'Erst kommt das Fressen,

Und dann kommt die Moral.'[164]

Nevertheless, it is not true. At the lowest point of our rejection 'Moral' did remain.

We are becoming as filthy as cows and pigs: we relieve ourselves wherever we happen to be. And still there is public morality, people do not do as they please. There is thieving, much and often, and still it is not condoned but condemned. Social conscience has still *not* been broken.

Moreover, there are angels here. T., M., and others.

Oh, God let us remain together. You have tried us enough now.

20 December A new provocation. The working parties no longer return to camp at midday but must remain at work for their midday break. Great difficulties with the food distribution. Nevertheless, at three in the afternoon the plaiters were suddenly relieved by Polish Jewesses.

Apart from that: rain, cold, wet. Tomorrow it is winter. The shortest days of the year. They seem the longest.

22 December Yesterday was the official start to winter. The war is not over, on the contrary, according to the news that has reached us the Germans are on the offensive. It drives us to despair. The thought of it still lasting an indefinite time with all the accompanying risks makes us downhearted. And again we experience the nature of those risks.

---

[164] First food, then morality.

Yesterday S. F. died, an engineer. Oh, what an assimilator. How he used to deny everything that stood for the Jewish question. Forty-seven years old. Starvation. O. died, fifty-one years old, starvation.

And then there are new orders.

1. In the mornings, reveille at five. Naturally it is the greatest nonsense imaginable, for at five in the morning it is still pitch dark. And before half past seven there is no roll-call.

2. The beds are to be pushed together in groups of four. Impossible. The women crawl over each other. Imagine the fun when the person in the middle has to piddle or has diarrhoea! And we are sleeping two to a bed.

3. And finally, Albala and the *Ältestenrat* have been dismissed and *Häftlinge* have arrived to organise matters.

We are very worried, but must wait and see. By itself it is extremely serious, of course. Perhaps it will not be too bad.

How something like this happens? From one moment to the next without any opportunity to justify oneself. There is always someone higher up.

The judicial commission has been dissolved. Anyone who steals will die within eight days. That is the new justice.

Christmas I do not know if there will ever be a hand capable of describing the wretchedness of four thousand starving Jews in this camp on Christmas Day 1944. But even if there will be a hand capable of it, not an eye will be capable of reading it, not a heart equal to it, not a mind willing to suffer it. There is a sharp frost. For Christmas they gave some faggots to the huts. Now the women are crowding around the stoves for a little warmth, to make a small mug of porridge or heat some water. The children are walking about with frozen hands and feet, crying from the cold, snapped at by their nervous parents.

Christmas 1944. Today, Boxing Day, ten deaths. Yesterday, seven. The day before yesterday, three. And there are plenty more candidates. We reckon on at least ten a day, three hundred a month.

Thirty-five hundred *Kampinsassen* ... [165] But worse still is the political news.

Yesterday it was alleged: Brussels retaken. The Germans again forty kilometres from the coast. 470,000 Americans taken prisoner. Significant retreat in Holland. Probably it is all much exaggerated, but the fact of the German initiative and offensive remains.

How in God's name is it possible ... ?

Christmas 1944!

No one will ever understand the feelings that this news evokes among us, who had hoped to be liberated before the winter. It is not fear of death. But of *this* death, *this* torture.

A few days ago we lost the last of our privileges. Albala has been deposed. The *Kapo*s now rule. From five in the morning till late in the evening they walk through the camp. Armed with a stick or a riding-crop, they look for people to send to work and round us up.

Yet so far, it has turned out better than expected.

There is less corruption. And W., a German Jew with much experience of Holland, is in charge of the *Kapo*s. Much of the autonomy will probably remain now. Probably even the judicial commission, in a modest form.

But Hanke, the *Kapo* of *Kapo*s, has said: 'Wer stiehlt, stirbt.'[166] Theft of food is punished with death within twenty-four hours. Justice is a difficult thing. What shall we do, what will our responsibilities be?

Fortunately December is almost over now and also 1944. Away with it! All hope for 1944 has vanished. We seem to have been duped, disillusioned.

I shall speak to W. about the judicial commission.

We had slightly better food for Christmas. Pearl barley with gravy. Yesterday red cabbage and jacket potatoes. Today *Nudeln*[167] and potatoes. Tomorrow swedes again, swedes, swedes, swedes.

The food was better, but far too little. We got thirty-five per cent of what we need.

---

[165] Camp inmates ('Kamp' is Dutch, 'insassen' is German).
[166] Those who steal, will die.   [167] Macaroni.

Fine Christmas. A faggot and *Nudeln* – twenty deaths – frozen feet and the Germans on the offensive.

How much longer?

Boxing Day Evening. It is almost over. The great event here was the food. How good it was and how fat. It had bacon in it. But it was not even a third of what it should have been. On the three days there was also no work in the afternoons.

The news remains bad. The mood is wretched. The number of dead is increasing. Irritability is mounting. Quarrels are on the increase. Men quarrel with their wives, and wives bore their husbands. I had forgotten to mention that this year we also 'celebrated' Chanukah here. One evening, around a candle. The miracle of the oil did not repeat itself. I gave a talk in the *Altersheim*. Chanukah is very topical. (Chanukah is the Feast of Dedication.)

Oh, liberty, liberty, liberty. My children, may God preserve you from having to long for liberty.

28 December Today, seven deaths. A few days ago S. P.-S. died. He left two young children behind. Today L. His wife last week. A child of eight left behind. Mrs B. Her husband left behind. An invalid. M.A., one of our worst thieves. Hungarian. Convert. Y., a lawyer. Here he had stolen bread. Numerous thieves die here, or numerous candidates for death begin to steal.

It is better to remain silent now. Our hearts are filled with sorrow. And on top of that, bad news. How much longer?

This morning, I had to carry containers. I am worn out.

T. has diarrhoea – again. It is not getting better, it keeps coming back. Here, the truth is out: they have been empowered to adopt KZ methods.

There is much beating, particularly in the eternally disputed *Stubbenkommando*.

These are notes which need to be elaborated. There is much corruption now. Bread, food, cigarettes. Our feet are frozen, our hearts are dead.

6 January 1945 The first six days of the new year I have spent in bed, laid low by a horrible green dysentery. The doctor managed to get some *Cibazole*[168] for me which – though much weakened – helped me make a full recovery. A bladder infection from which I had suffered for many years was cured at the same time. That was the gain.

New Year's Eve already seems ages ago. In the past, too, New Year's Eve always seemed so long ago that one could no longer remember it. It is like sinking into the depths, the depths of memory, and as if it finds its expression in time.

The two of us sat on the bed, three tiers up in pitch darkness. There had been an air-raid alert. We could hear bombs falling in the distance ...

We avoided everything that might have seemed like 'reflection'. Everything that might have led to sentimentality and melancholy.

After the air raid, at around 9.00 p.m., I returned to my hut.

It was a beautiful winter's evening, yet even the brilliant full moon could not drive the sombre mood away.

It was freezing. It had snowed.

Meanwhile, better news has reached us from the front. The German offensive has been halted.

Now, though, everything has come to a halt. And we are weary, weary like dying people.

R., one of F.'s young daughters, has died. And every day more are dying. K. is dead, H. is dead, S. is dead. The first two were thieves, and how!

The old year had brought parcels: four hundred for the entire camp. We received four and can live now. We have great need of it because every day the food gets worse. Day after day swedes, sometimes twice a day. The swedes are frozen and bitter. We hardly see potatoes any more, if at all.

The extra food is distributed from a central point now. All in all, it is an improvement. The Greeks lost by it. They lost their privileges.

---

[168] A sulphonamide.

7 January 1945 The judicial commission has remained after all.

The *Kapos* are a problem though. They trade and traffic with the *Lagerinsassen.*[169] They also buy up stolen items.

I had a case yesterday. A lamp had been stolen and sold to a *Kapo* for half a loaf. We dealt with the matter, despite the risks involved.

Just now I heard that P. has died. They say old G. is also in a bad state. Eighty-seven years old. He had so hoped to see *Eretz Israël* (Palestine). P. was an outstanding *Misrachi* (orthodox Zionist). An excellent accountant. Old G. is a tragedy. Also E. v. d. L. I now hear. Thirty-three years old. Exhaustion. An excellent man. And so many, many others.

Next week we will have been here one year. 12 January. Last year the winter only started then. It dragged on till May. How we have suffered in that year.

The amount of bread we used to get for three days now has to last four days. Today is Sunday, until Tuesday, then.

Apparently, the military bakery in Hannover has been hit. They are requisitioning *our* rations now. It is always *us* who are the first to suffer. Afterwards, no one will understand any more the terrible impact of such news. Moreover, next week there will be still further cuts in our bread rations. W. 'hopes' that by the end of next week things will have returned to normal.

Indeed, who tells us there will not be more bombings. Surely, that is far more likely.

It is wet and cold. My feet are almost frozen. It goes together badly with cramp.

It is rumoured there are women here who consort with the *Kapos*. They receive them in bed.

I have just had a discussion about the matter of the lamp. I must withhold an entire loaf. I proposed a compromise of half a loaf. That is what it will probably come to.

I am too soft and sentimental for a judge. I leave too much to our Lord. That would not be so bad, if he did not leave everything to me. Bad colleagues.

---

[169] Camp inhabitants.

Mrs L. is suffering with oedema. She is having a rest now. I visit her, why? How can one love an old woman of seventy? Have I aged so much myself?

All kinds of IPAs are circulating. The camp is to be enlarged, we are to move to the Russian camp. The exchange is not taking place. The exchange will take place. The work is ending, is not ending. It is going to be turned into a *Konzentrationslager*,[170] one person says to another, believing it to be of interest.

What is certain, is that people are dying. The bread is getting less, the food worse, the mood still more desperate, illness is on the increase. We are dying in the filth, in the dark, in the cold.

That is how we start our second year. There is really no point in writing any more. It is a continuous succession of wretchedness, wretchedness, and more wretchedness. And if we must die – then better at once ...

8 January 1945 All day sleet has been dripping from a leaden sky. It is not going to get light today. The mood is the mood of death. It is impossible to imagine how sombre it is. It is midday, without light one cannot do anything. There is hunger, cold, illness, wretchedness, and death.

9 January 1945 Today the courageous Otto S. passed away. Exhaustion. *Kreislaufschwäche*.[171]

After not getting any bread at all yesterday, we were given half a ration today. You try to live on that!

It is freezing cold. We are starving.

13 January 1945 Yesterday marked our first year here. It has been a terrible year, far from home, from the children, without news from them, a year of disappointment. The transport to Palestine, the peace that did not come, a year of hunger, cold, hounding, persecution and humiliation. Fortunately, though, apart from a few bouts of dysentery, we have not been seriously ill.

---

[170] Concentration camp.   [171] Poor circulation.

The food is getting worse and worse. At midday, swede soup, every day without a single potato. The 'extra' food is distributed centrally now. Every day there are genuine punch-ups over a ticket. Some are given to the *Dienstbereiche* and some to the doctor for the weak and the sick. Recriminations about favouritism, at every attempt, of course, to be as fair as possible.

The extra food is distributed outdoors by a *Kapo*, accompanied by the inevitable blows with the ladle in every direction.

The *Kapo* system has existed for three weeks now. Its characteristics are: hounding with truncheons and sticks when there is work to be done.

Postcards dated early November have reached us from Amsterdam. Everything I had feared seems true. No gas, no electricity, two hundred grams of bread a day. Hunger and shortage. I fear it may be as bad as here. The game is lasting too long. Probably in Holland there will also be large numbers of deaths.

Here it is increasing all the while. Today J.H. Yesterday O.S., Dr C., dentist F., et cetera, et cetera, et cetera. Young B., nineteen years old, Anr. B., who therefore also did not help with preventing the hiring out of a camp blanket.

There is no news. No parcels either. We have reached the bottom, and are therefore facing the worst hunger again.

T. is bearing up extremely well. She keeps herself going and is full of courage. It is mostly men who die. If it carries on like this it will be a matter of a few months – then no one will be left.

People look pitiful. Literally living corpses. They are dropping with tiredness and wretchedness.

The *Stubbenkommando* is dreadful. Although they get extra rations, they also get extra beatings. Yesterday afternoon, another court case. A large quantity of semolina had been stolen, a bag containing ten to fifteen kilos that one of the Hungarians was keeping for a group of Hungarians. The accused were a Greek woman and her brother, who confessed. The woman we sentenced to five days' bunker and the man to eight (three days on bread and water) and assignment to the *Stubbenkommando*. The commandant changed this to: one month's assignment to the *Stubbenkommando*, *without any extra allocation*. If, after one month, he has behaved himself, the bunker sentence will be quashed.

This is all but the death penalty. At this time of the year *Stubbenkommando* without extra food is impossible. *Stubben* are tree stumps that must be dug up and dispatched.

The court sittings have become onerous. The *Kapo*s enter with their truncheons and sticks and stay to observe. One can imagine what remains of the independence of the bench and the rights of the accused. It is all unimaginably bad. Oh Holland, oh poor humanity! From time to time there is no bread at all here – from time to time (tonight, for example) we are not allowed to use the toilet. Those who have diarrhoea must go outdoors. We have procured some buckets for ourselves, discarded jam buckets.

This morning, my neighbour had to resort to them.

This morning his bunkmate discovered to his horror that his shoes were full. The other had soiled himself twice during the night.

We are living amid the lice. For months I have not been able to change into clean underwear, nor had a shower. Naturally there is also no heating here, we suffer terribly from the cold in the huts, which are draughty and where the door is never shut.

Deaths, deaths, deaths.

For how long?

Apparently, Westerbork was still in existence at the beginning of November. The persecution of the Jews continues. Nevertheless we are a year nearer to peace than on 13 January 1944.

15 January 1945 Fourteen deaths today. The death cart comes several times a day.

It is rumoured that everyone will get ten cigarettes, including the women. C., who had been assigned to the *Stubbenkommando* for theft, is out of it again. He had been beaten so hard that he was admitted into hospital.

There are IPAs. Russian offensive. *Machtübernahme*[172] by Keitel.[173] I do not believe a word of it.

Fourteen deaths. Even as they die people steal bread from each other. No soup this evening. There is no water and no electric light. They have locked the toilets. Conditions in Holland are said to be even worse now. It is not about who has it *worse*, we or the Dutch. It is *despite ourselves a different* fate. A different fate means being afraid of something different. And man is characterised by his fears, by what he is afraid of.

16 January 1945   The number of deaths rose to seventeen yesterday.

Among them the elderly, blind V. He used to have his children and grandchildren here but because they were *Doppelstaatler*, they were sent away. Where to? We do not know. The elderly blind V. remained behind by himself. The children here say: he was a proper grandpa! He was very good at telling stories and when evening approached, he would start to sing Jewish songs. One of his sons used to be a teacher – a pleasant fellow and an excellent teacher.

Then there is 'camp fever' here, another word for *paratyphus*. Raging fever, often lethal.

And to keep our spirits up, there is talk of spotted fever in the women's camp.

If I should manage to emerge alive from here, and if I should still have the mental and physical strength for it, I will write down the speech for the prosecution that I delivered against R. whom our little J. used to call *Onkel*.[174] *Onkel* is lying in bed with oedema, tormented by *Todesahnung*,[175] broken in spirit. He has twenty days' *Bettruhe* from the *Stabsarzt*, and when the bread cupboard stood open, stole a packet of bread from it. *Onkel* used to live on the second floor while we used to live on the third. In the evenings, during the anxious times when Jews had to be indoors by eight o'clock, we often sat together talking and waiting to see if the bell would ring and the Germans would come to take us away. One evening they did come, but let us stay in the house. And in the end

---

172 Assumption of power.
173 Keitel was at the head of the German Officer Corps.
174 Uncle.   175 Presentiment of death.

we ended up here, the spoiled millionaire's son with his beautiful wife, as bread thief, and I as public prosecutor. And I became like a prophet, sent out to curse, but who could only bless. Oh, if only I had been allowed to prosecute ... ! I demanded a conditional sentence of eight days. The bench wanted no 'weakness' but gave eight days' unconditional, to be served once he had recovered.

And we all know that this recovery is problematic, and how our path could be the same as his ... twenty deaths today!

And one candidate for death steals from another, and the third one pronounces judgment. My God, will we never remain silent?

News has arrived that we must move to the Russian camp. Much disquiet, extreme worry. What can we expect this time? And the move itself in the cold. How many deaths?

Now it is not going through tomorrow, on account of the lice, and the camp cheers. *Es leben die Läuse*.[176]

21 January 1945 Several days of great commotion in the camp lie behind us. Mös and Fräulein Schlottke arrived unexpectedly and composed an *Austauschtransport*.[177] A list with names on it, names off it, the most bitter disappointment. Why should they care?

In the end, three hundred people are leaving today, mainly South Americans. It is assumed they are going to Switzerland, to freedom. They are not told anything.

They have left now and a flat, low spirit hangs over the entire camp. It is dreadful having to remain here until everything – even life – is lost. Take V., for example, whom I have just visited, who together with another lies twisting and turning in the lice and lice wounds in a pitch-dark bed. He suffers from insomnia and has been prescribed bedrest. His wife and six children have to share three beds, likewise in perpetual darkness. By day without sunlight, by night without light. The woman is worn out. Yet these people do not lose confidence and hope in God. In God who has deserted us so.

---

[176] Long live the lice.   [177] Exchange transport.

Snow, snow and sharp frost. Nine deaths today.

22 January 1945 Hard frost and snow.

Last night *Rechtsanwalt*[178] H. died, a fine man, speciality: Roman Law. For eight months his wife had struggled for him, courageously and sacrificing everything. Her bread, her cheese, her jam, everything she could spare was for him. But for months on end the patient had to eat boiled swedes. H. is dead, together with eight others today. I read their documents. I see their photographs. It is a never ending tragedy.

23 January 1945 Hut 23B houses: a group of Hungarians who were sent here as skilled workers, and all one can say about them, is that they are like a gang of wild men. Partly *Chasidim*, partly converts, and at the same time thieves and robbers. Next, a group of French women, some of whom are mentally handicapped. One of them has stayed in bed for five weeks already, without leaving it. Calls of nature are all done in bed. Third, a group of *Doppelstaatler*, dégénérés[179] to the extreme.

And fourthly, in a separate section, the Ascher[180] diamond group – hanging on and around Bram,[181] whose condition, I fear, is most worrying. With the courage of a lion, the Ascher group fights against the general state of filth that dominates the rest of the hut. Not buckets, but cartloads of mud, rags, old tin cans, pieces of glass, the remains of shoes, rucksacks, boxes, an altogether sickening mountain of stinking filth, a hotbed of pestilence, cholera, typhus, spreads over the floor, is scraped together into a heap from time to time, after the Hungarians and the French women have first had an hour-long quarrel over whose responsibility it is.

The result of the quarrel was that at two this afternoon, during roll-call, a heap of filth was lying in the hut. The *Rottenführer* reported it to the *Lagerälteste*:[182] result, no food for two days. Two

---

[178] Lawyer.   [179] Depraved.
[180] Before the war, Ascher was one of Amsterdam's leading diamond merchants.
[181] Short for Abraham.   [182] Senior prisoner of a camp.

days without food while people are dying by the dozen from hunger and exhaustion. Two days without food when there is hunger oedema, camp fever and tuberculosis.

Yesterday, a group of people departed from here. Today, they will no longer remember what it is like here.

My former neighbour and eight others died today. Now his children can fast for two days. Diarrhoea and no food, frost and the entire day not a spark of warmth for the children.

31 January 1945 Today it is thawing for the first time after a very long period of frost. It has been bitterly cold – too cold to write, especially as we were not given any firewood and there has been virtually no heating in the huts. Except that from time to time a few faggots would be flung into the huts: those who were quickest could fetch a few branches with which to boil a little water, or reheat the previous day's food. It is crowded around the stove; it gives no warmth; the diarrhoea sufferers try to toast bread; one or two fortunate ones bake a cake.

In the meantime, the dying has continued. Here are a few names: F., v. B., Dr D., Dr L., N., the journalist, who was still in perfect health a few days ago. With this weather, everyone is ill.

The men from the diamond industry – at least some of them – have returned to the camp. From what we hear, they have suffered terribly. Many, many have died.

More and more *Häftlinge* keep arriving here, men from Oranienburg, sent here to convalesce. They find it an El Dorado here. It is raining. Already it is terribly muddy. I am very afraid of my feet getting wet.

There are approximately thirty thousand Jews in the camp now. Every day roll-call. One disaster after another.

There are IPAs. A Palestine transport is rumoured to be leaving. A Russian victory. Even Schneidemühl[183] is mentioned today. For

---

[183] Now called Schneeren, a small town approximately 25 km north-west of Hanover.

very many it has all come too late. Despite everything the mood is improving a little. It is rumoured there will be no more parcels. A disaster! Nothing less. The days pass by in an endless, endless, frustrating sequence. Days of dying. But the darkest days are over.

8 February 1945 I had hung my coat in a cupboard. Someone has stolen the buttons.

Mrs R. and her son took Veronal.[184] The mother recovered. Fourteen days later the son was despatched to the crematorium. Someone else cut his wrists with positive results: crematorium.

In the washroom of hut 17, which had housed transports, two corpses were found. R.M. is dead. *Chaluz*. Son-in-law of R.C. List of casualties: two brothers, a woman, a son-in-law. Mrs E. has died. List of family casualties: seven people.

A bestial meanness. We are being crammed into old huts with leaking roofs. The moribund *Altersheim* has to move. It is costing dozens of lives. Exhausted, they pack the little luggage they have. A whole ration of bread is being asked for moving a little luggage. I saw J.; oh God, it makes you weep. Such a move means death for dozens and its preparation for hundreds of others.

A cart with bagged *Häftlinge* corpses passes by. Europe 1945. What an outrage!

15 February 1945 For quite some time now Germany is being driven into a corner; it keeps having to clear more territory and at the same time surrender more and more concentration and Jewish camps. It seems not to know what to do with the livestock, and in the end decides to drag it all here. Sometimes for longer, sometimes for shorter periods. As a result we, who until recently numbered seven thousand people, have now risen to a total of forty thousand. For all kinds of reasons, including the enormously high mortality rate, our camp has gone down to twenty-seven hundred people. The space is becoming increasingly cramped. Last week, we had the long

---

[184] Name of a sleeping pill (a barbiturate).

threatened move which grew into a full-scale pogrom. What follow are some of the things that I witnessed with my own eyes.

The hospital and the *Altersheim* had to move simultaneously, as well as the women's huts and several men's sections. There were no bearers or stretchers for the sick and the *Altersheim*, despite their having been promised. The sick remained in bed and were promised help. Everything had to be completed by four o'clock.

The promise was not kept. There were no men or materials available to help. Some of the men had offered to help people move in exchange for bread. Only one or two fools did anything for nothing. In any case, most of the men were too tired to help.

The *Lagerälteste* had chartered a hundred *Häftlinge* to help. He himself was being chased by the Germans, he chased the *Kapos*, the *Kapos* indulged their sadism on the *Häftlinge*, the *Häftlinge* on the Jews. The result was the pogrom.

When things were not happening quickly enough, the *Lagerälteste* stepped in, and in no time at all the Jews were paying for it via the *Kapos* and the *Häftlinge*. In hut 13 they dragged out the half-naked men two at a time on top of one another in one bed. Moaning and groaning. In hut 12 – women's *Altersheim* – I witnessed the destruction of the three-tier bunk beds. The elderly women, groaning on the third tier and unable to leave their beds, were simply thrown out.

What interested the *Häftlinge* most was the bread. Whatever they could find they stole and gulped down. They behaved exactly like hungry dogs.

A woman, Mrs A., was laid up with diarrhoea, as well as being much affected still by five deaths in the family. I was to move her belongings and she would walk on my arm. The trouble with old people sometimes is their obstinacy. When the moment had arrived, it became apparent that she was quite unable to walk and could not even put her shoes on due to the oedema. She was thrown out of her bed. I found her lying on the floor among suitcases, mattresses and rubbish which covered the entire floor. When I entered, numerous sick people were already lying there.

I had been going back and forth carrying luggage to the new huts.

A few people lay dying on the floor, including a woman who was naked from the waist down. Powerless, we looked on.

Outside, a man was dying and his wailing wife begged us to fetch a friend, but at first there was no one available, and when there was, the friend could not be found. And so he arrived too late.

The sick had to leave the hut. Otherwise they would be beaten out with a truncheon. The *Häftlinge* stole whatever they could lay their hands on. Whatever remained was stolen by the Jews themselves. I lifted Mrs A. up and placed her outside. It had been raining heavily and the ground was one pool of mud. I found a mattress from somewhere. The blankets got dirty. I covered her up. When she was still feeling cold, I took a blanket from a dead person. I could not stay with her because I was humping luggage. I was also looking for a stretcher or for men willing to help. Everyone had worries of his own though; most were too tired or too lazy.

In front of hut 23 someone had been lying since early morning with frozen feet. He was unable to walk, exhausted, and stiff from the cold. He pleaded for help. I saw W. and passed on his request. W. did what he could. He was indeed carried away two hours later. He was covered in lice and afraid for his luggage. Possession is everything. That is what these people had learnt. And indeed, how can you manage without slippers!

Hours and hours later I managed to secure a bed and three bearers from somewhere, and at last we were able to carry Mrs A. away. We arrived inside the new hut of the *Altersheim* (formerly 18) where we put her down. The hut, though, was full of people and luggage, and the beds could not be brought in yet. In any case, there were insufficient beds, and for those that were there, no boards.

It began to get dark; it started to rain. An indescribable chaos ensued. The elderly lay dying on the floor and on top of the luggage. People walked over them, trod on them; they were too weak to shout. Besides, in the half-light one could not see them lying there.[185]

---

[185] (Author's note): One of the dying women was clutching a book in her hand, which, being curious about its contents, I picked up. It was the *Ethica* by Baruch d'Espinoza. Nice subject for a thesis: *Spinoza in Bergen-Belsen.*

Mrs A. was one of the fortunate ones. She had a bed, a bed with bed boards, mattress and blankets. Except that she was too close to the door. There was no room to place her elsewhere, though.

2 March 1945 The hut was crammed with beds, luggage, boards, transferred mattresses, filth and corpses. Everywhere people were sitting and lying on top of and across everything; for four days and four nights the elderly lived without beds or partly in beds without mattresses.

January, 186 deaths. February, 230 deaths.

After a few days, a little order was restored. Mrs A. was found a better place. Meanwhile her bed was used for distributing butter and cheese.

It became a deathbed. On 13 February at 5.15 p.m. In the final days T. had cared for her, cooked, made tea, some porridge. We were dismayed by this death. A death in rebellion. We had wanted to go to Eretz together. She had had courage, strength and energy. She had been fond of me. Something precious has broken. Something terrible, irreparable has happened. L. is waiting in vain. She had wanted to see L. and H. again. It is dire having to die here.

R. is dead. S., D. His wife, and many dear friends. A., B., N. On Friday D.'s wife died. On Saturday they were to have gone on transport. On Saturday evening the transport was cancelled. Shortly afterwards the Chief Rabbi died. He had been an honest, but not very strong man. At the end of February there had again been a distribution of parcels. The previous distribution had been on 31 December. The addressees had received a maximum of one parcel per three persons. The rest had been divided among the camp so that everyone received a seventh of a parcel.

Yesterday there was again a distribution. The food is appalling and gets worse by the day. Swedes in water, sometimes turned rancid, for the rest nothing.

I have been ill, eight days' high fever (evening temperatures of 39–40°). Everyone here gets ill from the weather. And there is no end in sight.

5 March 1945 Sleepless nights, filled, filled with the central problem: life or death, and when will it end? Filled, filled with the central
national problems, the place of Judaism in the world. Religion, the
concept of God. Constantly reaching back to the One eternal God
– its meaning and how mankind deludes itself with having van-
quished God. Will we manage with materialism? We cannot ignore
what has happened, but what really matters, is that we should stay
alive! I have so much to say still.

The dying continues. One thing: the pessimists were right.
Pessimists, optimists, they say nothing about the war. They all talk
about themselves. For lack of facts, no one has insight. At most
Ahnung[186] of the relative strengths. And I knew that Germany was
powerful.

Everything is getting less, forty grams of butter a week instead of
sixty. Half a piece of sausage, et cetera.

Starving, starving, starving.

Inspection of the *Aussenkommandos*[187] by the *Häftlinge* doctor:
three cases of spotted fever. The *Schneebaumlager* is leaving for
Liebenau[188] today; the Ascher group too. We are afraid of becoming
a KZ. It is very much like one already.

7 March 1945 Recently I have come to learn the meaning of despair.
I am ill again and have given up all hope of getting out of here. I
will probably get better again, but there is no permanent deliverance.

It is 7 March. Nothing is happening. Hunger is increasing, and
in the long run, the psychological burden in particular becomes
unbearable. If only there were a means to end it all. I am afraid of
the pain, of the death-struggle.

Every day the dying continues. I have fever.

11 March 1945 And still, and still we ate pancakes with jam on
9 March (T.'s birthday). One can do a great deal with semolina and

---

[186] A notion.   [187] Outdoor working parties.
[188] An internment camp (Abel J. Herzberg, *Kroniek der Jodenvervolging, 1940–
1945*, Em. Querido's Uitgeverij, Amsterdam 1985, p. 307).

water. The day's jam ration did the rest. Apart from that, it was a day of little cheer. We are not much looking forward to 30 March and 1 April. On 1 April A. will come of age.

16 March 1945 Every day now transports of thousands of people are arriving from concentration camps. Men and women, including Dutch people, acquaintances, friends.

Twenty to twenty-five per cent are dead, sometimes more. On the way to our latrines (the white house) there is a field full of corpses. And every day the carts trundle past filled with corpses and more corpses. It is a gruesome sight. And no one knows about it or will believe it. It makes us profoundly dejected and pessimistic. The corpses are being thrown into lime now. The crematorium can no longer cope with the volume. The mortality rate in our camp is declining slightly. Except that we have had the first case of spotted fever.

T. also has fever again, day after day. I am worn out and can hardly move. Almost the entire day I lie on the bed (if one can call it such). The filth is increasing. We are sick of it. For weeks I have been unable to make my bed.

17 March 1945 Saturday. After a few days of exhilarating spring weather it has started to rain again. The swishing of the rain on the roof of the hut makes us nervous, so far as we are not already nervous. As always, the *Häftlinge* must remain outdoors the whole day. The corpses are lying in the rain. To be more depressed is impossible. No news from the front. T. is ill. I am half dead with misery.

The rain is coming indoors. My shirt, which I had hung on a rafter, got soaking wet. It is half past seven in the morning. I am still in bed. Fortunately, with all our misfortune, we can rest as much as we want.

Psychologically, the ordeal is becoming very great, for many too great, I fear.

Sun, sun, God, give us a little sun at least. It is the least.

Reply: rain, rain, rain.

In the afternoon One of the worst things here is the lack of regularity. One day we eat at half past eight, the next we must wait till two, three, four o'clock or even later. Sometimes the evening soup arrives before the midday meal and at other times at half past nine in the evening, and sometimes not at all, that is to say, the next morning. It is little more than water. The waiting is killing. The camp is equipped for a few thousand people. Now there are forty-five thousand. It is an indictment of heaven. Five hundred, six hundred, seven hundred deaths a day! *Häftlinge* stay alive for only three months. The prisoners travel for five or six days in open wagons and without food! What takes place here is the most horrendous in world history. And there is no end to it, no end.

Dr A. has spotted fever. None of the doctors has ever seen a case of spotted fever before. I am tired and exhausted. Today I saw my old friend W. and got a shock.

God Almighty, put an end to our suffering. I beg you.

19 March 1945 Today, there is festivity in the camp. *Everyone* has received a parcel: one kilo of sugar, one pound of butter, one pound of pea-flour, one packet of crisp bread, two packets of stock cubes. To an outsider, the joy is incomprehensible. The most profound gratitude from us miserable beggars to the donors. The Joint? The Jewish Agency?

Today is F.'s birthday. Her husband offered ten thousand guilders, payable in gold in Amsterdam, for a shawl, a brooch, or something similar. No one gave it even a thought.

20 March 1945 There is no bread today. It is rumoured there will be no bread for three days, and probably even longer. The camp is getting larger and larger; the food supply worse and worse. There is terrible bombing, day and night; apparently bakeries are being destroyed and traffic is disrupted.

Aber: kapitulieren werden wir nie.[189] We, the SS, still have plenty to stuff ourselves on. The rest does not matter.

---

[189] But: we will never surrender.

The situation is very precarious. I am also ill again, fever and diarrhoea. How will it end?

22 March 1945 The weather affects the mood of the camp most profoundly. Had it not been such a gloriously fine spring day today, we would all be feeling as dejected as on our worst days.

Last night a transport of two thousand people arrived from Buchenwald concentration camp. The shouting, abusing, crying, taunting, groaning, cracking of the whips and thuds of the beatings could be heard throughout the night.

This morning, behind the former hut 16, where the former hut 15 used to stand, we saw hundreds of corpses being dragged onto a heap and stripped of their clothing. They also removed the gold teeth from their mouths. Never has it been as bad as this. All day, the heap of emaciated, naked bodies was left lying in the sun.

Their facial expressions are frightening. They seem to know what is being done to them.

Furthermore, all over the camp it stinks all day of the crematorium which is unable to devour the large mass of corpses. Men, women and children sit in the stench making soup or cakes with the pea-flour from their parcels.

Now that the weather has improved, we are not such regular customers of the crematorium any more. On average four a day, against nine to ten in February. Those who died today include N., L.'s youngest child (born in Westerbork), the twelve-year-old son of W., himself also admitted into hospital now, as well as his wife. In the huts there are numerous patients with temperatures of thirty-nine or forty degrees. Is it typhus? Is it influenza? Some die.

But the weather is fine. It is splendid weather. Admittedly, it is the third spring of imprisonment; admittedly, there is not a single flower, plant, or blade of grass in sight – it is splendid weather though.

And there are constant air-raid alerts.

Apart from that, we got one ration of bread after two days without any. Who knows for how long?

The *Häftlinge* were kept waiting at Celle station for two days. We happened to have been paid a visit by an inspection committee who apparently were not meant to see them. During those two days the people were given nothing to eat. And here there was no bread.

30 March 1945 Today is E.'s birthday, and A.'s is the day after tomorrow. A. comes of age then. Best wishes, my dear children. I no longer dare to speak about next year. But maybe, maybe we will see flowers again. Today F. died here; he had played an important role in the judicial commission as head of investigations. It had not protected him against spotted fever.

For five months we have not had a shower. On Sunday we suddenly had to have a delousing shower. Our hut was to go first. Reveille at half past three, fall in at five. Everyone had to go. The blankets and clothes had to be bundled up. Even the suitcases had to be emptied and the contents disinfected.

At five o'clock we were herded to roll-call, experienced extreme difficulty with clearing the hut, were kept waiting for an hour and then heard it would take 'another hour or so'. We decided to take everything to the disinfecting machine which was standing inside the camp in front of the hospital and the *Altersheim*. For the rest, no one gave a thought to the delousing shower until five in the afternoon when we were suddenly summoned for it. I went and ... returned at eleven at night. There had been no 'Posten'[190] to take us back, so we were kept waiting for hours. The treatment was carried out with sticks. Whoever had to go to the toilet was refused permission. The shower gave me a nasty surprise. I noticed that I had oedema in my feet. Apart from that, the delousing shower was a great success. The next day, I again found lice in my clothes.

At least half the camp has not been deloused. Last Monday Mös came and we learned what it was all needed for: transports.

For the time being we have been saved from those transports. We are in quarantine. A serious outbreak of spotted fever has erupted here. In the hut of the Albanians there are more than a hundred

---

[190] Guards.

suspected victims. The hut has been isolated. I had to leave the hut again in great haste, first to 33, which was without light, without a proper roof, and was dripping with rain. Half in hope I went to the *Altersheim* where I now have a temporary bed.

Our prospects are truly brilliant. A choice between spotted fever or transports. What transports mean we learn here daily from the *Häftlinge* ... Corpses, corpses, corpses.

Our mortality is rising rapidly again. Spotted fever, typhus, and thrice weekly a piece of bread ...

How will it end? People here feed themselves on good hopes for the war ... I still cannot share their optimism ... There will be months and months still of the worst torments.

Despite everything, we celebrated *Seder*[191] last night. Oh, oh ... ! A historical *Seder*. There was no need for bitter herbs.[192] Nevertheless, it was more than last year. People had baked *Matzos*[193] with the flour we had been given and they had tasted quite good.

1 April 1945 Sunday. A. has come of age. The first day of Easter. No bread, not for days now. Tomorrow we will get the last half ration. After that – so we have been told – there will be no more bread. By way of compensation we have each been given half a swede. Raw swede lies heavy on the stomach. At midday there was soup consisting of water and a little flour. Tonight we are getting swede soup. There will be famine in the heart of Europe. People will die by the dozen. In the *Häftlinge* camp they are constantly dragging naked corpses through the mud. In March there were seventeen thousand deaths in the entire camp out of forty-five thousand people! We had a hundred and eighty. Prospects: spotted fever, hunger, typhus, transports. People console each other with good news and say that the war will end this week. They do not know Hitler. Easter – Peace – God, oh God!

---

[191] A ceremonial meal eaten on the first or first two evenings of Passover.

[192] One of the prescribed foods eaten at Passover to remind Jews of the bitter days when their forefathers were slaves of the Egyptians.

[193] Wafers of unleavened bread.

There are no more roll-calls. Also no work. There is only death. A little flour is distributed and a few people receive some oatmeal. It is all nonsense.

2 April 1945 Our food consists of raw swede, and even with that we must be sparing. Yesterday they distributed cigarettes; every man and woman got ten. Even raw swedes are being traded. There is no more wood in the kitchen, let alone coal. Old shoe soles are being used for fuel. As a result, the food arrives hours too late again, or not at all. All we will get today is a spoonful of swede soup. Maybe a piece of bread. Originally we were to get half a ration, but 'thanks' to twelve hundred dead *Häftlinge* they are giving us a full ration. Perhaps again on Thursday. We are overcome by a great weariness. Will we be saved? IPAs, IPAs, IPAs about the war situation. We know nothing for certain.

W. is very weak. B. too. They look terrible. T. lies in bed all day. Today they are giving us a pat of butter. It is two o'clock now; apart from raw swede, we have had nothing to eat yet.

8 April 1945 Last week the tension mounted and mounted and finally became unbearable, all in connection with the political news, or rather rumours, which were getting wilder and wilder. It was even claimed that Hanover and Bremen had been taken, and that we were about to be liberated. The big question, of course, was whether we would be evacuated. We know that when they are in retreat the Germans always take their prisoners with them. The question, though, was generally answered in the negative because of the outbreak of spotted fever and the large number of other sick and exhausted people.

Yesterday, Job's tidings arrived: evacuation! The first to report were the 'Transportfähige'.[194] A few hundred people, who did indeed leave yesterday. According to reports today, the transport is still at the station. We have no idea yet what will happen with us. We know

---

[194] Those fit to travel.

even less where we will be evacuated to. Eight hundred Hungarians have also left. The rumours continue. One says we are surrounded, the other that Hanover has not fallen yet. The latter is probably true. Are we or are we not leaving? The lives of hundreds of people depend on it. What is in store for us? Meanwhile, an active trade has developed across the fence with the Hungarians. It is a wonderful sight to see all who still have something peddling their wares. Doctors with old suits which they are trying to sell for a couple of potatoes. Today (it is two o'clock now), we have had nothing to eat yet. Raw swedes are arriving now. The tension is mounting to impossible heights. Our nerves seem about to break and burst. Hunger.

I tried to sell a tweed suit for twenty potatoes. The police in the Hungarian camp forbid all transactions. Risk of spotted fever ... And whatever is left is stolen. The huts have emergency toilets which are in constant use and stink. The weather is beautiful, but cold. An IPA says we will be 'released' and no one will look after us. From tomorrow – it is said – there will be no more cooking in the kitchens. What then? What if we are sent into the woods? What are we meant to do with our luggage? And with our blankets. Oh, oh, the sick, the sick!

10 April 1945 Yesterday, the evacuation of the camp continued. There was uncertainty at first. To leave as quickly as possible, or to remain as long as possible. The first had the advantage of securing the best place, the second, the possibility of surprises and a last-minute rescue by the Americans. Because on one thing we are all agreed: this was to be a new extermination of people. At first, everyone held back and the evacuation took place in quite an orderly fashion. The sick would leave first, then those who were fit and able to walk. The sick were to be transported by lorry. The distance to the station is six kilometres, which is quite a long distance in our state of exhaustion, for women and children burdened, moreover, by tens of kilos of luggage. The insolent own half the world and also grabbed the first lorries. We had worked out that few people were fit, but in the afternoon the entire system began to avenge itself. The Germans said: so many people have now left, that is the number of sick and infirm. All who remain must therefore be fit. An enormous scramble ensued for places in the lorries which drove up and down. The SS meted out blows, the Jews thronged. The *Kapos* were also in attendance. Those who had to walk were formed into groups. T. and I had the misfortune to fall among them. They included children, a poor old woman, a worn-out old man, sick, completely exhausted people, et cetera. It became a *marche funèbre*. Terrible. T. and I have oedema in our legs. It became an unprecedented torment. The weather was beautiful and warm.

On the way, we met all kinds of interesting things. Large groups of *Häftlinge* from Auschwitz, of every nationality. We saw various acquaintances again. They did not look as bad as we were accustomed to. As usual, the sick trailed behind. The dead we saw later at the station, in a heap. These *Häftlinge* are transported in open coal wagons, sometimes covered with a tarpaulin, sometimes also without such a covering. We were already counting on having to leave in their wagons. The *Häftlinge* had their orchestras with them and were in good spirits. As we left the camp, the orchestra of the *Kapos* was playing jazz music. It was a remarkable parting from fifteen months' incarceration and wretchedness.

On the way, we saw people camping in the woods. We saw prisoners of war, with carts and tents. And large groups of soldiers.

It took us hours to walk the six kilometres, repeatedly having to rest. The SS soldiers were in an easy-going mood. Except for one who hit out with a stick, because T. had wanted to give something to the *Häftlinge*. A plate and a pan, which she had removed from her luggage to throw out as ballast. Everything was so heavy that we threw away the swede we had been given as our only rations ... An anxious heart ... We had no idea where the journey would take us, nor even an approximation of how long it would take. We had been told eight to ten days; what were we to live on during that period?

When we reached the train, it appeared we would have done better had we left earlier. There were no places left. By chance, we managed to secure two, right next to the toilet.

That is how we have been sitting in the train now for two long days. The loading of *Lagerinsassen* is continuing. The sick have remained behind. They will die the death of *Häftlinge*. It is awful. There is also talk of people having fled – to be precise, French women who spoke German. In the train there are typhus patients, victims of spotted fever, and bacteria carriers. The wagons are over-full. We have third-class coaches and a number of goods wagons. The question is, which is better? In the latter you cannot sit, there is no toilet and no water; in the former you cannot lie down, and by now the toilets are one big heap of dung and a source of stench, filth and infection. The entire station has only one water tap. People throng for a little water with which to cook and wash themselves.

As far as the cooking arrangements are concerned, the fires are made with organised[195] wood, and the camp bowls serve as utensils in which the organised beetroot and turnips are cooked. A large heap of them is lying beside the endless train. The SS are allowing the 'organising'. This afternoon they cut off the water because of an air-raid alert.

What sort of adventure lies ahead? There is virtually nothing to eat. They gave us one loaf of twenty-four centimetres for eight days. We were promised butter and some sausage. We have seen nothing yet. It is all we shall get. How long will the journey last? Where to? To Theresienstadt, they say, later to be exchanged and sent to Switzerland. No one believes it, except for the optimists who need to have their dream. During the night we were told that most of the camp – as far as they were not present yet – would remain behind. We got furious at the thought that *we* had fallen for it.

This morning the report proved to be false.

How long will we travel for? We are already worn out with fatigue. Naturally, we did not sleep last night. How can one sleep, with two people sitting on a narrow bench? Bombs from above, sickness inside, uncertainty, yet despite everything, no fear.

On the contrary. We are in good spirits. We had been confined for fifteen months. For the first time in fifteen months we saw trees,

---

[195] 'To organise' – a much-used euphemism during the war meaning to obtain by artful methods, e.g. by stealing.

grass and a stretch of land again. After fifteen months we were sitting in a train again. Whatever happens, it will be a journey. My legs are swollen, my head aches and only God knows if we will reach a destination. But we are off on a journey. Right through warring Germany, together with the enemy deep into the country. No one knows when we are leaving. Perhaps tonight, perhaps tomorrow.

Even so, we are not as unhappy as in the camp. But we have not reached the start yet ...

11 April 1945 The night is hell. We are sitting on our bench, folded double, rolled up, with pain in every muscle, and get in each other's way. Aggression – bad as it is already – is mounting. The wagons are packed now. In our coach, which has seating for forty-eight people, sixty-two must live and sleep. Last night they gave us butter, one pound per four persons for four days. It is a lot, relatively, and we are not dissatisfied. The promised sausage – for which we are longing – has not arrived yet.

The night dragged by. First we experienced a heavy bombardment at Bergen station. Then suddenly a jerk and our journey had begun. Supposedly to Theresienstadt and Switzerland. The train crept forward. The sky was filled with bombardments and combat. It thundered and cracked. The night was cold and dark. I was constantly quarrelling with the woman facing me because of our feet. We were unable to sleep. From time to time someone would doze off and after a few minutes wake up with a sigh. That was the second night. How many more will there be? We are dreading it.

The day turned into a feast, though. It became a splendid spring morning. Cool and bright. We seemed to have been shunted into a siding in Soltau. We were allowed off the train, fetched some water, stood talking to one another, and went to cook something. Everyone still has some carrots, turnips or beetroot.

Suddenly an order: *einsteigen*.[196] We drove to Soltau station and a

---

[196] All aboard.

little beyond. Again we stopped. All at once we slowly drove on again. Ten minutes later the station was heavily bombed. Had it been anticipated?

It is deathly quiet in Germany. We see nothing but soldiers and SS. It is dismal in Germany. Everyone expects the end any day now, the political catastrophe.

We travel around through forests. From time to time we stop for half an hour or an hour. We go into the woods then and lie in the sun. For a prisoner a piece of luck and a real pleasure. In consequence, we feel as happy as on an outing. Now that we see nature again and are in direct contact with it, we feel free. Although our situation is full of danger, we are hopeful and cheerful. Where are we going? Towards Hamburg, they say. Tonight, they say, we will be in Uelzen. That means twenty-five kilometres from Bergen after twenty-four hours' journey. It seems we are being sent ahead towards the enemy, and will simply have to live on the train for want of other accommodation. Apart from what we had been given, there is almost no food left, and nobody knows what we are meant to live on. No one in his senses believes the story about Theresienstadt and Switzerland.

We passed a station. A train was waiting there with ... the Hungarians, who had left a day earlier. They were supposed to be heading for Budapest.

Everything seems to have gone mad. A few people have remained behind in the camp.

14 April Two hundred people are said to have remained behind in the camp, including E.M., the son of M.P., E.P. and others. We fear the worst for them. For that matter, our own future is not so bright either. There is *nothing* to eat. The *Zugführer*[197] has gone to Luneburg, to forage, he is alleged to have said. The question is, what the outcome will be, assuming he had spoken the truth. We still have two beetroots. We will have to live on those for an indefinite time. I have diarrhoea.

---

[197] Guard of the train.

On 12 April we remained in one spot. A thirty-six-hour stretch. The Jewish leadership held a collection and bought potatoes. We got forty-five small ones. They were finished in two days. The leadership are trying to buy more. Things are going badly. The locals no longer accept money.

W. is ill. The normal sign of the dreaded illness. K. has just died from it. Endless air raids. Yesterday we endured an attack by machine-guns. Fourteen lightly wounded. I took the opportunity to visit a farm. I got two eggs and a little milk. Unbelievable. Yesterday we ate fried eggs. All night, I had an upset stomach and today, diarrhoea.

From Soltau to Uelzen we travelled at an average speed of three kilometres an hour. Repeatedly stopping, waiting for hours, and each time the same image. Camp fires along the track. The biggest problem is water. Sometimes we have to fetch it, at other times, like yesterday (near Uelzen) and today near Luneburg, there is a brook. Naturally, it is a relief. We wash our hands, can rinse the pans, and cook the beetroot and potatoes that we still have.

Today I was given half a rotten swede and was delighted with it. Tomorrow's breakfast. Yes, air raid upon air raid. Especially frightening at night. The women and children are getting nervous. The nights are hell, blood and mayhem. Everything seems bewitched then. The weather is wonderful. Till now, the days have been like holidays, despite all the worries, despite air raids, et cetera. Sometimes, one is overcome with fear. Spotted fever. Will we make it? After six years of war! After all we have experienced, to stumble at the threshold? For how many has there been no mercy? And will there be no mercy? All afternoon air battles, sirens, attacks.

There are no trains to be seen, no people to be seen. Everything here is war, war, war.

The population, that is to say the few people we meet, are friendly enough. The farmer did not want any money for the eggs and the milk. He had had enough of that, he said.

We have now gone to Luneburg where we are in front on the track. Theresienstadt does indeed seem to be the official destination, followed by Austausch. No one believes it any longer, not the *Zug-führer* either, who happens to be a very decent fellow. What will happen with us then? God only knows.

There is no news. Everything is just rumour. Küstrin[198] retaken by the Germans and the death of Roosevelt. We do not know if it is true. All in all, it is enough for the mood to plunge far below zero. What do they want from us? Where must we go? A devil had come to God and had said, Bergen-Belsen is a marvellous business. It would be even better, though, if it were put on wheels and driven around. Travelling misery. The nights are unbearable to live through. Spotted fever on wheels. Six deaths today.

15 April Last night we arrived in heavily bombed Luneburg. An anxious night. They had driven us into the station. Naturally, there was an air-raid alert. Our breakfast consisted of swedes. No water for washing. Next ... direction Lubeck, as far as Büchen. Their intentions are still unclear. Our hunger is becoming very noticeable. *No food* has arrived. From Büchen onward again, allegedly towards Berlin. We are just wandering about. The night was quite calm. It has got very cold. And already it is 15 April 1945. G.L. lies dying on the floor of one of the coaches. Nobody had given a thought to her. Not even she.

15 April, 2.30 in the afternoon, Hagenow. I cannot make out the route we are taking.

16 April Yesterday they had promised us there would be bread, butter and coffee in Ludwigslust, the station after Hagenow. When we reached Ludwigslust towards ten in the evening, the train drove on, as if the engine was hungry, not we. Meanwhile, something like a miracle has happened. The train with the Hungarians caught up with us in Hagenow and came to stand next to us. It had spent the previous night in Luneburg. The ladies and gentlemen had been less particular than we had been, though, and had taken whatever there

---

[198] Now Kostrzyn, about 25 km north of Frankfurt an der Oder.

was to be taken. It was quite a lot. Wagons with potatoes, packets of honey, et cetera in the bombed station. Threats of death had not bothered them.

As a result, they had enough foodstuffs with them and were able to do business. In no time at all a brisk trade had developed. The most favoured counter-offer was cigarettes, but they also accepted salt, gold rings and all kinds of other objects. Occasionally someone sold for money. I traded my wedding ring for thirty-five potatoes and paid ten Dutch guilders for fifteen more.

They brought us two days' relief from our worries. Providing we are careful, we will make it. In the meantime, during a pause, a farmer gave me a further forty potatoes. We have already cooked them all today. *In essence*, the worries of the transport are not lessened by such strokes of luck. And for numerous people (for example the sick and exhausted), practically not at all. For the latter are unable to obtain anything for themselves. Large families are also badly off. What is done about it? This morning we were in a partly evacuated village. Result, plunder. People returned with all kinds of delicious things: herrings, potatoes, macaroni, et cetera. Removed in part from a couple of wagons. Somebody brought me a packet of maize flour.

For the rest, attack upon attack with machine-guns. My feet have started to hurt terribly.

At the moment it looks as if – barring accidents – we will finish up in Theresienstadt after all. Today, twenty-five people died who could not be buried because of the air-raid alerts. I only saw a father and mother digging a grave for a dead child.

The weather remains wonderful. The nights are frightening. Everything becomes different, eerily large.

18 April Yesterday we spent the night in a Berlin station. We went round the entire city and saw the terrible devastation. On the walls we could read 'Berlin kämpft, arbeitet und steht'[199] and other such

---

[199] Berlin fights, works and stands.

resolute phrases. For the past two days there has been no food; last night we finally received one kilo of potatoes, seventy-five grams of soup vegetables, half a swede and a hundred grams of curd each. Today there would also be gherkins. The leadership is much taken with itself. We begged and partly plundered and have become fully fledged gypsies. For all that, we are eating much better than in the camp. The Hungarians are selling us their stolen goods.

Death is on the increase. Spotted fever seems to be decreasing. The lice infestation is terrible. The nights impossible to get through. Last night, thunderstorm. Today, the most marvellous weather on earth. It helps us get through the difficulties. Barring accidents, we will probably make Theresienstadt.

In Berlin we also met the Hungarians again. They had sustained a heavy attack – fifty-six casualties, more than 250 wounded. A dangerous enterprise indeed! Yesterday I begged potato peelings from a soldier and cooked an excellent soup with them.

19 April 1945　The misery seems about to begin. We left Berlin, and after all kinds of vicissitudes, stopped in the wilderness yesterday afternoon. To our utter surprise here of all places we were given a ration of bread which we polished off immediately, of course. We were also given sauerkraut and a third of a gherkin that had already been foraged the previous day. Today each person got two more rations of bread that 'Eiserne Reserve bleiben muss'.[200] Last night it was announced we would not be moving from here, but would wait for further instructions. It seems there is no contact with Berlin any longer. Transit to Theresienstadt seems out of the question. The Russians, they say, are positioned thirty kilometres from here, the British 120 – (or the Americans). We are in the midst of the mire. Machine-guns as well as bombs. No damage, no casualties. *Pourvu que ça dure.*[201] We have just heard that the Russians have been beaten back … It can take a few more days, then. The problem is food, and especially something to drink. In fact, nothing has been arranged.

---

[200] To be kept as iron rations.　　[201] If only it lasts.

They do show concern (even the *Scharführer*), but one cannot eat that, or wash one's hands or pan with it. There is a brook nearby. They do not want us to go there. We go all the same. And suddenly it is allowed.

There is a forest fire. They are laying a smoke screen. Sigurd A. has died of croup, after two days' illness. It is a tragic business. Our pan has burned through. A rucksack got burnt. T.'s warm coat got singed. Today it was stormy and cold. It was difficult to cook.

Yesterday, thirty deaths. Dr A. and G. have died. About Dr A., nothing but good. Only this morning I saw G. He died in the toilet; his head and hands were lying in the filth. Tonight, there are nine sick people in our coach. People fight for a place to lie down. Things could not be worse. And God knows what still lies in store. The mood has plummeted; we are very worried. There is nothing to be foraged. I went to farmers. They refused to give anything. I have lost a gold ring.

21 April 1945 After we had remained stationary for twenty-four hours or longer, had heard the distant bombardments at the front increasing and decreasing, had ourselves been regularly attacked by machine-guns and bombers, fortunately without any losses, the order was suddenly given: *einsteigen*[202] and departure. With utmost haste we brought the pots and pans inside – and before we knew it, we were moving again. Since yesterday we have been standing somewhere in a beautiful forest without provisions, except for one kilo of potatoes this morning, and this evening a spoonful of salt and nine hundred eggs, for which lots were drawn, and some given to the sick. Naturally there are mutterings about corruption. We got three eggs (one on the grounds of being on the sick list), one of which we traded for twenty potatoes. People are doing much buying in the neighbourhood. The farmers are very forthcoming and anti-National Socialist. Now at least. How they were before, I cannot say.

Foraging is forbidden, but happens all the same. The guards are

---

[202] To board the train.

being sidestepped. People return with meat, ham, chicken, but above all potatoes. Unfortunately I cannot go with them for my legs are so swollen that I can no longer wear my shoes. I am walking around in galoshes and have severe cramp in my calves and stiffness in the back of my knees. As a result, we are living on potatoes. We have been cooking for almost the entire day and look like charcoal burners.

This afternoon the weather broke. It is raining and in consequence, our life changes completely. We are confined to the train. Cooking has become impossible. The firewood is wet ... T. is ill and feels feverish.

We got hold of an American newspaper from 17 April. A veritable relief because we knew hardly anything for certain. We are somewhere near Dresden now. It may be the last point and therefore still take a long time. God have mercy upon us! Life is getting difficult. Sleeping on the bench is becoming an increasing torment. Last night I tried to remain outdoors, but it started to rain.

Probably Holland will be free even later than we. By 1 May, though, everything is likely to have ended.

For the romanticists: this morning S. struck his wife *coram publico*.[203]

More money was collected for foraging.

There are many deaths. S. has died of exhaustion, and so it goes on. Death train.

26 April 'Alle marschfähigen Männer, Frauen und Kinder sofort mit Bagage antreten.'[204]

Now we are in for it!

Almost no one appeared to be *marschfähig*. Two hundred out of the twenty-four hundred were prepared to leave. For the rest, not a soul paid the slightest attention to the order. A great joy overcame us. It seemed the train would go no farther, that was the main thing. The end was in sight. How? remained the exciting question, but that

---

[203] Publicly.
[204] All men, women and children able to walk, fall in immediately with your luggage.

was of lesser importance. Would there be fighting? Would the train come under fire? It seemed hardly believable that it would not happen, for our train looked exactly like a military train. Except that it was bedecked with white flags on which we had built all our hopes even though they had not protected us against the constant attacks by machine-guns.

We went to do what we always did, cook alongside the track!

Suddenly: 'All aboard, extinguish all fires!' No evening meal, then.

There were rumours that perhaps we could all stay together. And then nothing happened. And after that, again nothing. And then, after nothing, again nothing. We waited. The entire train was filled with singing. Everyone felt as if it was the eve of some festival. It could bring death or freedom.

It took hours. Then a small engine arrived. The train was divided in half. The engine was not powerful enough to pull the entire train. Deep disappointment. Announcement: we had to leave because our woods were about to become a battlefield. They were taking us four kilometres farther. The announcement seemed quite remarkable. We ended up somewhere on a track close to a village, apparently called Tröbitz-Niederlausitz.

To our left, a thin line of trees. To our right, woods. It was evening. It became deathly quiet. Nothing happened. We went foraging and I returned with a thick pancake and some bread. We had had nothing to eat.

And then again nothing happened. Night fell, it got misty. A pale moon shone. The sleepless hours dragged by. Silence, silence, except for the intermittent popping of anti-aircraft fire and the sound of explosions. Occasionally, the crackle of gun fire. We were waiting to come under attack. Nothing happened.

Russian armoured vehicles had already been in the village, people said.

And early in the morning, very early – Russian sentries stood farther along the road. Liberty!

Tovarischi Svoboda. Comrades, liberty!

They gave us cigarettes.

Up till now, though, 26 April, they have not bothered about us.

They show no concern for us, apart from leaving us the local inhabitants to plunder. And this plundering was carried out thoroughly and without mercy.

We have nothing. We are ill. We were billeted on farmers. The train is empty. My legs are swollen and inflamed. T. has bronchitis, diarrhoea and fever. Nothing is happening.

Nine of us are living in one house. Our room is on the first floor. A woman has come to help us in exchange for food. We slaughtered two piglets. The woman is a good German Catholic, from the Polish part. A marvellous woman, twenty-six years old, filled with melancholy and belief in God.

Dr F. used to live downstairs, a Hungarian, a scoundrel. He moved house and stole a pig and a calf for himself.

We are ill. Tired. How is it in Holland? Outside, the birds are chirping.

I lie awake at night and count the strokes of the clock. Is this freedom?

Postscript

When the *De Groene Amsterdam* was preparing to publish the diary, the last few pages had gone astray. Later, they were found again. As will be seen from their contents, they were written partly in the train and partly in Tröbitz, a village located sixty kilometres east of Leipzig, where the train was intercepted by the Russian army. The Russians did what they could for the former prisoners, but they could not prevent the spotted fever from spreading virulently and claiming hundreds and hundreds of victims.

Our stay in Tröbitz lasted two months. In the warm flowering spring, heavy with melancholy, people would walk shivering with fever, illness, sadness and longing through the few deserted village streets. There seemed no end to the dying. With help from the Russians, infirmaries were set up, and two extensive Jewish cemeteries. The mood was one of dejection.

Gradually the illness diminished and disappeared. After two months, the handful of people who had managed to survive began to be repatriated to their various countries in Europe.